Staging Memory and Materiality in Eighteenth-Century Theatrical Biography

ANTHEM STUDIES IN THEATRE AND PERFORMANCE

Anthem Studies in Theatre and Performance takes a broad, global approach to cultural analysis to examine and critique a wide range of performative acts from the most traditional forms of theatre studies (music, theatre and dance) to more popular, less structured forms of cultural performance. The twenty-first century in particular has seen theatre and performance studies become a major perspective for examining, understanding and critiquing contemporary culture and its historical roots. In addition to traditional theatre studies, then, the series takes as its subject international folk performances, minstrel and music hall shows, vaudeville, burlesque, ballroom dance, rock concerts, professional wrestling, football and soccer matches, snake charming, American snake-handling religions, shamanism, street protests, Nascar or Formula 1 races, tractor pulls, fortune telling, circuses, techno-mobbing, the gestures of painting and writing, and even the performance that denies itself, that pretends that it is not play(ing). Performance is thus a vital manifestation of culture that is enacted, a form to be experienced, recorded, analysed and theorized. It is among the most useful and dynamic foci for the global study of culture.

Staging Memory and Materiality in Eighteenth-Century Theatrical Biography

Amanda Weldy Boyd

ANTHEM PRESS

Anthem Press
An imprint of Wimbledon Publishing Company
www.anthempress.com

This edition first published in UK and USA 2018
by ANTHEM PRESS
75–76 Blackfriars Road, London SE1 8HA, UK
or PO Box 9779, London SW19 7ZG, UK
and
244 Madison Ave #116, New York, NY 10016, USA

British Library Cataloguing-in-Publication Data
A catalogue record for this book is available from the British Library.

ISBN-13: 978-1-78308-666-5 (Hbk)
ISBN-10: 1-78308-666-1 (Hbk)

This title is also available as an e-book.

CONTENTS

ACKNOWLEDGMENTS

The most difficult part of a book-length undertaking is narrowing down the field of people to whom I am indebted. When you think about the amount of effort on the part of so many people, you realize that every book is a miracle of sorts! I am grateful, then, to have the opportunity to thank many of these miracle-makers who have helped in the fruition of this project.

First, and most immediately, I wish to thank my mentor, Emily Anderson, who guided me through grad school and then into "the real world" and made it look easy. I hope that you see your continued mentorship reflected in this text, and that I have done justice to the hours of discussion about this project that we have shared. I so fondly remember you imitating Colley Cibber's cry of "A harse, a harse, my kingdom for a harse!" during one of our meetings with such immeasurable zest! May my words and delivery in the upcoming pages be similarly inspired by the exuberance of the eighteenth century and of its present-day fans.

I wish to thank Joseph Dane for his clear-eyed insight, wisecracks, and wisdom, as well as Leo Braudy, Heather James, and Thomas Habinek, all of whom have provided helpful encouragement and criticism. My research skills have greatly benefitted from conversations with Bruce Smith, Rebecca Lemon, Anthony Kemp, and David Roman. I additionally thank the English Department at the University of Southern California (USC), which has funded research projects at the Folger and at the Houghton, as well as numerous conference presentations. I'd like to thank Peter Mancall and the USC-Huntington Early Modern Studies Institute for supporting me through a summer fellowship during which I first worked on theatrical biographies of Charles Macklin.

I am appreciative of the assistance of many librarians and library staff who helped me secure materials for this project: USC's Special Collections, the Houghton Library, the Huntington, and the Folger Library each provided inspiring workplaces in which to interact with the past. My particular appreciation goes to Melanie Leung, the Folger Image Request Coordinator, for her assistance in navigating the use of images for the collage that comprises the cover of this book.

My gratitude goes to Craig Svonkin and his annual Pacific Ancient and Modern Language Association (PAMLA) conferences, through which I have gotten key feedback on aspects of the present work. I also celebrate with this project the celebrity/performance studies group at the American Society for Eighteenth-Century Studies (ASECS), rather newly formed as an official caucus, for offering a network of scholars whose questions always lead to more questions, as it should be.

It was through a paper given at ASECS that I met Mark Pollard, then a commissioning editor for Pickering and Chatto, who, by showing early and sustained interest in my research on Macklin, led me to consider how my ideas might resonate with a larger audience, and whose enthusiasm for my project led him to find my manuscript a home at his next job with Anthem Press.

I am grateful to Tej P. S. Sood for offering me this opportunity, as well as Katy Miller, Abi Pandey, and the rest of the editorial staff at Anthem for having faith in my project, for designing clear expectations, and for making this adventure in publication so pleasant. I wish also to salute the three anonymous colleagues who provided encouraging and detailed reviews on an early chapter draft, and the three additional anonymous reviewers who commented upon a later full draft: I hope I have done justice to your insights. Additionally, this manuscript has benefitted heartily from the efforts of Annalisa Zox-Weaver and Isabel Stein, delightfully detailed copy editors. I am confident that any errors herein remaining are my own, for which I apologize to the reader, all six reviewers, and to Annalisa and Isabel.

I wish to thank Steven Edgington and Cora Alley at my present institution, Hope International University, for encouraging me as I worked on this project, and to my colleagues at Hope for providing a friendly environment for teaching and thinking. My gratitude goes to Robin Hartman and Katy Lines of the Darling Library for their generous assistance and support.

Among earlier influences that deserve my heartfelt gratitude is Helen Deutsch of UCLA, whose seminar on Alexander Pope illuminated the eighteenth century and introduced me to the joys of archival research. Karen Cunningham was also instrumental in teaching me how to craft a sustained argument and encouraging me to work within my own writing style to do so.

My friends at First Presbyterian Church of Orange have cheered me on, supporting me with a scholarship and continual encouragement. My thanks also to the members of the Church of the Valley, as well as several early teachers who encouraged my interest in someday becoming an author, especially Stephen Collins, Patrick Schlosser, Ann Hampton, and Brenda Martin.

A tip of the hat to several good friends and colleagues who perhaps have heard (and read) more than they ever might have wanted to about Garrick, Macklin, and Kemble: Amanda Bloom, with whom I have been lucky enough to travel, through laughter and tears, lock-step with through the eighteenth century in grad school and beyond, and to Kenni Palmer, whose Amazonian appetite for debate and discussion complemented by unflagging generosity of spirit makes her a cherished friend indeed. Andrew T. Post and John Kaucher each have provided a much-appreciated analytical eye for style and content. And, finally, to the best of friends, Beth Grimm, who found me in a library in the first place, and who has since provided a consistent sounding board for my ideas, responding with the perfect blend of humor and perspective.

To my family—Jennifer, who stimulated the competitive desire in me that helps me get things done; Shelby, who is wise enough to know when to take a break for the day; and my extended family, who has cheered on my writing career from the very beginning, I thank you. As for my parents, Jonathan and Lisa, here is the book that you always said you knew would happen. Our day has come, and I hope you feel a great deal of accomplishment in having helped shepherd me (and my manuscript) in countless ways. Thank you for your steadfast belief in me. And a tip of the hat to Eric and Evan, whose presence during revisions was a constant source of delight.

Finally—finally—to Jonathan Boyd, my husband and my constant champion, whose excellent examples of creativity and industry (seen in the form of the book cover's collage of six meaningful pieces of theatrical miscellanea) are only matched by boundless goodwill and humor, and whose words brighten the heart as well as the mind—I am so glad that you have been riding the bus side by side with me every step of the way. I offer you this book and my love forever and always.

INTRODUCTION: COMPETITION AND LEGITIMACY

Colley Cibber's Complaint as Generic Demand

In 1735, Charles Macklin, a comedian, put out another actor's eye with a cane in the green room at Drury Lane, claiming that the lesser actor had stolen his prop wig. The offending actor, Thomas Hallam, died shortly thereafter, much regretted by Macklin. Incredibly, Macklin recovered from this scandal and enjoyed a lengthy career delighting the British public. Possibly more incredible was the apocryphal claim that many potential witnesses were unable to supply testimony about the skirmish because they had been too engrossed in reading a draft of the riveting autobiography of a fellow actor, Colley Cibber.[1] Thus, legend has it that Nero played the fiddle while Rome burned, and actors read Cibber's autobiography while Macklin lay in the center of the green room, weeping over the disfigured body of young Hallam.

Before the story goes much further, it seems important to include that the source of the above story was none other than Colley Cibber himself, who, along with his duties as actor, stage manager, playwright, and poet laureate, appeared to be his own best publicist. Yet the popularity of Cibber's *An Apology for the Life of Colley Cibber* (published in 1740) was—and is—undeniable, having outstripped all other accomplishments of a remarkably accomplished man.[2] While small attempts at theatrical biography already existed, the above anecdote indicates the novelty of Cibber's book.[3] Although it was technically an autobiography rather than a biography, Cibber's book was revolutionary within the nascent genre, particularly because Cibber spent so much of the *Apology* functioning as a biographer of other actors in order to fulfill his stated desire of providing, concurrently, a history of the stage from the Restoration through 1740. As the bellwether of this new genre, Cibber attempted to describe both the need for, and the limitations of, the biographical project as specifically applied to thespian subjects: "Pity it is, that the momentary beauties flowing from an harmonious elocution cannot, like those of poetry, be their own record; that the animated graces of the player can live no longer than the instant breath and motion that represent them; or, at the least, can but faintly glimmer through the memory and imperfect attestation of a few surviving spectators."[1] Evidently the impulse for those "surviving spectators" to commemorate, critique, and compile was stronger than the fear of confronting the ephemera of performance.[5]

Despite Cibber's dubiously sincere call for approaching theatrical memoir with a sense of futility, and the sentiment's popularity with biographers and critics thereafter, I would like to suggest that theatrical biography of the period does, to a certain extent, succeed in overcoming obstacles to representation because of unique formal features (such as *points*, which were a specific means of analyzing performance in the eighteenth century) and uniquely applied features (such as anecdotes and letters) that became ensconced in the "archive" available to theatrical biographers. With time, this archive broadened due to an increasingly competitive field for biographers, who were interested in finding new ways to claim their subject's stories and, in effect, to overcome to Cibber's seeming pessimism about the biographical enterprise.

William Hazlitt, writing in 1817, expands upon Cibber's observation by directly linking the ephemerality of acting with the need for a surrogate presence, or for a new presence entirely: he notes that "the genius of a great actor perishes with him, 'leaving the world no copy.'" However, he adds, "This is a misfortune, or at least an unpleasant circumstance, to actors; but it is, perhaps, an advantage to the stage. It leaves an opening to originality [in the form of a new actor who, while replacing an old one, does not seek to be an exact copy]."[6] A careful reading of theatrical biography, with a focus on what the biographer is doing, and how, shows that the theatrical biographer is caught in the bind between Hazlitt's temporally bound call for a "copy" of the actor and for a later occurring "original" to supplant the need for that earlier actor. Ultimately, biographers seek to copy (or reproduce) the actor through the individual author's "original" approach to the subject's life.

This line of thought rests on the belief, buoyed up by close reading of these texts, that theatrical biographers are subject to concerns about temporality and nonpermanence that might otherwise appear to be solved, or at least mitigated, by the existence of a tangible textual artifact (the written biography) in contrast to a fleeting performance on stage. In *The Archive and the Repertoire* (2003), Diana Taylor argues that scholars pay too much attention to the supposed "rift between the written and the spoken word," where from the sixteenth century onward the problem in fact lies with the Western preoccupation with a fixed, reliable (written) archive, in contrast to an ephemeral (performed, bodily) repertoire.[7] In characterizing the written archive as reliable, readers might miss how performative the act of writing can be. Taylor herself alludes to this by noting that an individual entry in the written archive requires a framing device, fashioned by the specific author, and thus never is devoid of political, cultural, or social implications. She observes, too, that repertoire can be self-sustaining, but is less often in the case of individual performers (and never with individual performances); thus, individual performers rely on a written archive as presented by a framer or framers.[8] The present book argues that the framing device, rather than acting adversely against the archive, works alongside it to create a product that functions on multiple levels to record not only the actor, who might otherwise be at risk of being "lost" to time, but also the anxiety of his biographer. In other words, it seems that the theatrical biographer, confronted with the difficult task of preserving a specific thespian and confronting the limits of his own genre and, in some cases, a cadre of rival claimants to his task, became exquisitely aware of his own ephemeral relation to time, and sought the assurance of his own reputation or legacy through his role as biographer.

Marvin Carlson, in *The Haunted Stage* (2001), explains that all performers must confront the "ghosts," or memories held by the audience and by the performer himself, of the previous persons who have played a role, of the previous roles the particular actor has assayed, and of other conditions that overlap with prior performer or spectator memory.[9] He notes that all theatre is thus retrospective, because the audience evaluates the current performance based on past experiences. By amplifying and recontextualizing the temporal concerns of actors, the act of biographical writing becomes a performance more closely allied with theatre itself than with other types of writing or representation. Because theatrical biographers, in the process of completing their projects, are attuned to the actors' temporal challenges as well as to the biographer's own difficulties in trying to contain the actor's performance within the text, the biography preserves two layers of artistic anxiety. These time-related concerns, shared by actors and their biographers, manifest in biography primarily through concerns about originality and competition: the theatrical biographer recognizes the need to be perceived as an artist, and with that, recognizes the threat to an individual's relevance and artistic legacy posed by other practitioners.

Theatrical Biography as a Legitimate Concern

Is theatrical biography subject to a competitive spirit that is not encountered in literary biography or in fiction writing? Many scholars have suggested that the competitive basis of originality can be seen in most artistic genres, but I believe that the theatrical biography treats this conceptual quandary in a special way, both by virtue of its historical conditions and its generic goals.[10]

Although I call upon performance studies scholars, this monograph is primarily one of theatrical and literary history: I am interested in what the biographer is doing, how he perceives his role, and how his readers received these efforts. My project takes its roots from my own challenges in finding criticism that deals with biography outside of literary biography, or the study of famous authors. In the rare instances that the eighteenth-century biographer is afforded any attention as author of the work, the investigation is either fleeting or is focused on Boswell.[11] A survey of the field clearly indicates that biographical studies hold a tremendous bias toward literary biography, and within that, toward more modern biographers. Nonetheless, even very modern literary biography cannot escape the suspicion of generic illegitimacy in the realm of original artistry. In 2000, critic Tom Paulin (who is also a poet and a biographer, notably, of Hazlitt, "the first modern historiographer of fame") attacked Richard Holmes's *Sidetracks: Explorations of a Romantic Biographer* (2000), asking: "Is the biographer an artist who can and should exist on equal terms with the dramatist, fiction writer and poet? The short and robust answer is 'certainly not.'"[12] Currently, many biographies are treated as permanent (if frequently flawed) vessels conveying important knowledge about their subjects rather than as dynamic texts worthy of aesthetic study. Jean Marc Blanchard (1978, p. 668) speaks to this problem by assuming in his criticism that "autobiography is a literary genre, whereas biography is not." Laura Marcus, in *Auto/biographical Discourses* (1994), comments on biography's strange position between history and literature,[13] noting that whereas autobiography is approached as a literary genre, biography "remains very largely untheorized."[14] This division calls to attention the interplay between originality and truth, wherein autobiography is seen as "original" because of its remarkable authenticity, even if it is not always particularly authoritative regarding the truth. In fact, since a remarkable vogue for autobiography in the 1970s, that genre has enjoyed a great deal of scholarly attention, to the point that the majority of theoretical books preferentially focus on the author who writes of herself rather than of another.

My task, then, is at least partially to examine theatrical biography as a proper scholarly concern, to supplement the myriad accounts of autobiography and literary biography. In attempting to account for how the theatrical biographer succeeds and fails at capturing his subject, I hope to reconsider the biographer's potential role as artist rather than as rote recorder. In effect, my project's theoretical makeup combines Jack Stillinger's 1991 attack on the myth of the Romantic author, *Multiple Authorship and the Myth of Solitary Genius,* with Leon Edel's call in his "BIOGRAPHY: A Manifesto" (1978), which claims a spot for the biographer as an artist whose self is recorded within his work. Edel's work is hardly finished. In 2012, biographer Stacy Schiff wrote an article entitled "The Dual Lives of the Biographer," in which she expresses the difficulty of comprehending the unstructured present events in her own life while simultaneously attempting to recreate a seamless narrative of another's (finished) lived experience. Despite Boswell's clearly not strictly applied maxim that the biographer should use solely the subject's words or correspondence to round out the historical record, the reality that the biographer uses himself to fill in gaps in the subject's life—factual or interpretative —is understood. How the biographer might resonate through the absent subject, rather than within pockets of the subject's absence, is less considered.[15] Diana Taylor argues, "The repertoire requires presence"; the authors of theatrical biography, in seeking to enshrine the repertoire within the archive, offer their own presence, to varying effects.[16]

Joseph Roach discusses the public intimacy that arises with the concept of celebrity, a desire that leads to "the general circulation of their images in the absence of their persons [...] a mental mélange of half-remembered public appearances, painted or graphic portraits and bits of anecdotal gossip."[17] He equates the acting process itself with the fans' obsessive attempts to claim access to the entertainer through material trappings vaguely associated with the artist: just as fans substitute images and items for celebrity presence, acting itself is an endless process of auditioning surrogates for an inaccessible original—the character as written, before the first interpretation in live performance.

Both Roach and Carlson, by virtue of their focus on performance studies, are highly attuned to the temporality of criticism and standards: in assessing trends of "natural" acting through several decades of acting theory, Carlson notes a repetitive practice wherein "the father's ghost is passed over but only to summon the ghost of the grandfather."[18] Reviving an old precedent can be an effective technique, as a new performer can do something that has already been done—but has not been seen by the present audience—under the guise of novelty. Thus, even after Davies seems to establish particular criteria for successful theatrical biography, later practitioners such as Congreve will jump backward to a prior precedent for general life writing. The difference is the ease of comparison between fathers and grandfathers when the written text still lingers, even if its popularity has faded.

In staking its own claim for significance as a genre, and within individual efforts to establish lasting supremacy over a given thespian's story, theatrical biography often sought novelty (and, ironically, distinction) by its association with other forms of art, especially the novel, painting, and newspapers. Before examining individual cases of innovation and hybridization (and, in some cases, regression), it may be useful to briefly consider theatrical biography's relation to these three guiding presences, all of which provided inspiration to early practitioners.

The novel as a genre achieves its ascendancy during the lifetime of my project, which spans from 1740 to 1833. The earlier date represents Cibber's *Apology* and the approximate beginning of David Garrick's and Charles Macklin's mainstream London careers, and the later date is determined by James Boaden's final biography of an eighteenth-century thespian. Both the novel and theatrical biography come into focus as genres during the same period. The novel becomes heavily invested in mock biography, and biography borrows from novelistic techniques in order to compete with pure fiction.[19] Moreover, in a quest for perceived authenticity, both genres become interested in material artifacts, taking shape in the novel and in theatrical biography as epistolary correspondence. This trend would eventually mushroom into material collections of letters and artifacts inserted into *Lives* by fans intent on "expanding" the reach or comprehensiveness of their copy of a favorite thespian biography.

Just as novels and theatrical biography seem to have a symbiotic relationship (see, especially, Chapter 1 and Chapter 2 of the present work), painting emerges as a key facilitator of and competitor to theatrical biography's project of preserving the actor's memory.[20] The relationship between the two genres was not just theoretical, but formal, based upon a shared vocabulary. Shearer West argues that the change in acting styles and acting expectations (a circuitous relationship) was greatly affected by the establishment of the Royal Academy of Arts in 1768 and the subsequent development of a critical vocabulary with which to evaluate painting.[21] West's argument extends to the possibility that acting styles shifted partially because of the remodeling of the theatres during actor and theatre manager John Philip Kemble's tenure (a larger space meant more emphasis on sound rather than on facial expression or gesture), but also because periodicals liked to spark competition between actors who might otherwise assay a role very similarly, especially as the vocabulary for critiquing acting began to coalesce, and this vocabulary equally benefited theatrical biography and further linked it to painting and newspapers. It would stand to reason, by extension, that turn-of-the-century biographers got more competitive as their subjects, the actors, sought innovation in their field, and as painters encroached ever closer on biographical prerogative.[22] The fraught but often productive relationship between the two genres will be touched on in Chapter 1 and explored at length in Chapter 3.

A third and particularly advantageous partnership arises between theatrical biography and periodicals. Stuart Sherman, whose work is on newspapers and their effects on eighteenth-century perceptions of time, singles out periodicals as the place "where diurnality and immortality converge."[23] Theatrical biography often started as germs in newspapers, and returned to circulation as bite-sized reductions of a full-length work. It is not coincidental that a surge in theatrical biography occurs in the 1780s, a time when the newspaper obituary becomes a fad; conveniently, 1779 marked the year of the actor David Garrick's death. Garrick carefully curated his own image in newspapers and in other media, and the success of his campaign for immortality became apparent.

Sherman sees in the efforts of Garrick and other thespians a quest to avoid obsolescence: "At stake is the question not only of what press and player might do for each other tomorrow and tomorrow and tomorrow but also of whether the not-altogether-poor player's reputation might outlast, in any way and to any extent, his corporeal hour upon the stage."[24] With the newspaper as Garrick's perpetual-motion machine, print achieved a reputation as a safeguard of reputation, a testimony of having existed and created art. This material documentation is also, I believe, why literary biography seems more legitimate—the art that spurred the biography, and that serves as an extension of the biographical subject's person, is still easily referenced. Furthermore, although newspapers were often thrown away, and easily replaced (an asset for keeping new information circulating about an actor), full-length theatrical biography increasingly became crafted and marketed as a collectible, permanent good—a fixed monument to the actor.

The interest in generating an archive, and the potential to use contributions to that archive as a way of asserting one's own presence in addition to that of the archive's subject, can be seen in readers' interactions with these texts. The final sections of Chapters 1 and 2 investigate readers' responses to a particular thespian biography as manifested in annotations, extra-illustrations, and scrapbooking. Scrapbooking, the most visually stunning and strange of the textual modifications under consideration, entails the cutting and pasting of miscellanea, often including playbills, signatures, portraits and, of course, newspaper articles and cartoons, the latter a further indication of theatrical biography's interrelation with newspapers. Extra-illustrating, an often cleaner and more dignified operation, involves pasting pictures into a copy of a theatrical biography or other work, frequently at an interval in which the subject of the illustration is directly discussed in the text. Finally, annotating is the act of making handwritten notes in the margins of the text, adding a running or occasional commentary to supplement the text. Each of these types of intervention allows a fuller or more focused composite to emerge, catered to the newest "artist's" interests.

I argue that even as they obviously signal investment in the text, these types of interchanges also mark the text as a permanent locus in which one could store objects of value, a repository intended to be preserved and, as we will see, in some cases bequeathed to family members as part of a material legacy. This revision changes, or perhaps opens up, the role of the biographer. Although this line of inquiry is certainly not the focus of the book, ultimately I see the extra-illustrating reader taking up the gauntlet thrown down by the biographer: the reader sees the biographer achieve some fame in his role as recorder and seizes some of that cultural authority and transcendent relevance for himself in becoming, through unauthorized but often passively encouraged material or textual interventions, a co-biographer. This impulse, more collaborative than competitive, not only adds to the fame of a given thespian, but centralizes the material archive, in miniature, within the pages of a given biography. Scrapbooking or annotation, as informal or inconsistent features of certain copies of particular theatrical biographies, complement the consistent formal features of the original text, further aiding the biographer in reaching his goal of preserving the actor.

Overview of Chapters

The study of theatrical biography as a success story necessarily starts with Thomas Davies. After carefully attuning himself to public tastes in biographical writing, Davies tied his product to his own reputation as a gentleman by publicly claiming authorship of his *Memoirs of the Life of David Garrick* at a time when such works were primarily anonymous. Thus, Davies solidified his personal legacy while raising up theatrical biography and establishing a baseline set of expectations for the genre. Simultaneously serving as a tour of trends in shorter theatrical biographical writings and evidence of Davies's genius by comparison, this chapter investigates what set Davies's biography apart from other biographical attempts, shows the state of biographical accounts of Garrick prior to Davies's arrival, and looks at the contents of Davies's work, contemporary reviews, and subsequent attempts by other authors either to unseat or amplify his fame. Davies, through the *Life of Garrick*, sets up an author-focused model for claiming the right to another man's story, which subsequent biographers take advantage of in forming their own conception of a biographer's work and due. The "personal" touches of Davies's biography invited expansion by scrapbookers and extra-illustrators; these new collaborators not only marked their own presence by participating in the text, but also expanded the material archive beyond the original bounds of the text, temporally propelling the narrative forward in time and spatially broadening its initial powers of representation.

As the centerpiece of this book, Chapter 2 examines three back-to-back biographies of the comedian Charles Macklin in order to determine the extent to which theatrical biographers were actually able to represent their subjects' onstage antics (the feasibility of which is limited by time and space). I suggest that the project of crystallizing a dynamic physical performance within a book is not quite as futile as it would seem, because of specific formal features of theatrical biography in the eighteenth century. Conventions in general biographical writing, such as anecdote, and in theatrical criticism, such as "points," engendered these moments of success. In turn, such success overturns, or at least challenges, the view of eighteenth-century theatrical biography as a rote compilation of facts and dates that necessarily fails to deliver the most pressing component of the biographical assignment. In re-presenting these onstage (and offstage) moments, the biographer becomes more closely akin to the actor as an artist himself. Moreover, he becomes more aware of the competitive nature of performance, and thus we see each of Macklin's biographers attempt to hybridize their theatrical biographies with different genres, including literary biography, the novel, and newspaper compilations of anecdotes in order to deliver the best version of Macklin's story. The final section of this chapter follows the work of J. J. Cossart, whose painstaking annotations to one copy of the *Memoirs of Charles Macklin* show how strongly readers identified with the enterprise of using anecdotes, especially, to further bring the stage onto the page.

Following the lead of Chapter 2 in considering that the biographer is an artist, and that the material archive available to him allows for some (limited) success, Chapter 3, rather than being centered on an actor whose story is performed, follows the career of James Boaden as a performer of theatrical biography. Boaden's value is not simply in his unprecedented fecundity, or in his continued relevance to scholars today, but in our ability to track the changes in his approach over five biographies spanning almost a decade (between 1825 and 1833). Boaden generated works on John Philip Kemble, Sarah Siddons, Dorothy Jordan, and Elizabeth Inchbald, as well as a prefatory biography with collected correspondence of David Garrick. Within that period, his subjects' personal correspondence becomes more prominently featured, creating two distinct phases in his biographical output and forcing Boaden to reflect, often quite self-consciously, on the balance between this increase in archival material and his role as biographer. Most importantly, Boaden's insistence on a material record as a hallmark of an increasingly professional school of biography underlines the emphasis on materiality that forms the base assumption of theatrical biography as a project: the translation of ephemera to finiteness, under the watchful eye of an authoritative biographer.[25] At the chapter's conclusion, seemingly having overcome some of the objections to the archive being able to contain performance, Boaden's (and biography's) representative laurels are challenged when Boaden's own son, a painter, declares supremacy of the paintbrush over the pen, questioning the archive's preference for written word over other forms of memory. Unsurprisingly, my book declares Boaden Sr. and biography the winner, but notes that combining painting and text, as so many scrapbooks at the time did, offers the fullest view of a thespian subject.

The epilogue brings the continued theme of materiality forward to the present day by calling to the forefront three more recent "experimental" biographies in which scholars seeking to capture ephemera instead produce a blend of academic study and personal memoir about the research process: these biographies not only participate in the handling the same types of material objects beloved by eighteenth-century theatrical biographers (including anecdotes and complicated schemes to capture a thespian's voice), but also demonstrate the efficacy of a strong authorial presence in helping readers make peace with what has been lost. If the actor is not fully there, whichever biographer is his newest representative is conspicuously, self-consciously, and cheerfully onstage to fill the gap.

Postscript: Forestalling Objections about the Decidedly Masculine Face of the Biographer

Of the biographers whose work I discuss, James Boaden is the name likely to evoke recognition among historians of the long eighteenth century. As a critic, his work surfaces most frequently in the form of brief anecdotes, quotes, and facts taken from his biographies. Even slightly sustained investigations into Boaden's biographies often dismiss him as inaccurate, biased, misogynistic, or tone-deaf.[26] Certainly, charges of Boaden's misogyny have validity, but the fact remains that Boaden's accounts are still in circulation, especially within theatre and performance studies circles. Moreover, in spite of evidence that even his initial audience perceived the problematic nature of his works, at least in part, his representation of the stage undoubtedly affected later readers' perceptions of the time period he covers. My work seeks to situate Boaden and his fellow biographers—especially Macklin's biographers, who are all but unheard of, excepting Cooke—in a deeper context than a quoted anecdote or cited inaccuracy. Additionally, I emphasize the extent to which theatrical biography, while theoretically a fact-based project, bears the permanent stamp of its maker, like so many other genres, and thus cannot be read as unbiased fact.[27]

I freely, if regretfully, admit that the present project all but excludes female voices from primary sources, but the omission is due, in part, to the relative scarcity of biographies about actresses.[28] The main accounts of eighteenth-century female biography are actually autobiographies, and thus do not participate in the same phenomenon of competition between subject and author. The dichotomy of women participating in autobiographical speech and biographical silence is explored in my third chapter, in which James Boaden acts as biographer to Sarah Siddons, Dorothy Jordan, and Elizabeth Inchbald, mediating each actress's presence differently, depending on the amount of autobiographical documentation available.[29]

In fact, a number of the biographers featured in this project made a conscientious effort to preserve female actresses in capsule-length biographies within the larger biography. While such capsule biographies often lack nuance and treat women in stereotypical ways, these moments provide some of the most concrete evidence of certain actresses who might otherwise have been lost to memory. Thus, Boaden and his cohort have become almost required fare for scholars interested in recovering minor female actresses. Actress's and biographer's names are thus forever intertwined in quoted material, preserving the actress at the cost of perpetuating the problematic but inescapable fame of her (male) biographer.

Chapter 1

"DAVIES'S NAME […] IN FAME'S BRIGHTEST PAGE SHALL ON GARRICK ATTEND": FROM ANONYMOUS TO PERSONALIZED PARTICIPATION IN THE *MEMOIRS OF THE LIFE OF DAVID GARRICK*

Johnson and Davies

In October 1780, a poetic review in *Town and Country Magazine* reflecting on the recently published and immediately popular *Memoirs of the Life of David Garrick, Esq.*, by Thomas Davies declared:

> As long as old Time on this globe shall remain,
> My Shakespeare and Garrick unrival'd shall reign […]
> While Davies's name as historian and friend,
> In Fame's brightest page shall on Garrick attend.[1]

This poem added a new twist to the established story of Garrick as Shakespeare's champion and preserver; namely, it created a space for Thomas Davies, promoting the role of the biographer as an artist who might be able to approach—and be worthy of—the fame of a Shakespeare or a Garrick. Such a conception established the possibility that the biographer could appear in the annals of time, as the life historian joined the pantheon of exalted British artists. Davies's name thus became a symbol of the fame to be won from biography. In these pages, I argue that this phenomenon led directly to a burgeoning politics of competition among biographers visualizing their work as self-advancing, professional art rather than anonymous, collaborative record-keeping (although, as discussed later, it would leave room for readers' participation).

By all rights, this chapter should be about Samuel Johnson's *Memoirs of Garrick*.

After all, the eventual *Memoirs of the Life of David Garrick, Esq. Interspersed with Characters and Anecdotes of His Theatrical Contemporaries* began as his brainchild. Johnson and Garrick had a long and storied history, having come from more humble origins to London together as teacher and student, respectively. Boswell suggests that Garrick's meteoric success, vanity, name-dropping, and affected ways irked the rather irritable Johnson, who jealously worried that his own fame, garnered as a literary critic, author, and man of wit, might be eclipsed by his pupil—an actor! Johnson was not a fan of theatre, Boswell speculates, especially after the failure of Johnson's play *Irene*; moreover, Garrick and Johnson's attempts to collaborate seemed to be star-crossed, likely due to neither man tolerating criticism well.[2] Nonetheless, the two men remained friends, and Johnson was known to have a particular soft spot for his onetime student.

His own close affiliation with Garrick, including his enviable advantage in tracing Garrick's early years, would seem to position Johnson as an ideal biographer. In fact, it was Johnson who authored *Rambler No. 60* and *Idler No. 84*, two of the most foundational documents of biographical theory, and he declared in *Rambler No. 60*: "The business of the biographer is often to pass slightly over those performances and incidents of vulgar greatness, to lead the thoughts into domestic privacies, and display the minute details of daily life.[3] It might stand to reason that Johnson demurred because he did not wish to dwell on Garrick's "performances and incidents of vulgar greatness," which would be required if he wished to comply with the Cibberian desire to re-create the actor onstage. However, the truth is infinitely more intriguing, and does not require Johnson to be unduly charitable or self-effacing: Gerald M. Berkowitz acknowledges that Johnson was "the logical choice for Garrick's first biographer," but explains that "Mrs. Garrick rejected him."[4]

Because he quite obviously believed not only in the general project of thespian biography, but also in the specific need to document David Garrick's life, Johnson hand-selected the very man to do the job—Thomas Davies, an unassuming, generous-spirited bookseller from Garrick's outer circle, whose name would ascend into "Fame's brightest page" as the author of the *Memoirs of the Life of David Garrick*.[5] Unlikely as it seemed, Davies's account not only answered Johnson's demand, but also held sway as the supreme biography of Garrick for well over two hundred years, surviving a number of attempts by other authors to capsize Davies's claim to Garrick's story. Many factors contributed to the success of Davies's biography, including the popular subject, the rise of cheaper printed materials, the subject's interest in self-promotion, and the choice of biographer, but this chapter will follow Johnson's lead in considering the last factor—the biographer—to be of greatest importance.[6]

This chapter situates Davies in the center of a continuum of biographical installations about David Garrick in order to show how Davies successfully mediated competing and developing theories about what should be included in thespian biographies, further formalizing the features that led to success. Succinctly put, Davies appeared to have learned valuable lessons from his predecessors: he reintroduces the "history of the stage" aspect that had brought Cibber great success but subsequently had been ignored by other biographers; presents specific moments of greatness in an actor's onstage presentation, thus better memorializing the thespian in question; and, most important, he attaches his name and reputation to the project, changing the former understanding of a biographer's relation to his work. Davies's innovations evoked numerous responses, many of which challenge the earlier-established balance of agency between a biographer and his subject and, eventually, his readers, who increasingly took Davies's cue in personalizing the narrative.

A brief sketch of Mr. Davies, and his motivations considered

If, as I contend, the biography was particularly successful due not just to what Davies actually produced, but also to the public perception of Davies, it might be useful to consider Davies's qualifications and the context in which the subject, time, and author came together under the watchful prompting of Dr. Johnson.

Davies was born in Scotland, likely in 1712. He was an actor by trade, achieving some recognition in London for his role as the original Wilmot in Lillo's *The Fatal Curiosity* in 1736. He began dabbling in bookselling during the immediate aftermath of the Licensing Act of 1737, having foreseen increasingly difficult working conditions for thespians. Davies maintained a presence onstage but, according to Johnson (as reported by Boswell), he was driven from the stage in 1762 based on a succinct but graphic critical appraisal by Charles Churchill in May 1761.[7] Davies returned to being a bookseller, a trade that, like acting, was still in transition as a less than gentlemanly profession, but which he must have viewed as a safe haven. It was at his shop at 8 Russell Street, Covent Garden (conveniently located in the theatre district), that he had the pleasure of introducing his friend Johnson to Boswell in 1763. As a bookseller, Davies maintained a high reputation for his general sociability and quality products.[8] Writing to editor John Nichols, Davies recalls writing "a silly pamphlet" in 1742, and subsequently "was smit with the desire of turning author," a task to which he did not really devote himself until the 1770s.[9]

The *Memoirs of the Life of Garrick* represents a break from Davies's earlier authorial efforts, not only in scope but also in terms of publicity. He had shown interest in Garrick as early as 1776, when he wrote a much-republished article on Garrick under the pseudonym "Leonato." In 1777, Davies anonymously wrote a pamphlet-like memoir of John Henderson, "The Bath Roscius," which sold for a shilling and required two editions.[10] A shorter biography, the *Life and Writings of Philip Massinger*, appeared—also anonymously—in 1779. Thus, the *Memoirs of the Life of David Garrick*, published in early 1780, was the first work for which Davies formally claimed authorship. The first edition of this two-volume theatrical biography, published barely a year after the great actor's death in January 1779, promises that, in addition to Garrick's life, it will supply a collection of interesting anecdotes and no less than the history of the English stage for the past thirty-six years—a remarkable undertaking that proved very successful. Cheryl Wanko notes that *Memoirs of the Life of David Garrick* was advertised for ten shillings; one shilling was the average price of a theatrical biography unless the text were particularly lengthy, already bound, or on a subject of great popularity. For reference, she adds, a ticket to sit in the boxes at the theatre around the same time was five shillings, so the price was still rather reasonable compared to other entertainment.[11]

Having emerged as an established and well-liked author based on the *Memoirs of the Life of David Garrick*, Davies wrote a final work, also under his own name: 1783–84's *Dramatic Miscellanies*, which appears to have been completed as a response to bankruptcy stemming from overly indulgent business practices.[12] Davies died on May 5, 1785, having personally overseen four editions of his *Memoirs of the Life of David Garrick*, a strong testimony to his success as a biographer.

From this capsule biography emerge some qualifications on the part of Davies, strengths that the author himself does eventually iterate, after effusive praise of Samuel Johnson, whose doctrines on biography Davies seems to have sought to obey. Davies cites his own "long acquaintance with the stage, and an earnest inclination to excel in the profession of acting [… which] afforded me an opportunity to much of plays and theatrical history."[13] His earlier (anonymous) biographical efforts, his shop's proximity to the Covent Garden theatre, and his own awareness as a bookseller about the public's interests go without reference. Later readers have recognized Davies's vocational advantages. Wanko states, "Davies was ideally positioned for accessing printed material about Garrick, for knowing what readers wanted from biography, and for being able to provide the commercial support his venture required."[14] Davies, as a bookseller, could have anticipated the market for a Garrick biography by grangerizers eager to connect more closely with Garrick, two samples of which we will see at the end of this chapter.[15]

It is this relatively modest, but perceptive man, known as "honest Tom Davies," who steps in as the father of theatrical biography, building on a heritage established by the genre's grandfather, Colley Cibber. Cibber's auto-biographical *Apology for the Life of Colley Cibber* promised—and delivered—a history of the stage from the Restoration until the book's publication date of 1740. A key feature of the comparatively high attraction of Garrick for thespian biographers is the way in which his narrative conveniently maps onto Cibber's timeline. Readers could take in the entirety of the London stage as mediated through Cibber from 1660 to 1740 (Cibber arrived onstage in 1690), and immediately segue into the next year, 1741, with Garrick's debut at Goodman's Fields Theatre, up through his death in 1779. Thus, the two works taken together represent over one hundred years of British theatre history, clustered around two seminal figures. Certainly, a prospective biographer would be intrigued by the obvious temporal tie-in with the beloved *Apology*—a chance to join his own book to Cibber's established masterpiece.

In the tradition of biographers being seen as hack writers who compiled huge unrelated volumes of material about a recently deceased person for easy money, references to Davies's biography of Garrick frequently remark on the author's financial difficulties. James Boswell cattily recalls that Johnson gave Davies the idea of writing a Garrick memoir in order to secure the financial stability that the well-intended bookseller could not seem to find in his trade, noting that Johnson had looked down on Davies's short-sighted decision to abandon his rather lucrative acting career in 1762.[16] It is evident from Davies's comments that Johnson commissioned him to write the biography, but based on Mrs. Garrick's attitude toward Johnson, the task would hardly be easy money for a potential biographer, even with Johnson's support.[17]

Wanko seems to suggest that Davies's motivation—and, indeed, any theatrical biographer's motivation—for writing about a chosen thespian is to absorb some of the subject's cultural authority. As David Garrick held the greatest amount of cultural authority among contemporary thespians, Davies would thus stand to gain the maximum transferable allotment of that authority. Theoretically, cultural authority would then be a means to one of two ends: riches—already discussed and, to a certain extent, conceded to—or "immortality." The applicability of this latter goal can be assessed based on the ways that Davies does or does not allude to future readership or to his own intended reputation, especially in light of Davies's use of a pseudonym in an early Garrick biographical effort. Fame is a motivation to be seriously pondered in the context of the much-publicized *Memoirs of the Life of David Garrick*, as Garrick would, on the surface, be one subject who would seem to practically guarantee long-lasting relevance.

George Winchester Stone Jr., who in 1979 became Garrick's fourteenth biographer (alongside coauthor George M. Kahrl), identified another possible motive for Davies's investment in Garrick in a 1975 paper in which he attempted to address the sustained interest in versions of Garrick's life story. Remarking on the contrast between Davies and Arthur Murphy, author of Garrick's second full-length biography, Stone notes, "Davies sought, but not very hard, to counteract the impression, saddled upon the actor by contemporary detractors, that Garrick was over-vain as an actor, avaricious and mean as a manager. Murphy destroyed the Davies defense."[18] Certainly, as will be discussed later, Murphy's biography was written not only as a monument to David Garrick (and to the author himself) but also as a conscious rebuttal to Davies.

As we will see from contemporary responses to Davies's biography, some readers felt that the author was unnecessarily generous to Garrick to the point of denying character weaknesses that were quite thoroughly documented by other sources. This last motivation—that Davies was attempting to create a positive and lasting tribute to an admired actor—seems in keeping with his generally well-tempered treatment of Garrick. Davies and Garrick worked alongside each other as fellow actors and then as actor and actor-manager; Davies had direct access to Garrick and had an intimate knowledge of his professional decisions that would not have been available to other potential biographers. He was capable of describing what Garrick did onstage not just from the vantage point of an audience member, but as a trained colleague. Furthermore, Davies might have recognized in himself a superior cache of personal knowledge and access to etchings, playbills, and other materials that made the approach to that particular subject easier or more preferable to other potential subjects he might have chosen. Ultimately, Davies proved he had superior knowledge and understanding of generic expectations when contrasted to the main biographical materials available about Garrick prior to 1780.

The Earlier Biographies of Garrick

As we have surveyed Thomas Davies in brief, it may be useful to get a picture of the biographical subject, David Garrick, both in terms of our retrospective knowledge of the actor and in terms of the publications circulating prior to Davies's account, in order to see not only why Garrick made an ideal candidate for those with a biographical impulse, but also why Davies's book—and Davies's name—achieved such ascendancy within theatrical biography.

An enduring trope of theatrical biography, when dealing with an actor whose work might not have been seen by the reading audience, is to compare

him to a present-day actor.[19] It is safe to say that there is presently no congru-
ent turn of the twenty-first century thespian, as, if accounts are to be believed,
he would need to have the facial elasticity of a mid-1990s Jim Carrey with the
credibility of a Philip Seymour Hoffman and the proprietary control over his
own career like a Ron Howard.[20] He would also have to be responsible for fostering the cult of a well-liked but hardly sacred actor-author, as Garrick did for
Shakespeare. Fundamentally, there is no immediate parallel to David Garrick
because of the almost universal acknowledgment of his contemporaries that
he was the most popular and gifted actor to stand on the stage during his century. Although a small number of present-day thespians rise to the top of the
profession, we can claim no such consensus as the eighteenth century could
about David Garrick.

Garrick was constantly yoked to the adjective "natural," as his acting style
represented a "revolution" from the loudly artificial declamations of James
Quin's generation.[21] Not only was Garrick the foremost actor, innovator of acting theory, manager of one of the two most successful playhouses in England,
and author of a number of well-received plays and adaptations, he was also
one of the first "modern" celebrities to diligently control his own image, propagating an astonishing number of portraits and other "Garrickiana" (artifacts
including letters, pendants, statuettes, and the like) and working alongside the
newspapers to shape his reputation. Remarkably friendly, if understandably
egotistical, he was also known for being quite entertaining offstage. Kalman
A. Burnim, offering a brief introduction to viewers of the permanent Folger
Shakespeare Library online Garrick exhibit, describes Garrick as "one of the
most astonishing British personalities in a time and country brimming with
astonishing personalities."[22]

If comparisons to other actors were one lodestar by which eighteenth-
century writers described their thespian subjects, another was the anecdote: a
brief and frequently representative story designed to catch the essence of a
character's attitude (and, not infrequently, movement). In the tradition of
long-winded anecdote tellers, the reader surely won't mind if I supply this
delightfully telling anecdote about David Garrick:

> The last time that Garrick was at Paris, Preville [considered to be the
> most accomplished comedian in French theatre] invited him to his villa.
> [...] Our Roscius being in a gay humour, proposed to travel in one
> of the hired coaches that go to Versailles, on which road the villa of
> Preville was situated. When they got in, he ordered the coachman to
> drive on, who answered he would do so as soon as he got his comple-
> ment of four passengers. A droll whim immediately seized Garrick, and
> he determined to give his brother player a specimen of his art. While

the coachman, therefore, was attentively plying for passengers, Garrick slipped out of the door, went round the coach, and by his wonderful command of countenance, a power which he so happily displayed in [the role of] Abel Drugger, palmed himself upon the coachman as another passenger. This he did twice, and was admitted each time as a fresh passenger, to the astonishment and admiration of Preville. He [Garrick] whipped out a third time, and addressing himself to the coachman, was answered in a surly tone, "that he had already got his complement" – and would have driven off without him, had not Preville called out, that as the stranger appeared to be a very little man, they would, to accommodate the gentleman, contrive to make room.[23]

In attempting to identify who David Garrick was through this anecdote, we can gather that Garrick traveled extensively, rubbing shoulders with other renowned actors. He obviously had a particular sense of humor, enjoyed showing off, and was extremely convincing in his ability to try on different personae without a costume change or much in the way of a pause. Physically, the anecdote notes, Garrick was "a very little man"; this detail is verified by a number of sources that attempt to make amends for this shortcoming. Socially, we gather that his friends appreciated Garrick's company, as Preville could have chosen to leave Garrick behind once the show was over. There is also a sense that Garrick might not have known when to stop a joke, so keen was he on the opportunity to outdo himself. These impressions seem accurate in light of much more extended biographical readings. Thus, the anecdote achieves its goal of amusing and illustrating: we can imagine the slight Garrick "whipping" out of the coach to ply his trade in pursuit of Preville's approval. Moreover, even in such a brief snapshot, one can see that Garrick must have been a figure of enormous interest to his audiences and contemporaries. In fact, it was not too long into Garrick's arrival on the London scene that he began popping up in novels, slowly edging from existing in a group of anecdotal encounters or character sketches to being the subject of full-length biography.[24] There were undoubtedly numerous accounts of Garrick's life in the form of small stories in the newspapers and gossip around town, and four particularly prominent instances of life-writing about the famous actor predate Davies's biography and appear to have been widely read; they would have formed a core of examples, facts, and approaches for Davies's consideration as he wrote his biography.

The earliest Garrick protobiographical attempt, *The Juvenile Adventures of David Ranger*, from 1757, is actually an initially anonymous novel designed to be taken as a biography. Later it was revealed to be written by Edward Kimber. This "biographical" novel not only confirms Garrick's popularity as

a potential biographical subject, but also limns the struggle of theatrical biography against being subsumed by other genres. The second effort, upon the
event of Garrick's retirement in 1776, is a newspaper article that enjoyed wide
distribution. It is attributed to "Leonato," which, as mentioned earlier, was a
pseudonym adapted by Davies solely in the context of writing about Garrick.
As such, this biographical writing serves as an outline for the later full-length
work and establishes Davies's investment in writing about Garrick well before
the traditional time that ushered in would-be biographers, the subject's death.
The third example, published in the initial aftermath of Garrick's passing
in 1779, is a pamphlet, *The Life and Death of David Garrick, Esq., the Celebrated
English Roscius,* written by someone called the "Old Comedian." Here, we see
an extending of the shorter narratives into a more sustained attempt at theatrical biography, and an obvious understanding of some of the key features
that biographies were expected to possess by audiences growing more familiar
with the genre (and more demanding of its authors). The final example is a
serialized newspaper piece on Garrick that appeared around the same time as
the Old Comedian's pamphlet. This newspaper "obituary-biography," titled
"Biographical Anecdotes of the Late Mr. Garrick," produced under the auspices of John Nichols, editor of the *Gentleman's Magazine,* appears to be one of
the first sustained biographical farewells to a deceased celebrity, and it highlights the helpful yet competitive relationship that both aided and threatened
the production of theatrical memoir books.

While tracing a teleology from the hint of a Garrick biography expressed
by Kimber's *Juvenile Adventures of David Ranger* to the outline by Leonato, and
then to the two more realized but nonetheless rather bare-bones accounts
offered by the Old Comedian and the *Gentleman's Magazine*—efforts that would
eventually find fuller iteration in Davies's memorable *Memoirs*—a catalogue of
these early short biographies also reveals that each attempt was either anonymous or employed a pseudonym, including the 1776 writings of Davies himself. Such uncoupling of an author from his work would seem contrary to
my earlier argument that theatrical biography was not only a project in com-
memorating a favorite fallen thespian, but also one in securing a bit of the
limelight for the author. In fact, a survey of thespian biographies that were
written prior to 1780 reveals only a handful of biographies explicitly boasting
an author, and of those, a number turn out to be pen names.[25] In an inter-
mediary position is the unscrupulous publisher Edmund Curll, who identified
himself at various times as author, compiler, or publisher of several theatrical
biographies and pseudobiographies in the 1730s and in at least one instance
used a pseudonym.[26]

Not only did theatrical biography primarily occur under conditions of anonymity for its authors, but it also occupied a less legitimate generic position,

as many of its practitioners, once revealed, turned out to be hack writers (the idea being that the compiler hacked large chunks of extant documents and facts into a barely coherent whole, rather like the process of producing a hot dog). With the liminal context of theatrical biography in mind, we can now consider the first attempt at a theatrical biography of David Garrick.

Generic conflation: The Juvenile Adventures of David Ranger (1757)

The first example of earlier biographical efforts to feature Garrick is actually a novel. Although not technically a biography, the *The Juvenile Adventures of David Ranger* is crucial not just for seeing how similar novels and theatrical biography might be, but for highlighting the surprising eighteenth-century perception of the less-developed genre of theatrical biography's supremacy over the novel. This preference is surprising when we think of today's popular perception of the supremacy of fiction (especially novels) over fact (biography).[27] The permeability between novels and biography not only suggests biography's tendency to mirror or cull from other literary traditions as it finds its own generic footing, but also, in this context, indicates a sustained interest in Garrick as a subject through whatever literary means were available.

George B. Bryan's *Stage Lives; A Bibliography and Index to Theatrical Biographies in English* (1985) identifies *The Juvenile Adventures of David Ranger* as the first chronological full-length biography of David Garrick, obviously imagining "Ranger" to be a code name for our thespian. Garrick had indeed played a character named "Ranger" onstage, so the name would have been associated with the actor. Upon perusal, the work is a picaresque novel playing into an understood public interest in information about David Garrick, who had been the ornament of the London stage since 1741. This confusion is not surprising.[28]

The novel was written by Edward Kimber, an established author of "ramble" novels in the spirit of Henry Fielding; Kimber's novels were always presented anonymously but were rather easily identifiable as his work. His anonymous approach allied him with the conventions of theatrical biography at the time. By withholding his name and the immediate association with ramble novels, Kimber contributed to the potential illusion of the work as legitimate biography.[29]

A reviewer from the *Monthly Review* acknowledges the duplicity of the piece's author in hitching his novel to Garrick's coattails and periwig: "The title of this Novel seems to have been contrived to prepossess the public with expectations of its containing anecdotes relating to the celebrated Manager of one of our Theatres Royal; but this, to borrow a late fashionable phrase, was all a Humbug."[30] A second review of the *Juvenile Adventures* in the *Critical Review* of November 1756 echoes the frustration of Kimber's bait-and-switch tactics, which include, most obviously, the title of the piece. The reviewer proclaims Kimber's technique as "a mean artifice apparently made use of to mislead the reader into an opinion, that these are the secret memoirs of our modern Roscius."[31] (Indeed, a secret memoir would not be out of character: Garrick had a tendency to write his own reviews and criticisms anonymously, including, most famously, a 1765 fable called *The Sick Monkey*, in which he grievously insults himself for his prolonged absences from the theatre before anyone else has the opportunity to do so.) The Article XIX reviewer grudgingly acknowledges a few rather general similarities between Garrick and Ranger: both are leading actors who become managers. An instance of more specific homage sees Ranger marry a "Miss Tulip," surely in imitation of Garrick's bride, Eva Maria Violetti. Beyond these unsubtle parallels, according to the reviewer:

> The character hath not the least resemblance to the person so artfully squinted at in the first page of it, being nothing but a heap of ridiculous adventures, and some bad poetry by the author; with scraps of plays, ballads, &c. quoted to eke out a trifling and miserable performance; food for idle templars, raw prentices, and green girls, that support the circulating libraries of this learned metropolis.[32]

The accusation of random documents compiled under the guise of relevance is not out of place among actual theatrical biographies. However, a reader who sampled even the first few pages of the novel (after the prolonged, hyperbolic invocation of the muses, no less) would have known it was not a true biography, as some of the most basic facts of David Ranger's beginnings did not correspond with known facts of Garrick's, such as the year of his birth.

Yet at times it would be easy for a reader to lapse into considering what he read to be about Garrick, as Ranger occupied a similar space in the world as Garrick did. Filling in a potential fantasy about how David Garrick was "discovered" before he was an established actor, Kimber offers an anecdote about how David Ranger's unique talent came to be onstage. A stage manager, overhearing Ranger rehearse a few moving lines of a play in a coffee shop with his friends, "struck with hearing him [...] broke into the coffee-room, with G – d – n me, gentlemen, what have you got a *Powel* or a *Booth* amongst you, or has *Betterton* once more revisited these earthly mansions?"[33] Such a situation is believable based on the historical records about Garrick and the type of content ideally to be found in a theatrical biography. However, while the verisimilitude is intentional, it is not designed to foster any lasting confusion, relying on far-fetched coincidences described in purposefully overwrought romantic language.[34]

An argument can—and should—be made that theatrical biography took many of its cues, including its often overblown rhetorical style, from ramble novels and epistolary pseudoautobiographies. Nonetheless, it seems that magazine critics felt a significant threat from books that professed to be of one genre and then unabashedly betrayed that genre's stated intent, and books that ranged over a series of genres to become a miscellaneous collection while purporting to have unity. We get the impression, too, that biography was seen as superior to the novel at the time, with the reviewer from the *Monthly Critic* reflecting a rather unstrained admiration for the intelligence of the author's generic ploy, which interested the reviewer initially and led him to discover a tolerable story line despite the absence of the biographical Garrick:

> The work is by no means the most contemptible of the kind we have lately been obliged to peruse: It abounds with adventures, and is not altogether ill-written; the Author for being so much of a Scholar, as to understand Latin, which is more than the generality of our modern Authors, in that branch of Literature, especially, can boast.[35]

This reviewer singles out *David Ranger*'s author as being unexpectedly learned for the "branch of literature" his work occupied, and the second reviewer denigrates the *Ranger* novel as suitable only for the most unsophisticated readers, which is historically unjust.[36]

Besides the feeling of defensiveness that arises from the uncomfortable proximity of biography to novels, the significant conclusion to be drawn from these reviews is the evident desire for biographical material about David Garrick, an attraction that is consistently painted as diametrically opposed to what is mistakenly perceived as the low-brow desire for poorly written novelistic entertainment. The purity of the generic expectations underlying the reviews is undercut by the first reviewer's thwarted desire for anecdote, rather than a true narrative, and the second reviewer's obvious fascination with a "secret diary" of David Garrick, the reality of which would constitute a brutal exposure of the parts of the thespian's life specifically coded as private by many of the "gentlemanly" biographers. It is notable, also, that *David Ranger* appeared so far in advance of Garrick's death (twenty-three years earlier than that event), since another generally observed understanding up to that point was that biographies were most appropriately issued shortly after a subject's decease. Even if *David Ranger* was not a true biography, it did perhaps put into the mind that biographical treatments need not always be reserved for the dead; moreover, its critical response supported a hierarchy that, for a time,

ranked biography as superior to the novel. With the importance of technical theatrical biography growing, the next notable effort to co-opt a piece of
Garrick's fame would be a timid effort by Davies himself.

Testing the waters: Leonato/Davies's "Eulogium on Mr. Garrick's Leaving the Stage" (1776)

The indignant clamor for a sustained biography of Garrick would not be
answered for some time, but its future author capitalized on a surge of interest
above the usual appetite for all things Garrick when the actor announced his
retirement. In July 1776, a three-page article, "A Eulogium on Mr. Garrick's
Leaving the Stage," appeared in the *St. James's Evening Post,* and shortly thereafter appeared five more times—two occasions in the *Gentleman's Magazine* and
once each in the *Lottery Magazine, Hibernian Magazine,* and the *Scots Magazine*—
in identical or slightly altered forms under the same title of "Eulogium," simply "Garrick," or "A Review of the Theatrical Career of the English Roscius."
The author, in all instances, signed his work with the pseudonym "Leonato."

Leonato's brief biography of Garrick is significant not only in the volume of replication or the number of magazines in which it appeared, but
also because, as mentioned earlier, it was the work of Thomas Davies, and it
foreshadowed some of the formal features to be found in the later full-length
biography.[37] A comparison of the July 1776 article and Davies's book-length
Memoirs of the Life of David Garrick of 1780 shows definitive proof that the article served as an outline for the book, contributing not just opinions and talking
points, but also specific phrases and entire paragraphs that can be seen having
a second life in the famous biography.

As a short article, the "Eulogium" attempts to include the basic narrative
of Garrick's career arc and his character as actor, author, and manager—a
capsule biography, indeed. Its purpose is forthrightly announced: "How he
[Garrick] acquired and preserved the applause, love, and admiration of the
people, we shall here endeavor to recollect."[38] The article's narrative begins
in what will be Chapter Three of *Memoirs of the Life of David Garrick*, explaining the state of the theatre as Garrick found it. Davies's early opinions on
Garrick's immediate predecessor, Quin, are unchanged in *Memoirs of the Life.*[39]
Similarly, Leonato and Davies describe Garrick's rapid ascendency identi-
cally: "The coaches of the nobility filled up the spaces from Temple-Bar to
Goodman's-Fields. Not to admire Garrick, would have argued not only want
of taste, but the grossest stupidity."[40] Garrick's ability to transition through
emotion is painted as his highest virtue by both authors.[41] That "his first care
was to restore Nature" by reviving Shakespeare appears in both writings, similarly phrased.[42] The latter half of Leonato's work shows the budding of a

conciliatory, sometimes defensive, attitude toward Garrick's perceived faults, and while the opinions are the same as in the character sketch and body of the *Memoirs of the Life of David Garrick*, Davies seems to have broadened his analysis with examples to the point that close paraphrase or direct quotation from the compressed "Eulogium" were not functional choices. Nonetheless, a reader can certainly see a distilled version of the categorization of Garrick's life and opinions thereof that would be writ large in the later, less spatially restricted, *Memoirs of the Life of David Garrick*.

While the chance to see an outline of the *Memoirs of the Life* in the "Eulogium" of four years earlier is interesting in and of itself, especially in terms of those details that Davies felt were worth the space in the remarkably compact article, the evidence of sustained interest in Garrick's life is significant. It is quite possible that Davies had already, at this point, begun to give thought to a *Life of Garrick*.[13] Of course, Davies ultimately relegated Leonato to the 1770s, boldly proclaiming his authorship with the first edition of *Memoirs of the Life of David Garrick* in 1780 and eventually advertising his status as Garrick's biographer on the title pages of other works. The relationship between Davies's named and anonymous works suggests a very conscious decision about when to associate a work with his own name, and a burgeoning understanding of how Davies could build his own fame through his works.[44]

Defining moments in genre: Garrick by the "Old Comedian" (1779)

By the time David Garrick died in January 1779, the conception of what should be included as part of theatrical biography appears to have been manifestly clear: there should be a primarily chronological narrative, in which anecdotes feature heavily, followed by a character sketch. Most importantly, there should be some sustained effort to describe *how* the actor worked his magic in particular scenes—something that earlier biographers tended not to attempt, but which the "Old Comedian" (the pen name of our third representation of biographical Garrickiana) strives to do in two shining sustained examples that seem to have resonated with Davies when he went forward to extend his biographical sketch of Garrick into a book-length work. The work of the Old Comedian shows a struggle toward a yet-unrealized unity between the expected components of a theatrical biography.

The Life and Death of David Garrick Esq., the Celebrated English Roscius by the Old Comedian offers—in addition to the life—a number of documents related to Garrick, as well as "Anecdotes, Bon Mots, &c." of many theatrical performers, along with the *Life of Edward Alleyn*, the Roscius of Shakespeare's time, as a sort of B-side feature, now supplanted by Garrick as the present-day Roscius.

Alas, the Old Comedian, assuming the title of editor, more closely approaches what Wanko calls "the familiar Curllian compilation method" than what I will term Daviesian synthesis, where the same basic features are more consistently and proportionally blended together.[45] The Old Comedian's biography is a motley assortment of primary sources, the actual narrative of the biography spanning nine pages, two of which are a transcript of Garrick's speech as he retired from the stage, and four of which focus on Garrick's great moment of Bardolitry, the Stratford Jubilee, a multiday festival held in Shakespeare's hometown that both celebrated the Bard and, as Toothill claims, highlighted Garrick's status as his closest living embodiment.[46] The Jubilee was a significant milestone in Garrick's life and public perception, but the Old Comedian greatly overemphasizes mundane details of the proceedings, such as "Mrs. Garrick danced a minuet in a most graceful manner, and joined in the country dances."[47] More intriguingly, the Old Comedian figuratively dissects the deceased actor, with brief sections devoted to his figure (short), face (expressive), voice (clear, resonant) and education (cultivated). Garrick was able to separate his characters, says the Comedian, and his passions were, such that "If he was angry, so was you; if he was distressed, so was you; if he was terrified, so was you; if he was merry, so was you; if he was mad, so was you. He was an enchanter and led you where he pleased."[48]

This abbreviated biography shows the strengths and weaknesses endemic to the genre. The dissected character sketches provide moments of vivid description, while the narrative tends to get bogged down by some "necessary" digression. But the Old Comedian shows a glimmer of inspiration in assessing what made each character of Garrick's stand out, even pointing to a particular line in *Hamlet*: "In that picturesque display in Hamlet, of the poor parade of vestimental mourning, compared to the general grief of an affected heart, who could hear him without sympathy repeat, 'But I have that *within* which *passeth* shew.'"[49] This attempt to isolate how Garrick worked onstage, particularly in terms of vocal emphasis, is a matter of no small struggle to good theatrical biographers, a difficulty remarked on in detail in the second chapter of the present work.[50] Intriguingly, the Old Comedian also cites a particular point of weakness in Garrick's delivery, "a way of resting in the middle of a line, where the sense is continued":

We have a striking instance of it in King Richard, where, in the heat of his fury, he calls out to his archers, "Draw, archers, draw, your arrows to the head." This line ought to be spoken with rapidity, and the whole force of the voice reserved for the last word; instead of this Mr. Garrick bestowed so much breath on the three first, that he was forced to pause to get in more to speak the rest with, and accordingly he always pronounced the line with an unnatural gap in the middle, "Draw, archers, draw – your arrows to the head."[51]

The Old Comedian additionally comments on Garrick's occasional stiff prolixity, and courtship of laughter "where the author never intended it."[52]

The Old Comedian's contribution to the body of knowledge about Garrick and strategies of presentation and organization seems principally to be in his analysis of how Garrick actually spoke and moved in a specific scene. As I have suggested, two key features that seem to mark Davies's biography as superior to prior attempts are the synthesis of materials into a cogent narrative and the treatment of actors' onstage antics. The Old Comedian provides a cautionary tale of the importance of the former, and a fleeting example of excellence in the latter. Apparently the Old Comedian's efforts were not sufficient for an audience that was developing a more keenly delineated appreciation for—and expectation of—the genre. A review in the *Westminster Magazine* in April 1779 features an unusually succinct verdict: "It would not be worth anyone's while to have lived or died, to be so biographised."[53] It seems that audiences wanted a comprehensiveness that not only sustained the focus of its main character, but also included a whole host of extras; readers expected a narrative arc that made room for capacious flights of fancy that nonetheless did not overwhelm the main through line. In short, Davies's task was to enter an underdeveloped field populated with rather flimsy models and contradictory expectations.

Serialized anonymous "Biographical Anecdotes of the Late Mr. Garrick" (1779)

A novel early in his career, a eulogium upon his retirement, and a short biography at his death showed the audience's interest in Garrick throughout his days on the English stage. Lacking a true full-length biography of the intriguing actor, readers looking for anecdotal reports of Garrick would have found plenty of reports in the newspapers. To the pleasure of Garrick, these accounts were forthcoming even during his lifetime, incrementally memorializing the actor in anticipation of his eventual absence. As Stuart Sherman points out in his article on the brilliance of Garrick's media manipulation, newspapers were one of Garrick's preferred sources of propagating his own reputation, and he envisioned for himself immortality through periodical coverage. Thus, it should be unsurprising that a third and entirely different generic contender for the title of the "first full-length biography of Garrick" should appear as a serialized biography-obituary, billed as an "anecdotal life."[54] What might be surprising is the extent to which the "anecdotal" life followed the narrative through line of Garrick rather than providing a boisterous cameo of the subject in the midst of a whole cast of characters. As we will see in Chapter 2, later anecdotal biographies tended to be loosely related anecdotes about friends and colleagues rather than an actual biography of the titular character, but as newspaper obituaries were just coming into being, these anecdotes cleave to a more traditional understanding of brief newspaper biographies.

The "Biographical Anecdotes of the Late Mr. Garrick" appeared, starting in March 1779, in four installments (March through June) of several pages each. N. D. Norman's 2008 study of the rise of biography-obituaries in London newspapers cites the *Gentleman's Magazine* as the originating entity of the subgenre. John Nichols assumed editorship in 1778 and almost immediately decided to magnify the regularly occurring obituaries that had begun to run in the publication during the 1770s into "full-scale memoirs" when the deceased was considered extraordinary.[55] This line of thought challenges current understandings of how "full-length" biographies might have been classified by eighteenth-century readers, and points to the importance of Garrick in cementing this trend, as his death in 1779 made him one of the first London figures to receive such treatment at the hands of Nichols in the *Gentleman's Magazine.*[56]

The "Anecdotes" represent an important development in theatrical biography, not just because of their vanguard position in newspaper-obituary, but also because of the words "Biographical Anecdotes" replacing the traditional "Memoirs of" or "Life of" form. Although theoretically, the foregrounding of anecdotes would better suit Johnson's insistence that minute particulars are the lifeblood of biography, the taglines of anecdotes increasingly referred to a series of often tangentially related bons mots featuring a "gathering" or main character and his interactions with other people in society. Several examples of this construction will be seen in Chapter 2. Although Nichols's piece on Garrick gestures toward this divergent development in biography, these "Anecdotes" actually present a unified narrative life, including several anecdotes about Garrick within the teleology of his life.[57] However, the majority of the anecdotes are about other people, heavily skewed toward the first installment, and almost entirely in the form of footnotes. The only truly novel piece of insight about Garrick in one month's section is that he lost his voice during a play and was restored by the juice of a Seville orange.[58]

As the installments develop, we can see the newspaper attempting to work out a system of incorporating anecdotes without overwhelming the text, evidently having perceived that the proportion of stories focused on Garrick rather than on other people in his orbit as needing adjustment. Although the biography was limited by spatial constraints, the work is useful in considering the contents of theatrical biography and the distribution of those contents over the space allotted, and how the medium of any biographical work might lend itself more readily to some aspects of theatrical biography than others. We will see some striking differences between book-length and newspaper-length biography with Davies's memoirs, which, after appearing in full form, were then compressed into two installments for the newspaper and presented as "anecdotal." In that instance, Davies's lively social narrative is stripped of the exciting or witty insertions of the supporting cast of characters, the same cast of characters that had threatened to overwhelm the biography-obituary discussed earlier. It appears that theatrical biography as a mode including sustained narrative and cameos from the theatrical world around the subject demanded a book-length production so that neither feature was ignored or eclipsed.

Works like those of the Old Comedian and the *Gentleman's Magazine* represented the strongest biographical efforts of Garrick up to the point when Davies launched his biography. The comparative weakness of the Old Comedian's spotty account and the *Gentleman's Magazine's* lopsided relation between narrative and anecdote—not to mention the disappointment and intrigue stoked by the fictionalized pseudo-Garrick of the *David Ranger* story—might help to explain why Davies's admittedly flawed tour de force biography achieved supremacy (but doesn't provide evidence for the work's continued success when forced to contend with later substantial accounts such as Murphy's 1801 *Life of David Garrick*). Having laid the foundation of Garrick biographies and pseudobiographies prior to Davies's full-length *Memoirs of the Life of David Garrick*, it is now time to investigate the work that so thoroughly cornered the market on the remarkable actor, author, and manager.

The Main Attraction: Davies's *Memoirs of the Life of David Garrick* (1780)

This section considers what made Davies's *Life of Garrick* exemplary: specifically, how he reacted to the conventions of the genre, the actual content of the book, and the initial critical evaluations in relation to established precedents. Davies's biography personalizes the genre, shifting its boundaries to allow the biographer to play an increasingly significant role as an authority supporting—and sometimes competing with—the titular subject for the public's attention. I argue that because of the comparatively pronounced "absent presence" of Garrick, the fully present nonanonymous biographer slips into the void, changing the balance of agency within the narrative *Life of Garrick*. Such focus means that Davies's own person is critiqued simultaneously, or even in place of, the work that he wrote. As time goes by, this "absent presence" will be more directly filled by biographers such as James Boaden, who introduce themselves as participatory characters in the text, an inheritance from Cibberean autobiography but also from Davies's precedents of theatrical biography as innately tied to the person and reputation of its named author.

As we glance back at the four precedents of Garrick's biography before *Memoirs of the Life of David Garrick,* we see that Davies's main contributions to thespian biography included making a "history of the stage" part of the expected fare, which allowed him to include, in the main text rather than in footnotes, anecdotes not only of Garrick but also of his contemporaries.[59] This solved some of the shortcomings of the Old Comedian and of the newspaper biography-obituary. Davies also benefited from the subject and time of his work, because of Garrick's interest in media as legacy management and the much vaster information networks from which to glean fact and anecdote. In addition to normalizing an anecdotal history of the protagonist's social circle, which had obviously been part of the expectation but unevenly realized in some of Garrick's earlier lesser biographies, Davies also attended to the matter of *how* actors achieved their craft onstage—and this was, in large part, why Davies's *specific* account, rather than just the *structure*, has persevered. Finally, Davies's success seems to have been brokered by his own reputation as a gentleman. As one of the first thespian biographers to claim authorship of his biography, Davies ushered in not only a new era of personalization on the part of the biographer, but also the beginning move toward the professionalism of the genre and, eventually, the cult of the biographer.[60]

In many ways, Cibber is the grandfather and Davies is the father of the great works in the theatrical biography tradition. There are indisputably large works of thespian biography prior to 1780, but none seems to have staked such a strong claim alongside Cibber's as Davies's did, not only in the proud unfurling of a real name and reputation underwriting the text, but also on the level of synthesizing a remarkable depth and breadth of material.[61] Wanko, writing in 2003, describes Davies's biography as "the longest, most thorough, and most balanced biography of an actor to this date."[62]

Although any number of anonymous biographers gesture toward the responsibility of the biographer, one of the distinguishing marks of Davies is the sustained act of considering his task as a biographer, paying careful attention to preexisting generic requirements and to readerly preferences in order to improve upon, and not just meet, the expected conventions. In his remarks on the failures of Mr. Ralph, a historian, we can gain some insight into what Davies would consider a successful biography (keeping in mind that biography was, at the time, also referred to as a history of someone, and the terms *biographer* and *historian* both were used to describe Davies in the context of the present *Life of Garrick* enterprise). He writes: "But the author has taken effectual care to defeat the end he proposed, of making his work universally read [...] To the general reader it is intolerably tedious and disgusting: the narrative is almost continually interrupted by a commentary three times as large as the text; and the margin is loaded with extracts from a thousand pamphlets."[63]

Davies's remarks suggest that a biography should be widely applicable, easy to read, and focused on a compelling narrative comprehensiveness rather than on the other connotation of "comprehensiveness," which might lead to the inclusion of every potentially or passably relevant document or insight. The goal of universality explains both his desire to make the text a "history of the stage" rather than merely a biography and his commitment to bringing anec- dotes up from the footnotes into the narrative. He displays some restraint in including anecdotes, which he understands are expected and enjoyed by his readers, but which also might overtake the underlying narrative if not con- trolled. In each instance, he relays one anecdote that he considers to be exem- plary (which is, after all, the original point of an anecdote).

Just as Davies negotiates the balance of anecdote and plot summary, show- ing his awareness of audience expectations, he also carefully observes what he has decided is a rule about when to insert capsule biographies (brief snap- shots of a paragraph to several pages in length) of secondary characters, and notes: "It will perhaps be expected, after having written so largely on their theatrical abilities, that I should speak of Powell and Holland as members of society."[64] Such agreeable but ultimately proscriptive language cements cap- sule biography as an inalienable feature of thespian biography; Davies's stan- dard here is around six pages, which seems reasonable, if on the long side. Holland's description illustrates the turns of phrase that made Davies's biog- raphy endure the onslaught of other, less particular, biographies:

> [Holland's] two admired patrons, Foote and Garrick, were men justly celebrated for genius; but when he retailed their bons mots, he made wild work; he rendered that pert vivacity, which was originally sterling wit. But though Holland was by nature denied that shining talent which he aimed at, he had something to boast of which was more valuable; he had a mind exempt from all meanness, and was ever disposed to do acts of kindness.[65]

Davies had a knack for weighing a man, describing his faults in an easily relatable instance, and yet making almost everyone but Samuel Foote, mean- hearted trickster that he was, into a good person. Davies's facility with brief, several paragraphs long biographies undoubtedly aided the transmission of his work into later thespian biographies: Macklin's third biographer, Cooke, quotes Davies's treatment of the actors in the *Beggar's Opera* at length, noting that "Davies (Garrick's historian) [...] knew Walker personally," suggesting that one reason for Davies's supremacy is the supposed truthfulness of his observations, since he was not recycling descriptions taken from someone with greater access to the stage.[66] And, indeed, Davies benefited from the perceived authenticity of a "known" author in a sea of anonymous hacks.

Paradoxically, but predictably, based on Johnson's rules for biographical excellence, Davies's biography has proved its universal appeal through minute details. It resonates through time most prominently in the moments during which the biographer isolated a specific line or lines from a play and then described the minute action and expression of the actor in the role. Cooke, writing in 1804, frequently summons Davies as a guide to great thespian biography and, as a result, only he among Macklin biographers quotes lines and pinpoints precise moments of descriptions rather than supplying unmoored general observations on a specific actor's onstage persona (though he calls upon Davies's *Dramatic Miscellanies* and *Life of Garrick* interchangeably, as though the *Miscellanies* were an appendix to the biography). For example, returning to Cooke's citation of Davies's firsthand knowledge of Tom Walker (known for being the original Macheath in *The Beggar's Opera*), Davies describes the moment in which Walker, as Faulconbridge, responds to Salisbury's taunt from Shakespeare's *King John*:

You had better gall the Devil, Salisbury.
If thou but frown on me, or stir thy foot,
Or teach thy hasty spleen to do me shame,
I'll strike thee dead.

Davies follows the line with his description: "Walker uttered these words with singular propriety: he drew his sword, threw himself into a noble attitude, sternly knit his black brows, and gave a loud stamp with his foot." The "Player's commanding look and vehement action" resulted in applause, which "confirmed the energy of his conceptions."[67] We may recall that the Old Comedian's short biography featured one such moment of isolation and explanation. Particularly if one merges the *Dramatic Miscellanies* with the *Memoirs of the Life of David Garrick*, Davies sustains the excellence hinted at by the Old Comedian.[68]

Although there are moments evidently aimed at posterity as well as at an approving audience that can confirm the validity of his observations, Davies's book has moments of raw immediacy in service of training present-day actors and audiences. Describing the comedian Parsons, he says, "If he would be more simple and chaste in drawing Old Foresight's character, and not imitate the action of a sailor pulling up his trowsers [*sic*] so often, he would not perhaps gain such loud applause, but he would find more judicious approvers."[69] Davies excels at painting a figure in brief. His decision to give acting advice directly to a still-living actor adds vitality to the narrative that centered on a man now dead. Furthermore, his criticisms of actors are often specific rather than general; for example, he shows the repetitive gestures upon which Parsons overrelied, rather than simply noting that Parsons courted applause at the expense of nuanced acting.

As much as Davies liked to give instruction to future artists and biographers, he practiced what he preached, showing evidence of learning from past models. He expressed open enmity toward biographers who simply stitch together what had already been said, but he was also willing to acknowledge at least one or two authors from whom he had borrowed a relatively small amount. He quotes other sources infrequently, notably referencing Victor's *History of the Theatres of London and Dublin*, which had been printed for sale in Davies's shop (but not referencing Victor's anonymous *Memoirs of the Life of Barton Booth*, printed for John Watts). Voices of the age—theatrical and literary—inhabit the book, but only one voice connected to theatrical biography can be heard: Colley Cibber's.

Cibber's *An Apology for the Life of Colley Cibber* is still readily recalled by Davies, who appropriates Cibber's description of Nokes to describe Kitty Clive[70]; though paraphrased, and only forming a portion of Davies's treatment of Mrs. Clive, the borrowing of Cibber's sentiment stands out because Davies rarely appears to find recourse in others' ideas. Davies's estimation of Cibber can be intuited by the predictable though infrequent invocation of his name, precedent, or opinion. Toward the end of the work, Davies locates Cibber in a line of English actors able to contend with Garrick's primacy (alongside the more expected Betterton and Booth): his point in including Cibber is to rank Cibber—earlier referenced as author of that "excellent *Apology*"[71] as the better dramatic author, Garrick the better actor.[72] Earlier still, Davies tipped his hat outspokenly toward Cibber as an author:

> All lovers of genius and friends of learning will pay homage to the criticisms of Mr. Gray; but will his remains, though embalmed by his friend, the elegant Mason, be longer admired than some of the comedies of Colley Cibber? The *Apology* of the same author for his Life is one of those original performances that scarcely ever was excelled, and will last as long as our language.[73]

Such a strong endorsement not only marks Cibber as an obvious role model for Davies, but also indicates that Davies has inherited Cibber's interest in permanency and can see theatrical biography as a means to that immortality.

Davies's approach to posterity, or the extent to which he expected his account to be read in the future, is not straightforward. On one hand, he certainly seems to be writing with an eye toward continuing relevance, and indeed explicitly justifies a long digression on the actor Havard as useful for the education of future actors.[74] On the other hand, he directly addresses the then-performing comedian Moody with advice on how to improve Moody's portrayal of Sir Sampson Legend, so that "he would not perhaps gain such loud applause, but he would find more judicious approvers."[75] Even as he acknowledges the difficulty of the passage of time, Davies falls into the trap of cognitive egocentricity, advising his readers to summon an impression of Weston in order to imagine how Johnson, a bygone actor, without considering how irrelevant such an implied rather than explicit description would be within a few generations.[76] Davies was writing for posterity, and his frequent references to Cibber would tend to suggest that he envisioned his biography as joining Cibber's in a new tradition of nondisposable theatrical biographies.

Evidence suggests that, outside of the *Life of Garrick*, Davies was interested in crafting some literary immortality for himself. In the very newspaper that the final narrative segment of Garrick's "Anecdotes" biography played out just one year earlier—*The Gentleman's Magazine*—a review of Thomas Davies's *Life of Massinger* (1789) appears, in which the commentator, in the persona of Sylvanus Urban, declares the identity of the then-anonymous author: "From the name subscribed to a short inscription of this *Life* to Dr. Samuel Johnson [...] we learn that the writer is Mr. Thomas Davies, who, as we remember, for his very generous treatment of the late Mr. Granger, Dr. Campbell said was 'not a bookseller, but a gentleman dealing in books.'"[77]

We see a rather consistent portrait of Davies as gentlemanly, elevating his tradesman's profession, wielding an appropriately genteel pen in his biographical endeavors. Again, we witness his strong devotion to Johnson, and might wish to make something of the fact that he revealed his identity only in the context of the letter to Johnson at the beginning of Davies's *Life of Massinger*, rather than on the cover of the work—a slow unfurling of his identity.[78] Thus, we discover that, as early as 1779, Davies has begun contemplation of his *Dramatic Miscellanies*, and we already know that he had written an article (under the pseudonym of Leonato) about the actor, the "Eulogium on Mr. Garrick's Leaving the Stage," in 1776. Davies's identity as an author begins to build: with *Massinger*, he introduces *Dramatic Miscellanies* as forthcoming; with *Life of Garrick*, he reinforces the *Dramatic Miscellanies* as a supplement to the biography. Finally, upon publishing *Dramatic Miscellanies*, he justifies them based on the popularity of his *Garrick*, and even wrote upon the title page, "By Thomas Davies, Author of Memoirs of the Life of David Garrick, Esq."

The increasing identification of authorship in Davies's works, particularly as a biographer, suggests mounting pride in a literary career, and the understanding that Davies's name itself had come to possess commercial value, signifying a reliable author.

But although the readers gain innumerable tightly written and evocative portraits of the leading thespians from the *Beggar's Opera* up until 1779, several succeeding generations of theatrical biographers received an exemplary model of the genre and a source-text from which to borrow, and Davies gets his most significant foothold into fame, alas, there is, at least for this reader, a notable void. David Garrick himself is barely described in character, the most sustained description of a character being that of Hamlet seeing his father's ghost. Davies writes, almost painfully linking his own project as a biographer to Garrick's as an actor, "Hamlet was a part which he knew the public expected from him," a part for which every reader would have expected that Davies supply a detailed critical report.[79] "I have promised to give a review of his principal characters in another place, and shall therefore here only give a short draught of Garrick's playing Hamlet, with its effects," he offers.[80]

Davies recognizes the audience's expectation, but he separates the key grain of theatrical biography that distinguishes it from other forms of biography. The *Dramatic Miscellanies* ("another place") do not do justice to audience expectations of a surrounding narrative, and the *Life of Garrick* suffers for it. (This is why Cooke quotes indiscriminately from the *Life of Garrick* and the *Miscellanies* as if from one unit.) The beginning of the "short draught" is promising, as Davies writes that Garrick, upon initially encountering the Ghost, instantly impressed his terror upon the audience: "His expostulations with the vision, though warm and importunate, were restrained by filial awe." Alas, Davies does not elaborate, and dwindles to what seems to us to be general praise: "The strong intelligence of his eye, the animated expression of his whole countenance, the flexibility of his voice, and his spirited action, riveted the attention of the admiring audience."[81]

In sum, Davies does a far superior job describing supporting characters than depicting his main character, and while Garrick abounds factually in the narrative, he does not receive the lion's share of anecdote or description that one would imagine for such a commanding physical presence and personality. It is an interesting omission, one that the immediately succeeding biographer, Murphy, would strive to correct, but not succeed in doing. Perhaps Garrick was too remarkable to be fully described. Perhaps Davies assumed that his readers were universally familiar with Garrick's motions and characterizations. The strange ever-present cipher of David Garrick perhaps accounts for some of the most pervasive criticism about the *Life of Garrick*: Davies's financial motivations and the work's lack of organization. The former we have briefly addressed; the latter perhaps is explainable by the difficulty in pinpointing Garrick himself, but also by a trend that is carried over in later biographies, as we will see in the next two chapters.

Reviews of the Life of Garrick *as extensions of* Davies's character

With Garrick himself an absent presence in the work, the more visible named author received a surprising amount of personal criticism. Just as Davies's work benefited both initially and ultimately from his personal reputation and from the connections that he had made in his private life and his profession, his personal character, as well as his professional talent, were also fair subjects of debate and critique. In turn, Davies's shot at immortality increased, as newspapers discussed not only his name, but also his salient personal characteristics in reference to his writings. The technical craft of biography was, of course, also discussed.

In May 1780, one particularly truculent review appeared in the *Westminster Magazine* by a critic who appears to take issue not just with the composition but with the composer himself. He writes: "The Author [...] not having the abilities to delineate so extraordinary a character as that of Mr. Garrick, has thrown together a farrago of anecdotes and circumstances relating to those theatrical personages who had any connection with the hero of his work."[82] The critic contends that Davies's farrago is directly related to his incessant praise of Dr. Johnson, which is categorized as too much panegyric at the expense of eloquence, and, additionally, as misdirected.

Despite Davies's obvious belief in Johnson as the "greatest English author," the reviewer is unconvinced, crisply noting two potential motives for Davies's adulation, both ultimately economic: "Dr. Johnson has compiled enormous volumes; which are great objects in the eye of a bookseller, when they are saleable: he [Johnson] also suggested the plan of the present work for the Author's emolument. The conclusion therefore must fairly be, that he is the greatest man of the age."[83] The reviewer slyly suggests not only that Davies would benefit from Johnson's patronage of the lesser-known man's writing career, but also that Davies, as a bookseller, would support Johnson in the insincere craft of "compiling" (here meant in the Curllian sense of an unethically loose gathering). The conclusion to be drawn is that the bagginess of Davies's narrative is a technique for achieving more money, one that Davies learned from Johnson's supposedly underhanded method of compilation (which, it is worth noting, is more frequently praised than derided by contemporaries).

Having dispensed with the veil of purity surrounding Davies's allegiance to Johnson, the reviewer moves to an earlier benefactor, Garrick himself. Davies, "as a decayed Actor," should have access to the unemployed or financially struggling actors' relief fund that Davies so grandly touts David Garrick as having graciously initiated.[84] Either Garrick's relief fund has been overstated by Davies, or he is a fool to bother the public for relief via the current book; since the book should not be a financial necessity, as determined by the *Westminster* critic, "We are therefore under no temptation to spare a faulty work, [just] because it has been projected for the Author's emolument. Truth is in no case more important than in Biography."[85]

Davies's character is excoriated by the reviewer: his literary sensibilities are corrupt, he has rapaciously written a biography larded with irrelevant stories, he lavishes faulty praise on his heroes, and has betrayed the good name of biographer for economic advantage born about by poor management of Davies's acting career not only by Davies—but also by Garrick through the apparently defunct actor-relief program.[86] Although money is, evidently, almost always a strong motive for thespian biographies in this period (especially in the case of cut-and-paste artists looking to capitalize on a death), the reviewer is particularly biting about the state of Davies's personal finances. Just as the cult of the actor under Garrick produced additional scrutiny of the thespian's personal life, so too did the increased ownership and presence of a "real" author seem to allow for the probing of the biographer's character and circumstances.

But if Davies's good name received some tarnish from the *Westminster* critic, his reputation also went up in the estimation of many readers. Representative of this opposite end of the spectrum is a fanciful piece, one more in keeping with the view of Davies that circulates in later literature. As mentioned at the beginning of this chapter, in September 1780, *The Town and Country Magazine, or Universal Repository of Knowledge, Instruction, and Entertainment* published a poetical piece by J. R. called "On Reading Memoirs of the Life of David Garrick, Esq., by Mr. Davies." In this fanciful depiction, we find Shakespeare and Garrick strolling "arm in arm" on Pindus, a mountain range in Greece almost certainly meant to evoke the mythical conception of Parnassus, home of the Muses and resting place of poetic talents. While discussing "the drama and Nature's laws," they are interrupted by Truth's goddess, who appears with a copy of Davies's *Memoirs* which she presents as a gift to Garrick:

> This present accept; when perus'd you will own
> That justice impartial is here amply shown;
> And all those great talents that rais'd you so high,
> Are painted in colours that never will die.[87]

It is worth noting that Truth's goddess, in contrast to the *Westminster*'s critic, specifically lauds the "justice impartial" of Davies's account, which speaks directly to the critic's concerns. More important to students of biography in general, the goddess praises Davies for achieving the ultimate goal of good biography: to preserve or immortalize a subject, a task that, I will argue in a later chapter, is particularly important to biographers of thespian subjects, but difficult for them. Davies clearly has succeeded not only in the impartiality, but also in the vitality of his representation. More specifically, Truth's goddess acknowledges that part of the power of Davies's memoir was tracing the "shades" of Garrick's weaknesses, "without which a portrait's mere outlines at best." Having explained the technical features that set Davies's memoir apart, she confides in Garrick:

> As Davies sat writing, I warmly inspir'd him,
> And Phoebus with wit, sense, and eloquence fir'd him;
> Poor soul! He still thought, from himself sprung those flowr's
> That dropt from his pen, but indeed, they were ours.[88]

Nature's goddess joins Truth's goddess in conference with Shakespeare and Garrick, who are presumably still arm in arm; the new goddess embraces her favorite students, "loudly" declaring,

> As long as old Time on this globe shall remain,
> My Shakespeare and Garrick unrival'd shall reign,
> As Poet the one, and as Actor the other,
> To both whom exulting, I hail myself mother;
> While Davies's name as historian and friend,
> In Fame's brightest page shall on Garrick attend.[89]

While the first several lines from Nature's goddess are predictable, this last couplet is significant to Davies's standing. He is not Nature's goddess's child, and he does not have a place on the tour of Pindus, but his work is significant enough for the Goddess of Truth to interrupt the summit of geniuses, and for the Goddess of Nature to grant him mention on the same page of fame that belongs to Garrick.[90] Davies is respected by Nature, but he only receives provisional membership to Nature's club (his connection to Nature is through Garrick). Nonetheless, his *name* lives on; the gamble to "own" the biography by throwing aside anonymity or the guise of Leonato appears to have paid off richly.

If Davies has allied himself by name to Nature, Davies's relationship to Truth is arguably problematic, for although Davies is listed without qualification as Garrick's "historian," Truth's goddess openly says that she and Apollo actually deserve credit for the brilliant verisimilitude of Davies's work. Divine inspiration was not an uncommon trope, though reserved as an indication of highest praise in the context of a review. The poem does evoke a strange sense in which Davies is the agent, and then again maybe only the vehicle, for the *Life of Garrick*.[91] Nonetheless, the poem fundamentally narrates the fame of Davies as permeating not only the book of Fame, representing posterity, but also the very ears of the deceased and much-idolized Garrick and Shakespeare as stewards of the treasured past. In sum, this poem makes a remarkably high endorsement for the significance and predicted enduring power of Davies's *Life of Garrick*, and, by extension, the reputation belonging to the name of Davies.[92]

Taken together, the May review and the September poem might not provide a uniform report of Davies's success or failure, but they do make a powerful case for the importance of a work's specific author. Davies's memoir, according to the reviewer from the *Westminster*, fails predominantely due to the character weaknesses of its author, which translate into an unpalatable quagmire of a book. To the poet in the *Town and Country*, Davies's memoir succeeds on the basis of his association with Truth and Nature as embodied in the *Life of Garrick*, which so accurately immortalizes Garrick and simultaneously immortalizes Davies's own virtue and name for future generations. To write a biography is not only to open oneself to biographical examination, but also to potentially snatch a footnote of fame.

Davies acquired more than a "footnote" of fame—in fact, his biography lived well into the twentieth century as the unquestioned primary biography of Garrick. In the next section of the chapter, we will consider four texts responding to Davies's biography: an anecdotal compression of the *Life of Garrick* as serialized in the *London Journal* in the spring of 1780, which will hearken back to the anecdotal "life" that formed a biographical commemoration of Garrick earlier in the chapter; a memoir of Garrick by the playwright Arthur Murphy in 1801, quite obviously designed to snatch the laurels from Davies by readjusting the baseline narrative of the previous author to better fit what Murphy thought audiences wanted; the first edited edition of Davies's biography in 1808, which, by virtue of the editor's extraordinarily light hand, can tell us much about what was considered "sacred" in the text; and, finally, two scrapbooks made from copies of Davies's biography, representing a dilettante participation in theatrical biography from the pinnacle of the social pecking order and, in contrast, a much more modest attempt.[93] These latter two texts suggest the depth of personal participation in these biographies that seems to have coincided with the "personalization" of Davies's approach to the genre.

Editorial and Readerly Interventions

This section, in approaching a range of published and unpublished responses to Davies's *Life of Garrick*, indicates how individual readers responded to the biography by desiring to make their own mark on the work; they did so by participating in a range of phenomena from adding portraits, to cleaving together multiple accounts by different authors, to making numerous observations in the margins of the work. Particularly in light of the clearly iterated (but not always clearly distinguished) taboo on authors who compile materials without sufficiently blending them into a cohesive whole, editorial and readerly play allows for semisanctioned rewriting to happen under the cover of cut-and-paste techniques. These same techniques, when applied by someone claiming to be an "official" biographer writing a "legitimate" biography, would be cause for excoriation. Thus, different standards and expectations emerge for the official and unofficial, even though the original author and the "editor" both aim to preserve a favorite figure—or, for those adding to an existing text, to preserve a particularly significant text about a favorite figure—through intervention. This readerly play shows an interest not only in adding to the monument of a favorite actor, but also in expressing one's own individual connection to the actor or history through evidence of participation.

Serialized Life of Garrick (Davies's edition)

In the second section of this chapter, I suggested that the newspapers had a cooperative but at times adversarial relationship with books. Newspapers have the great advantage of a much shorter turnaround time, but they also operate within a significantly more conscribed space. The "anecdotal life" of Garrick, serialized in two chunks for the *Universal Magazine* in May and June 1780 under the title "Anecdotes of the Late David Garrick, Esq," appeared right after the full-length text had been made available.[94] In a remarkable instance of regression, Davies's longer *Life of Garrick*, having expanded from the original three-page article into the two-volume phenomenon, was condensed back into ten densely printed pages, but with a much sharper focus than the original sketch by Leonato.

Although it is not clear whether Davies himself or an editor made the selections of the material that would constitute the "anecdotes," when juxtaposed with the longer text, the very act of abridgment makes a claim about what parts of the narrative are important and, conversely, what parts are unnecessary. The *Universal Magazine* "Anecdotes" come almost verbatim from Davies's *Life of Garrick*, but without much of the context, character sketches, and incidental observations that make Davies's text such a delightful Cibberean read. Indeed, the "Anecdotes" does not offer more than a handful of anecdotes in the true sense. Instead, it is a narrative that has stripped away much of the action between Garrick and his contemporaries, and all diverting stories of other people in which Garrick does not feature. Such small nuances round out the characters, and in fact form a large part of the portions from Davies's work that are in more frequent circulation today. Characteristic is an apparently frivolous sentence in a paragraph about Garrick's Dublin tour in the unseasonably hot summer of 1742, in which Davies claims that packed audiences experienced "epidemical distemper," nicknamed "the Garrick fever," a detail that proves irresistible to present-day scholars.[95] Similarly, while two excellent bons mots of Quin and Cibber reacting to Garrick are included, sacrificed to the editorial pen is Garrick's excellent epigrammatic response to Quin's accusation "that Garrick was a new religion; Whitfield was followed for a time; but they would all come to church again."[96] Garrick's ensuing ten-line epigram captures his playful arrogance; the last four lines catch the characteristic sting and significance of Garrick's wit:

> Thou great infallible, forbear to roar,
> Thy bulls and errors are rever'd no more;
> When doctrines meet with gen'ral approbation,
> It is not heresy, but reformation.[97]

In the interest of space, perhaps, the omission of Garrick's epigram allows Garrick's wit, unrepresented, to be eclipsed by his aggressors'. In other instances, events of Garrick's life that might be considered canonical, such as his much-publicized rivalry with Spranger Barry, in which both men played Romeo in opposing playhouses on the same night, appear unimportant based on their absence. In the context of the *Universal Magazine's* abridgment of "Mr. Davies's ingenious Life of that celebrated performer, just published," the "Anecdotes" were a marketing device designed to sell copies of Davies's book—to give away all of the material would not only be spatially unwise for the magazine, but also commercially preposterous for Davies, who was not only the author but also the printer and the bookseller of the *Memoirs of the Life of David Garrick*.

While the flavor of Davies's phrasing remains largely intact, the reader of the serialized abridged version of the *Life of Garrick* misses Davies's detailed examinations of specifics and rich connections between Garrick and his world. The focus remains on Garrick, yet rather than emerging from the sea of detail intact, the actor seems to be playing to an empty stage. Ironically, we will see in the next chapter that, by the turn of the century, a newspaper's cut of an "anecdotal" life neither focuses exclusively on its purported subject, nor makes much semblance of a narrative through line, an almost exact reversal of the "anecdotal" life presented of Garrick in 1780.[98] Acting as a double-edged sword, greatly abridged newspaper versions of a longer text both publicize the work and, in the process of abridgement, allow the reader a seemingly much clearer, but often skewed, perspective from which to critique the entire work, primarily sight unseen. However, a book as popular as Davies's *Life* of Garrick generated a startling number of relatively direct engagements with the text in the form of critique and commendation, both implicitly and explicitly rendered. The most prominent of those responses came from Arthur Murphy in the form of a brand-new biography of Garrick.

Improving on the original: Murphy's Life of David Garrick (1801)

While some readers were content to add personal touches to Davies's biography, Arthur Murphy, renowned playwright and member of Garrick's outer circle, chose to write his own version of Garrick's life in 1801, some twenty-one years after the initial appearance of Davies's work, and twenty-two years after his protagonist's death. I propose that the latter biography is largely a reshaping of Davies's narrative, driven by Murphy's attempts to improve upon those faults in Davies's biography that had been noted and disapproved of by critics. The rhetoric surrounding Murphy's publication pitted the two authors against one another in a contest of character just as often as they evaluated the men's writing skills. In other words, the creation of a new, rival biography was the immediate occasion for a review, but the ensuing critique frequently functioned as a referendum on the men themselves.

Later competitive models of authorship, as we will see in Chapters 2 and 3, expose a politic of ignoring one's predecessor rather than calling attention to his existence. Murphy, however, is almost painfully aware of Davies's precedent, even though Murphy was a significantly more established author and, notwithstanding the lapse of time between Garrick's death and Murphy's account, arguably better equipped to tell Garrick's story because of his existing reputation as a writer and a keen observer of life. A talented man, Murphy practiced law, wrote plays, acted, and wrote for newspapers. Today, Murphy can occasionally be encountered through a play during eighteenth-century undergraduate coursework, but even with the irresistible subject of David Garrick, Murphy has not achieved Davies's prominence as a biographer.[99]

Although Murphy could claim the literary chops that Davies did not initially appear to have, contemporary reviews reflect a consistent preference for Davies's *Life of Garrick*. A review from the *British Critic* in June 1801 complains that Murphy offers nothing new to the story of Garrick.[100] Admittedly, Garrick was a challenging subject for novelty, because he had made every effort to train attention on his public works and had painstakingly hidden the majority of details about his private life.[101] The reviewer continues: "The *Life of Garrick*, by honest Tom Davies, was so well received, as to pass through no less than four large impressions, and there will probably be many who will yet prefer that work to the present."[102] While Davies had the advantage of comparative novelty and the immediacy that comes with publishing a work in the wake of the subject's passing, the reviewer makes it clear that Davies's work survived not on novelty, but on sustained interest, as testified by the number of editions it required. "Honest Tom," we might assume, is a nod to Davies's humbler literary pretensions and his background as an actor and printer—it also juxtaposes him with the privileged, cosmopolitan Murphy, who is accused of lifting the majority of facts about Garrick from Davies.

The *Critical Review*, also appearing in June 1801, carries an assessment that struggles about its disapproval of Murphy's biography. The reviewer, sensitive to the heightened expectations for the work based on its subject and author, describes with considerable pathos that "two old favorites stand before us" (Davies and Murphy), suggesting the potential pressure—and sincere desire on the part of the critic himself—to present a positive review.[103] The *Critical Review's* article is more specific about Murphy's failure to deepen Davies's account: Murphy's account was much closer to that of a "hackneyed gazetteer" than for a closer associate of Garrick.[104] Additionally, the author expresses displeasure with the sheer amount of space devoted to plot summaries of the plays that featured onstage during Garrick's lifetime, but credits Murphy for being modest about his own achievements, as he necessarily reviewed some of his own plays that Garrick's company performed.[105] The increasing textuality—performance as words rather than bodily gestures—of Murphy seemed to be essential to his conception, in line with a desire for concrete evidence of stage happenings, but frustrating to his readers nonetheless.[106]

The highest point of criticism about Murphy's biography was his failure to incorporate occurrences in Garrick's life abroad during the actor's hiatus from the stage. He belatedly iterates his purpose in his second volume: "We have now gone through the history of our great Roscius *in his public capacity*" [my italics].[107] Murphy's straightforward interest is in the public Garrick, whereas Davies maintains the illusion of displaying the private Garrick up to the point of appropriateness but not one iota past it.

Murphy's willful exclusion of life "in the round"—that is, not just in the theatre—extends to his treatment of other famous figures. In the extended statement of his purpose at 2:152–54, Murphy explains that he did not feel the compunction (as did Davies, he implicitly seems to say) to follow each auxiliary character to his or her death in defiance of the chronological narrative; rather, he allows characters to interweave at their moment of relevance and then fade back into the ether. However, Murphy talks in terms of authors, rather than actors, as the most important characters, a distinct departure from almost all other thespian biographies, where fellow thespians populate the account, and are advertised as an integral part of the work. Wanko accurately describes Murphy's approach: "He picks up and drops characters as he needs them," which he says he does so to avoid an unwieldy length and "a motley mixture," which also allows him to shine the spotlight the two main characters: Garrick and Murphy.[108] Wanko, who devotes a chapter of her book to comparing the two *Life of Garrick*s, claims that Murphy, as an author and playwright himself, was much more interested in immortalizing a literary Garrick than the thespian Garrick that Davies recorded. This theory is borne out in many of Murphy's choices, and, I argue, contributed heavily to the perceived inferiority of that work, as it led to too much plot summary and anecdotes about writers, when the attraction of the genre was the ephemera associated with actors.[109]

In keeping with his spurning of Davies, Murphy also takes umbrage at Cibber's biographical crown, declaring that "though Cibber cannot be cited as a legislator in criticism, yet as a man of experience [...] he deserves the attention of all dramatic writers" for his advice that a great thought in a play must be inserted in the right place for it to count.[110] Murphy cites the *Apology for the Life of Colley Cibber* several times, in one instance to analyze where Cibber failed as a critic: "Colley Cibber was eminent in his profession, and a close observer of the talents of his contemporaries; but when he attempts to give a portrait of Betterton, he finds himself unequal to the task."[111] This is the context of Cibber's famous lament on the difficulty of theatrical biography, given in full here, as in Murphy's account:

> Pity it is that the momentary beauties flowing from an harmonious elocution, cannot, like those of poetry, be their own record; that the animated graces of the player can live no longer than the instant breath and motion that presents them, or, at best, can but faintly glimmer through the memory of a few surviving spectators. Could *how* Betterton spoke be as easily known as *what* he spoke, then might we see the muse of Shakespeare in her triumph, with all her beauties in her best array, rising into real life, and charming the beholders. But alas! since all this is so far out of the reach of description, how shall I shew [*sic*] you Betterton?[112]

Murphy refers to this genuine philosophical quandary as Cibber being "obliged to stop short." He adds that Cibber's problem isn't unique to Betterton: it's the same issue Murphy himself faces. Citing the single instance in which Cibber does "descend, as much as might be expected, into minute particulars"— Cibber's description of Betterton as Hamlet—he says that the description could equally be of Garrick. Indeed, Murphy tries to outdo Cibber by describing Garrick, while explaining how impossible it would be to describe Garrick:

His imagination was so strong and powerful, that he transformed himself into the man he represented, and his sensibility was so quick, that
every sentiment took immediate possession of him. Before he uttered
a word, the varying passions began to work, and wrought such rapid
changes in his features, in his action, his attitudes, and the expression of
his eye, that he was, almost every moment, a new man.[113]

Of course, even a mildly interested reader could point out that Murphy, too,
fails to provide particulars of Garrick's acting, at least in this instance. Yet he
has done so here and there throughout the *Life of David Garrick*, but nowhere
as affectingly as in his description of Garrick as the distraught father Virginius
in *Virginia*, first shown in February 1754. After a tremendous plot summary,
Murphy focuses in on two words in a single line:

During that time, Garrick, representing *Virginius*, stood on the opposite
side of the scene, next to the stage-door, with his arms folded across
his breast, his eyes riveted to the ground, like a mute and lifeless statue.
Being told at length that the tyrant is willing to hear him, he continued
for some time in the same attitude, his countenance expressing a variety of passions, and the spectators fixed in ardent gaze. By slow degrees
he raised his head; he paused; he turned round in the slowest manner,
till his eyes fixed on *Claudius;* he still remained silent, and after looking
eagerly at the imposter, he uttered in a low tone of voice, that spoke the
fullness of a broken heart, "*Thou Traitor!*" The whole audience was elec-
trified; they felt the impression, and a thunder of applause testified their
delight.[114]

This description of Virginius, obviously an established and anticipated point
for Garrick, might be the most successful moment in Murphy's *Life of David
Garrick*, as it preemptively answers his criticisms of Cibber in Volume volume
2 and also seems in this instance to justify Murphy's slavish devotion to plot
summary, the other main criticism of his biography at that time.[115]

In the end, it is Murphy, and not Cibber (as Murphy had suggested) who
is known for his plays instead of his biographical writings. As the immediate criticism of Murphy's work suggests, Davies's *Life of Garrick* received the
laurels, a plaudit that was all the more impressive given the general consensus
that Murphy was better equipped to the task by proximity to Garrick and
literary bent.

The last lines of the *Critical Review's* assessment highlight what's at stake in
biography, as Garrick drops out from the conversation entirely, leaving the
spotlight entirely on Murphy: "We may not again meet him on such pleasing

ground: yet we are sorry to reflect that, on scenes so promising, he has not scattered the flowers around him which he might have culled, nor raised a monument of genuine criticism and more substantial instruction to his own 'fair fame.'"[116] For all the prefacing about "our old acquaintance," the critic makes clear that Murphy's failure is not just as biographer, or recorder of facts, but as author, critic, and instructor, suggesting the importance accorded to a biographer and the almost impossibly high expectations for him. Moreover, while the critic's appeal to Murphy's existing "fair fame" pays homage to his success as a playwright, it also highlights the missed opportunity of biographical immortality for the author, using language that is thematically similar, but tonally opposed, to the tributary poem that shows Davies's name attending as "historian and friend" to his subject on the brightest page of Fame. Biography proves a cruel mistress in the case of Murphy, whose work was not ignored, but never reached the acclaim of Davies's, always seeming to suffer by comparison. Thus, it was likely unsurprising when a new edition of Davies's *Life of Garrick* emerged in 1808.

Unobtrusive updating: An editorial approach to Davies's **Life of Garrick** (1808)

With Murphy failing to have toppled Davies, the 1780 *Memoirs of the Life of David Garrick* received the high commendation of being revamped by a professional editor, suggesting simultaneously and paradoxically the work's timelessness and its need to be kept up for sake of posterity. Davies's biography had enjoyed an unusual and often-referenced popularity, with four editions of the memoir in his own lifetime; the fourth one, in 1784, appeared with an improved index by the author. Murphy's 1801 biography, which I have suggested was undoubtedly intended to unseat Davies as "Garrick's historian," was challenged by a posthumous edited fifth edition of Davies's work (1808) and a sixth edition (1818) in the same vein. The editor who ushered Davies's work into the nineteenth century was Stephen Jones, who discreetly refers to himself only by initials, taking a surprisingly nonproprietary approach to his task.[117]

As we will see in other examples of post-publication interventions, the impetus to make a work more complete by adding in material that the author could not have possibly accessed appears to be widespread; immediate relevance is not always a feature of the eighteenth-century theatrical biography, and its readers appear to have had much more patience, and even enjoyment, for traipsing through a brief note on the historical happenings of even the most narratologically minor characters. As an editor, Jones bridged the gap between the original, official author, and the unofficial annotators, commentators, and extra-illustrators who had continued to promote the book's relevance. Jones's success was in the way that he mediated the demand for extra material without damaging or overwhelming the preexisting structure.

It is reasonable to wonder, however, after the example of Murphy, who seems to have largely relied on Davies's narrative to furnish his own, why Mr. Jones did not simply write his own competing biography of Garrick rather than reissuing Davies's and confining himself to footnotes (both literally and figuratively, considering the significantly less brilliant sheen of fame this editor received compared to Davies). He must have recognized an opportunity to enrich Davies's increasingly dated account by inserting some of Murphy's novel bons mots or updated facts, strengthening the first biography at the expense of the second. This transaction was, of course, precisely what Murphy had attempted to do in his appropriation of much of Davies's original text. Thus, the editor enacted poetic justice on behalf of the deceased biographer, but in an admirably balanced manner.[118]

Like Murphy before him, Jones appears to have been attuned to some of the criticism of Davies's original work. Underlying this entire chapter is a pervasive sense that, while critics frequently gave conflicting reports about a particular work, authors and editors did remain interested in readers' feedback. Jones exercises discretion in responding to the criticism: he treats Davies's wild chronology as a virtue not to be disturbed, but he must have found validity in accusations that Davies was too sycophantic to Garrick. Therefore, Jones inserts a handful of anecdotes within the footnotes that complicate or contradict the main text's assertions about Garrick's behavior. For example, Davies's innocent reference to the young Garrick as being "engaged for some time in the wine-trade" now links to a bon mot from Foote, who "used sarcastically to say, that he remembered Garrick living in Durham Yard, with three quarts of vinegar in the cellar, calling himself a wine-merchant."[119] Certainly, the effect—if not necessarily the intent—of Jones's insertions is to undercut the reader's reliance on Davies solely; Jones's intent was to present a more nuanced portrait, particularly as Murphy had revealed the same bon mot verbatim in his frequently less-flattering *Life of David Garrick*.[120] Jones would likely feel less need to shield Garrick from censure as they were not direct friends, as the taboo of speaking critically about the dead seemed to wane relative to years deceased, and, perhaps most urgently, because Murphy's rival *Life of David Garrick* was more than willing to depict the less attractive side of Garrick.[121]

Sometime between Davies and Murphy, some of the "gentlemanly" rules governing biography seem to have shifted. Testifying to the 24-year gap between the fourth and fifth editions of Davies's *Life of Garrick*, Jones more candidly remarks on the nature of Peg Woffington's amorous relationship with Garrick, adding in a suggestive anecdote that Davies obviously neglected, even as he dedicated an entire chapter of the *Life of Garrick* to Woffington.[122] As with his treatment of the Woffington affair, Jones recognizes the clash between Davies's desire as a gentleman to maintain privacy and Jones and Davies's mutual charge as biographer-historian-editor to make sure that the work remains intelligible beyond the first generation of readers, who can often fill in omissions based on popularly circulating knowledge. Thus, Jones shows no qualms in adding a footnote to identify the victim of a rather rude caricature by Samuel Foote: Mr. A– is revealed to be Mr. Aprice[123] and a slandered author, R. B. Esq. becomes demystified as Richard Bentley.[124]

Beyond splicing in Murphy when useful and being more faithful to the facts and less to the honor of the people involved, the largest alteration of Jones's is his decision to insert as footnotes the entire transcript of a small pamphlet war between Charles Macklin and David Garrick, the former of whom believed that the latter had betrayed him by going back on their agreement to boycott their theatre's unfair working conditions. These pamphlets traverse pages 83–115, sometimes leaving only a few lines for the body of the main text. Jones's largest systematic intervention is a number of letters used as supportive evidence for Davies's narrative, which is meant to bolster the authority of Davies. I believe that Jones is seeking to compete with Murphy's tremendous appendix at the back of the second volume of his *Life of Garrick*, at least with the parts that Murphy didn't import wholesale from Davies's narrative.[125] Notwithstanding Murphy's superficially better organization, his appendix, although associated with scholarly work today, should remind a critical reader of the less sophisticated patchwork of the Old Comedian and Edmund Curll.

In contrast, Jones's footnote insertion of full texts, while burdensome to the eye, more successfully weaves the source materials into the narrative than Murphy's disconnected sheaf of endnote sources, their contexts frequently forgotten over the span of many chapters' worth of narrative. Jones respects the original efforts of Davies both by not inserting his own "improvements" into the original text directly, and by adding them onto the proper pages rather than simply cobbling together an addendum or appendix at the end of the volumes. The effect is to treat the narrative as a cohesive whole that is to be respected while introducing additional materials where they are immediately relevant and useful in relation to the narrative. These details are important in establishing the increasing expectation of material "proof" in biographical accounts.

Of Jones's technique in managing anecdotes, facts, and criticism, an admiring critic from the *Gentleman's Magazine* declares: "We entirely approve of the Editor's reasons for confining those additions to notes in preference to incorporating them in the text, by which means the works of an author become in a series of years a book of scraps and ends, without method and in half a dozen different styles.[126] The reviewer promises to include a few of the choicest new anecdotes in the review after observing "The Editor [Jones] has faithfully performed his task"; his assessment connects the virtue of the editor to the virtue of the original author. Thus, Jones gets a footnote in fame, and provides a bridge between sanctioned and unsanctioned readerly participation in theatrical biography. As an editor, Jones elevates Davies's biography as a work worth preserving. He also provides a model of what types of document might be usefully added, as well as how those documents might be spliced into the existing book in such a way as to be unobtrusively illustrative.

A different book of "scraps and ends": Queen Charlotte's *extra-illustrated* Life of Garrick

As we saw, a second *Life of David Garrick*—Murphy's—incorporated much of Davies's first *Memoirs of the Life of David Garrick*. Later, Stephen Jones incorporates parts of Murphy's biography into a revised edition of Davies's original. The cycle might seem interminable, especially as greater numbers of biographers join the fray. As much as formal additions to the established biographies might have been encountered warily, unofficial additions flourished in the hands of individual readers. A particularly popular type of intervention was the extra-illustrated scrapbook. The trend, which originated outside of theatrical biography in the 1770s, was described by Stuart Sherman as "a nascent genre that, at least within the cloistered context of theatrical archives, can seem to have been born for the sole purpose of sustaining Garrick's memory."[127] He points out the prominence of periodical press material in these scrapbooks, firmly linking scrapbooking to Garrick's flooding of the market with his own image and letters with the intention to fashion a "periodicals-based posterity." If we look at two examples of extra-illustrated theatrical biography, we see that each serves as a monument to David Garrick, but also to their owners, with different implications about textually based legacies than that seen with Garrick and Davies.

Later additions to a text of this period are described by two main terms: "annotated" refers to marginalia or notes and is a readerly practice quite common today; "extra-illustrated" is a term that, in the late eighteenth century, referred to a burgeoning trend of binding or rebinding an individual copy of a book to include illustrations, newspaper articles, playbills, or other related phenomena that were deemed relevant to the text by the extra-illustrator. This was easy enough to do, for, as D. C. Greetham reminds us, booksellers often sold "books" unbound, as "binding was still considered as separate from the book itself and thus one area in which the idiosyncrasies of the individual owner could be indulged."[128] A less technical but widely accepted term denoting extra-illustrations is *grangerizing*, deriving from the last name of James Granger, whose earlier-mentioned *Biographical History of England* was specifically designed by Davies (as printer and bookseller) to encourage later illustration by individual buyers of the text.[129] A number of books of illustrations appropriate to the *Biographical History* marketed themselves as such, climbing in popularity through the 1820s.[130]

Just as every hand-annotated text will be different, each extra-illustrated copy of a text has a story to tell about how the text was read or used (or imagined to have been read or used). Each extra-illustrator thus greatly affects the understanding of the text based on his or her chosen amplifications or extractions. In acknowledgment of the role an extra-illustrator plays, the archival record lists the original and additional "author" of an extra-illustrated text when possible. It is comparatively rare to know the second author in such cases, as most of the books were altered for private consumption, and thus not labeled. Copies with acknowledged authors are particularly relevant to readers interested in peeping into the readerly practices of a biography's contemporary audience. One such person who did sign her extra-illustrated edition of Davies's *Life of Garrick* was Queen Charlotte of Mecklenburg, Consort to George III.

While the queen dates neither her receipt of the text nor her interventions, it seems reasonable to suspect that her additions occurred while the text was quite fresh. The two-volume, *Life of Garrick*, 18 cm (7 inches) tall, is expanded through Queen Charlotte's industry into four handsome volumes of 38 cm (15 inches), with expensive coverings and hand-drawn decorative borders on every page. Through several notes of provenance in the front of the first volume, Caroline Murray, who identifies herself as a former lady-in-waiting to the Duchess of Gloucester, elaborates on the significance of the text to the queen. Extra-illustration was the queen's pastime, including the "collecting and arranging of Prints, collating them with the page appropriately, and having these works, all relating to the Drama, rebound in this form."[131] The letter, signed August 1863, also lists a *Life of Colman* among Princess Sophia's literary inheritance of the illustrated *Life* from her mother, suggesting an assumption that theatrical *Lives* should be of particular note.

An additional, later note in the text, written in the pencil that so often indicates the work of a librarian, highlights the representative nature of the present copy of Garrick's biography: "Queen Charlotte, Consort of King George the Third, spent many leisure hours with books and prints about the theatre. This is an example of her handiwork in which she inserted appropriate prints in the text of a life of a famous actor, David Garrick."[132] Unlike later examples of annotators or extra-illustrator-annotators, Charlotte's practice precluded writing in the text beyond penning "The Queen" on the inside cover of each of the four volumes. She also commissioned a hand-drawn, multicolored title page for the third volume (actually the first half of Davies's second volume), in an attempt to "legitimize" her additions to Davies's work. For an extra-illustrator, what one chose to augment the text with, and how one went about it, left key clues about the illustrator's social status, preoccupations, degree of leisure, and generic expectations.[133]

Queen Charlotte's insertions change the phenomenological experience of the text, as did the work of an annotator, J. J. Cossart, on a copy of Cooke's 1804 biography of Charles Macklin, which I discuss in Chapter 2. Queen Charlotte's insertions change the phenomenological experience of the text. Each intervention affects our appreciation of a given text; Cossart contributed commentary and corrections to Cooke's writing, Charlotte's work is at first less invasive, amplifying rather than contesting the text that it seeks to illuminate. In all instances, Charlotte has selected pictures that are immediately relevant to the closest page: a portrait of the comedian Woodward complements the written portrait offered by Davies, confirming Davies's description of the man's appearance, with the effect that we can more readily imagine the movements of the figure pictured, as described by the accompanying text. In some cases, Charlotte has inserted several pictures of a single actor in multiple "characters," so that the motion is freeze-framed. She does not seem to have chosen portraits that contradict Davies's accounts. Because of the importance of visuals in theatrical biography, the queen's records are primarily helpful and, understandably, she is able to include a greater range of portraits of actors than might be available to collectors of lesser means.[134]

Charlotte's scrapbooks, of course, were for personal pleasure rather than resale, a window into her own world view. By virtue of her priorities, Charlotte's illustrations at times subtly overemphasize the part accorded to royalty, famous philosophers, and other bit players in the written record, as in the case of a portrait of Frederick, Prince of Wales, facing Davies's page 155 in volume 1 and George II in volume 3. Of course, portraits of actors and actresses were abundant, as evidenced not only from a sampling of granger-ized theatrical biographies at the turn of the century, but also by another helpful librarian's note identifying one illustration as "from Set of 12 portraits of Actors by Laurie." Charlotte's choice to have thespians mingle with royalty makes implicit claims for the role of actors, whose profession had come a long way from the earlier part of the century, when, Joe Roach reminds us, "players were despised."[135]

Pointon argues that the phenomenon of "collecting heads" rested on the "desire to [...] produce a complete map, which [...] would be open to tax-onomic investigation [... in which] the personal history of the illustrious in every rank, and in ever profession, will be referred to its proper place [...]

The collecting of 'heads' is thus an epistemology that can be understood as ordering society and making visible the body politic."[136] This does not seem to be upheld by the interplay between kings and actors in thespian scrapbooks. The "medieval bio-political schema of the *corpus Christianum*" that undergirded Granger's biographical classifications of heads deemed royal heads as "Class I" and "artificers" as Class X, along with "Painters, Mechanics, and all of inferior Professions."[137] So thoroughly does Charlotte mix Class I and X that, had Charlotte's creation been stripped of Davies's words, it might have been difficult to determine exactly whom the biography was about, as her collection is of Garrick's rather courtly world rather than of Garrick himself.

While there is a danger in abstracting too distantly the reading habits of an entire town based on a single book copy, Queen Charlotte's interest in theatrical biography is worth considering. Evidently, she had a well-known interest in extra-illustrating, and was known to direct this interest primarily, if not exclusively, to books about the theatre. To some extent, the ease of acquiring material representations—tickets, playbills, portraits, and other items commonly appearing in grangerized texts—makes theatrical books an obvious choice. On the other hand, Charlotte doesn't include tickets and playbills, which would have more concretely demonstrated her own presence at the theatre; she also demonstrates a focused interaction with the text, not sprinkling Garrick memorabilia indiscriminately between any two pages. It is obvious that she read and, presumably, enjoyed Davies's work; and that those around her realized the value of the texts to her by noting their later presence in Charlotte's daughter Sophia's library and iterating (and reiterating) the value of the text within the very pages of that text, lest later readers should miss the significance of Charlotte's work.

Objectively, Charlotte's approach to the text aligns her with the authorial practices of Curll and other hack writers who primarily piece together existing objects for the sake of amassing more material. However, her materials—fine art engravings—and method of placement based on a key word in the text are systematic rather than simply accretive, more akin to Davies's insertion of letters in the narrative than to those in Murphy's displaced appendix. But extra-illustrations belong on a continuum, and not all such "authors" have access to the time and materials available to a queen: in those volumes, the "scrap" in "scrapbook" may manifest much more literally.

Overwriting a Life: *An anonymous* Life of Garrick *scrapbook*

Theatrical biography seems to invite reflection upon one's own place in the world, a phenomenon that forms one of the strands of argumentation in Chapter 2. Suffice to say, the consideration of a thespian's impermanence onstage and our corresponding impermanence in the world's memory, not to mention the thespian's death as the occasion of theatrical biography, seem to yoke theatrical biography to death. We saw that Queen Charlotte valued her theatrical biography collections not just for their innate or market value, but for the investment in time that she made to augmenting them, enough to formally include them as part of her (explicitly regal) legacy to her daughter. The books thus became a stand-in for her, a physical artifact passed down in lieu of her physical presence.

Providing a remarkable contrast in appearance to Queen Charlotte's beloved *Garrick*, an anonymous scrapbook housed at the Folger Library also claims the title of *Life of Garrick*, and also serves as a glimmer of insight into the life of the scrapbooker himself.[138] Labeled as an eighteenth-century manuscript—for of course many of the engravings and text would have been made in the 1700s—the work looks to have been compiled in the first few years of the nineteenth century, certainly after 1801, as it makes use of documents published in that year, but probably not much later, based on the comparative meagerness of the collection and lack of scrapbooking technique. Notwithstanding its purposefully made binding, it is, as Garrick scrapbooks go, a notably philistine effort, a comparatively lean eighty-six pages in length, with ragged edges, readily visible tabs for edging in later additions, and clumsily pasted-in clippings that sacrifice one page of each leaf to the pasting process. More sophisticated scrapbookers, such as Queen Charlotte, would cut a frame into a larger sheet, enabling viewers to see both sides of a leaf. At first glance, it does not appear to be a *Life of Garrick*, but rather, the carcass of a French book offering a collection of capsule biographies of leading English public figures.

With the exception of the first few pages, a pattern emerges of a short biography on the verso, or the left side of the page, serving as "backing" for the recto, or right side of the page, which would have a scrap of Garrickiana pasted over the biography originally printed there. Thus, the left side of one page features part of Charles I's biography, while the narrative on the right side has been purposefully obscured by a handwritten bit about the year in which Garrick came to the English stage.[139] A fragment of Cromwell's biography faces off against a portrait of Garrick as Hamlet.[140] Biographies of George I and II are less than augustly opposed to a syncopated account of the Stratford Jubilee (syncopated because one side of every leaf has been pasted to the book).[141] Such juxtapositions invite the reader to consider Garrick not only as literally overwriting history, but also as having value before—or even in spite of—a number of traditionally more hallowed British figures, further collapsing the distinction between kings and actors. Although the book copy is far from perfect, with several pages bound upside down, and two pages of the original text appear in English rather than in French, the owner still went to some effort to create the scrapbook and willfully decided that a *Life of Garrick* was worth rendering unusable at least twenty-nine other "Lives."[142] This makes a strong case for the importance not just of biography, but of theatrical biography, as something to be experienced in an individual's life: the popularity of the genre may be a function of accessibility, as I will suggest later, as a regular Englishman might hope to meet a Garrick while attending the theatre but might not have felt such a connection to a remote member of the British royalty.[143]

The anonymous author—or more appropriately, compiler of this alternative *Life of Garrick*—takes a page (figuratively and literally) from Thomas Davies and Arthur Murphy's biographies, along with numerous popularly printed etchings of Garrick in costume and as himself.[144] The six leaves taken from Davies come from two different sections of the work: the account of the Stratford Jubilee, Chapter 45 of volume 2, and the account of David Garrick and Spranger Barry's competition over the part of Romeo, which occurs in Chapter 12 of volume 1. The proceedings in which Garrick attempts to route the sultry rival actor of Covent Garden by secretly mounting a production of the star-crossed lovers at his Drury Lane are immortalized in a pithy epigram, recorded by Davies and preserved by this anonymous scrapbooker, who speaks to the frustration of having to watch the same play at both playhouses for almost a fortnight:

"Well, what's to-night," says angry Ned,
As up from bed he rouses? "Romeo again!" and shakes his head;
Ah! pox on both your houses![145]

For reasons difficult to fathom, this anonymous scrapbooker follows three leaves from the Jubilee with yet another leaf about Romeo, returns to the Jubilee for one more page, and returns to Romeo for a leaf. Either because he had access only to these two "high points" or had selected these very "Shakespearean" moments as the two most essential parts of Garrick's life as told by Davies, the compiler then adds a single page from Arthur Murphy's biography of Garrick: the first page of Chapter 9, which comments on Garrick's status as "another Proteus, in the celerity with which he transformed himself into different shapes."[146] This addition suggests that the compiler did have some interest in what Garrick actually *did* while onstage, as Murphy mentions Garrick's ability to change "his voice, which was naturally clear and agreeable to the ear [but which, as John Brute] was changed to a rough and sullen tone." Even for the less materially sophisticated scrapbooker, descriptions of the actor receive priority. Turning back to the two incidences from Davies, the rival Romeos illustrates the potential for competition between actors (actually, Barry and Garrick usually practiced a peaceable division of audiences), and the Stratford Jubilee outlines the growing accessibility of David Garrick as someone available not just onstage, but offstage as well. One could, as Boswell did, attend the Stratford Jubilee, and even participate in the parade. Both incidents are larger than life, and yet accessible.

Scrapbooks (or extra-illustration, or annotation) are ultimately about participation: scrapbooking itself is an act of participation. Queen Charlotte's text and the anonymous text represent memorials to what an individual has witnessed and experienced during his or her life, and, more specifically, how these aggregated texts memorialize an individual's links with public personages via autographs and historical events.[147] While Queen Charlotte's extra-illustrations reflect a more sterile aesthetic of "I am immortalizing evidence that this happened," the anonymous scrapbook projects an ethos of "I am immortalizing evidence that I was there," as he may have stripped the advertisement of *Othello* from a wall, or acquired the signature of an actor in a coffee shop. Pointon notes that the desire for autographs came about in the eighteenth century, when more people wrote their own letters, and says that the vogue "marks the shift from a concern with the sign of the historic person to an interest in the trace of that person's actual existence."[148] Even in the case of Queen Charlotte, whose illustrations were undoubtedly taken from books, the act of intervening in the text is a testament to the inclination to devote an irreplaceable portion of one's life to the act of memorializing. The impulse to record something fleeting, in all instances, is at work, even if the announced centrality of oneself to the project of scrapbooking varies.

Like second and third iterations of an author's life, edited versions and newspaper abridgements, the scrapbook continues to demonstrate (often more radically) the sanctioning of readers to increasingly insert themselves into or otherwise play within the space of the memorialized life. So frequently, thespian biography was attendant upon death, and thus the rise of the newspaper genre obituary-biography and the inclusion, as early as Booth's first biography, of intimate details of the actor's autopsy—invasive, but mediated.[149] In a similar, but arguably more macabre vein, Garrick's anonymous scrapbooker appears to have attended Garrick's funeral in order to collect signatures of the mourners at this last public spectacle. This death register, helpfully labeled "the list of persons that followed the late Mr. Garrick's remains in 1779" is comprised of cobbled-together strips of tatty yellowing paper bearing individual signatures.[150] At least some of the signatures are certainly legitimate originals based on obvious variations in the hand; other signatures seem remarkably similar in penmanship, both in terms of letter formation and pressure of strokes, suggesting the author's commitment to making the register comprehensive.[151] The register can lift up to reveal the original text of the French capsule biographies: one of several pages on David Hume can be found underneath the third page of the register.

The signatures, which imbue cast-away paper with special significance, partially obscure the scraps of the French book that used to hold meaning. Thus, scrapbooking represents both the cure and the disease. In dissecting a book, program, or other memento to repurpose it, the original record is abridged, if not rendered unintelligible; the dismemberment of the prior artifact is committed in service of creating a new artifact designed to preserve or memorialize.[152] As I suggested earlier, scrapbooking in particular upends the paradigm established in theatrical biography of disdaining cut-and-paste: scrapbook is cut-and-paste to the exclusion of the cohesive narrative so prized in traditional biography.

Scrapbook culture, while an obvious extension of the biographical impulse, is not designed to result in great fame for the individual creator. Unlike the theatrical biographer, who must always worry about the obsolescence of his version of a story, the scrapbooker's own immortality is not a concern because a private scrapbook can less easily be rewritten, declared unimportant, or entirely replaced than an "official" mass-produced *Life*. Davies, who puts his name to the title page of his work, is at the vanguard of the "personalization" push for "official" biographies, shown by the abandonment of pseudonyms and anonymity. For expansions or alterations of a biography, the scrapbook shows signs of agency without identifying the agent: anonymity is the rule, not the exception. What emerges from the contrast of theatrical biography in the form of a continuous narrative versus scraps is a dichotomy between the named and the unnamed, the accountable and the free. The only reputation of concern in scrapbooking is that of the subject. Anonymous cut-and-paste biography is not thrall to the constraints that an attributed linear biography faces because the motives of self-directed fame or monetary gain do not apply, and only the preservation of the subject remains.

Extra-illustration as a practice continued to flourish into the 1900s, with pronounced activity on theatrical biographies in the last two decades of the century. While beyond the scope of this examination, the fact that readers continued to extra-illustrate biographies of eighteenth-century actors by eighteenth-century authors stresses the importance accorded to early works of theatrical biography and, not infrequently, to the original authors whose works were reprinted to accommodate interest some hundred years after their first appearance. Thus, the biography, its basic text sometimes unchanged, and sometimes even greatly abridged or fragmented, became a vehicle of transcendence even as the additional materials available to the extra-illustrator varied from period to period. Davies lives on, no doubt in some part due to the interest shown by a great number of less-effective fellow biographers or now-anonymous readers who felt a need to respond to his writings, and thus perpetuate his name, even if only in scraps.

Davies as an Enduring Figure of Theatrical Biography

Through personal participation, first his own, and then that of his readers, Davies acquired more fame. In turn, readers wanted to know more about the author. In Davies's case, we are able to recognize him in the cast of characters encountered during the *Life of Johnson*, as readers at that time would have been able to do. Davies's name is carried on in future theatrical biographies and in readerly additions. In short, biography functions dually as a memorial or surety for the author and the actor-subject. Because Davies was the first to achieve very solid success writing thespian biography (rather than autobiography), his ascendance provided a model to a number of would-be biographers with their eye on future fame.

The present day's ultimate cut-and-paste source for biography, Wikipedia, where the presence of a page indicates some level of fame, lists "Thomas Davies (bookseller)" among the other famous Thomas Davies of the ages.[153] The *Dictionary of Literary Biography* notes the "frequency with which leading literary figures of the day referred to the Garrick biography."[154] Both sources pay attention to Davies's participation in literary, theatrical, and social scenes, especially as involved Johnson and Garrick. I should like to argue that the interest in Thomas Davies (onetime actor, bookseller, biographer, and colorful personality) would not have maintained relevance if not for his biographical enterprise; he would instead be just another small cog in Boswell's grand biography, a capsule biography unto himself.

What is so colorful about Davies, a small man relative to the popularly known terrain of famous eighteenth-century authors, slipping among the giant shadows cast by David Garrick and Samuel Johnson? The biographer lives on not only through his own writings, but as he appears, quite jauntily and much more directly, in the *Life of Johnson*. It seems fair that he should receive a mention, perhaps a vote of gratitude from the author, as we have already discovered that it was he who facilitated the meeting between Johnson and Boswell (and, indeed, I suspect, one of several models of biographical fame after which Boswell modeled his anticipated biographical career). Boswell actually gives several views of Davies, beginning with a character assessment: "Mr. Thomas Davies was a man of good understanding and talents, with the advantage of a liberal education. Though somewhat pompous, he was an entertaining companion; and his literary performances have no inconsiderable share of merit," opines Boswell.[155] Davies was a master at mimicking Johnson, a talent that only increased Boswell's desire to meet the doctor for himself. Of Johnson's laugh, his acolyte says, "It was a kind of good humoured growl. Tom Davies described it drolly enough: 'He laughs like a rhinoceros.'"[156] Johnson loved Davies and was sorry when he quarreled with the "somewhat dramatic" bookseller who was "not without pride and spirit."[157] More unpleasantly, Boswell relates that after Davies gave a mutual friend an encouraging clap on the back, one observer said "he could not conceive a more humiliating situation than to be clapped on the back by Tom Davies."[158]

There is both irony and poetic justice that Davies should receive his most sustained biographical treatment as a supporting character in the *Life of Johnson*. In life, he seems constantly to have been immersed in Johnson's shadow, and certainly would have been so in death, had he not written the *Life of Garrick*, and even that is not free from his connection to Johnson both because of Johnson's role in the creation of the book and his participation in the actual life of David Garrick as an early travel companion and prominent social contemporary.

Davies's name primarily lives on in the context of Garrick's biography and his innovations to the practice of theatrical biography in the eighteenth century. Almost twenty years before Boswell hitched his fame to Johnson, Davies achieved what was then unparalleled fame in theatrical biography based on the twin poles of the unexpected maturity of his biographical world view and his willingness to associate the work with his actual name and reputation. As mentioned earlier, so central to the work was Davies's reputation and character that while Davies did not discuss himself as a subject within the biography, the reviews almost invariably commented upon the author and thus left incremental memorials to the man behind the *Life of Garrick*. Davies's character lived on after death. The *Gentleman's Magazine* comments on the popularity of the *Life of Garrick* as a function of Davies's appeal: "Such was the reliance of the literary world upon the amiability and integrity of Mr. Davies's character, that they approved, and the public admired."[159] Conversely, Percy Fitzgerald, who was perhaps the most voluminous and well-known practitioner of thespian biography in the latter 1800s, wrote contemptuously of the "faithless biographer" in his own *Life of Garrick* (1868): "It is a relief to be able to finish with one who has played so unworthy a part in Garrick's life—whose own life was such an alternation from bullying to fawning, from bluster to obsequiousness."[160]

Perhaps even more important than the effect of Davies's work on the representation of Garrick as a historical subject is his impact on the general practice of theatrical biography. The second chapter of my book, presenting three rival presentations of the life of Charles Macklin, a comedian, will expand upon the increasing competition between biographers, a situation we saw developing with Murphy's absorption and correction of Davies's account in his *Life of Garrick* and one that was subsequently played upon by editors and readers.[161] This competition is spurred on by the realization following Davies's success that a biography may serve as a memorial not only to the subject, but also to the author—thus, we see Davies's convention of naming himself become a norm, and an increase in authors inserting themselves more deeply into the action of the biography. The increasing understanding of theatrical biography as a profession unto itself leads to the application of the "cult of the author" status, generally denied to the genre up to that point. These changes, and the accompanying revisions to the theory of theatrical biography, will be discussed in the third chapter, which finds its center on the serial biographer James Boaden.

Chapter 2

HIS WORK, MY WORDS: ANXIETY AND COMPETITION IN THE POSTHUMOUS LIVES OF CHARLES MACKLIN, COMEDIAN

Establishing Expectations: The Biographer as Artist

"This is the Jew that Shakespeare drew!" So runs the most famous bon mot about Charles Macklin, comedian (ca. 1699–1797), supposedly spoken extemporaneously by Alexander Pope after witnessing Macklin assay the role of Shylock in the early 1740s. In 1968, J. O. Bartley introduced his edited version of Macklin's plays, *Four Comedies by Charles Macklin*, by suggesting that if any person could successfully make the transition from flesh to page, it would be Charles Macklin, due to the stodgy actor and playwright's strongly delineated characters, which he often wrote for himself, as versions of himself. This chapter seeks to evaluate the extent to which Macklin's early biographers were able to portray the man who drew the Jew that Shakespeare drew.

Certainly there was something special about Charles Macklin: upon his death in 1797, Macklin supplied the subject for three biographies in just six short years. Almost immediately, Francis Congreve's concise *Authentic Memoirs of the Late Charles Macklin, Comedian* (1798) appeared, followed by James Kirkman's strikingly inflated *Memoirs of the Life of Charles Macklin* (1799), and finally William Cooke's *Memoirs of Charles Macklin, Comedian* (1804). In contrast, the almost undisputed leading actor of the mid-eighteenth century and renowned pursuer of fame, David Garrick (1717–1779), had only two full-length biographies to his name in the same time period, spaced twenty years apart.[1] This chapter attempts to address the intersections of temporality and preservation that fascinated and repelled theatrical biographers. I will particularly focus on the extent to which biographers could hope to overcome the barriers of time and space imposed in the shift from live performance to fixed text, and the effects of those anxieties still legible upon the biographies themselves.

It is easy to accept Macklin, an actor, as an artist; he brings a character to life from a playbook. The theatrical biographer performs a parallel but inverse operation, bringing a character to life from the stage onto the pages of biography. However, an assessment of current criticism involving biography as a genre shows a pervasive tendency toward discounting biography as having literary value in its own right. Biography, with few exceptions, is equated with source texts that enrich or explain literary works, more akin to an encyclopedia than a novel.[2] Thus, when *The Guardian's* critic Tom Paulin was faced with evaluating Richard Holmes's *Sidetracks: Explorations of a Romantic Biographer* in 2000, he charged Holmes with overstepping generic expectations, writing, "Is the biographer an artist who can and should exist on equal terms with the dramatist, fiction writer and poet? The short and robust answer is 'certainly not.'"[3]

Although I believe that the time is ripe for a reconsideration of biography as an artistic genre, I wish to consider, in this chapter, the unique artistic challenges of the theatrical biographer in particular. There is little debate that many theatrical biographies in the eighteenth century were rushed, overstuffed, plodding tomes of miscellanea; however, this chapter urges us to consider not only the stated purpose of theatrical biography at the time, but also the extent to which the biographers achieved it, and by what means. In effect, it asks that we consider the eighteenth-century biographer as an artist, even in those instances where his art falls far short of expectations.

This chapter thus centers on two foci: first, it turns to theatrical biography as a test-case for my revised understanding of biography as an art, arguing that theatrical biography goes beyond a strictly factual account of which plays a performer participated in and to what acclaim as measured by tickets or audience commentary. The biographer also captures portions of the actual onstage activity because of the specific criteria of evaluating performance in the eighteenth century. Second, concentrating on Charles Macklin as my case study, I argue that the specific temporal conditions surrounding theatrical biography coalesce into the biographer and actor sharing similar anxieties in relation to their art, an anxiety that provides metacommentary on the particularly competitive nature of originality in the eighteenth century, even in genres that might initially seem to foster collaboration in place of contest.

I hope to highlight the unique struggles faced by theatrical biographers in terms of their own technique and, perhaps more important, their own understanding of challenges. I suggest a special role for theatrical "points" and anecdotes, in capturing the lifeblood of theatrical judgment at the time, and in bringing the stage to narrative. I note, also, that the use of anecdote both engenders and endangers the narrative, especially in the case of the Macklin biographies here under consideration. Finally, calling upon an annotated version of Macklin's third biography, I indicate that the reader response to theatrical biography was dynamic. Although readers recognized and responded to the idea that the actors could not entirely be faithfully recaptured in a static art form, there was ongoing engagement with the actors through theatrical biography and the accretion of layers of mythos.

Tracing the parallels between actor and author

Marvin Carlson's contention in his book *The Haunted Stage: Theatre as Memory Machine* that all performers and audiences face a stage crowded with ghosts (or memories held by the audience and the performer himself) of the previous persons who have played a role, of the previous roles the particular actor has assayed, and of other conditions that overlap with prior performer or spectator memory can easily be applied to theatrical biographers.[4] Because the biographer's task of assessing an actor was so frequently comparative in nature, he could not help but be attuned to the competition that he himself faced from other biographers (and from his readers' comparisons). Thus, the biographer's temporal concerns amplified those of the actor, while recontextualizing them into the new medium of translation.

This section argues for a shared experience between actor and biographer as the biographer, in effect, joins the long line of people who have "performed" the roles of a chosen thespian, while also competing with other biographers for the right to tell the story. Overarching this chapter is the claim that theatrical biography is worthy of study simply for discovering the extent to which, and how, biographers sought to preserve what the thespian did onstage—as well as for the ways in which that task affected biographers as fellow artists. We can see these anxieties first in the general story of the actor Charles Macklin, as he struggles to become known and remain relevant, and again in the retelling of that story by multiple biographers who must battle the ghosts of their predecessors and ensure their own relevance in the face of newer, forthcoming biographies.

Charles Macklin, the subject of this chapter—or more appropriately, the subject once removed, as I primarily am interested in Macklin through his biographies—achieved prominence in London when he appeared as Shylock in Shakespeare's *The Merchant of Venice*. Both true to, and complicating, Carlson's theory of returning to the grandfather at the expense of the father in the pursuit of novelty, Macklin introduced three innovations to the role. First, Macklin restored Shakespeare's "original" version of *Merchant*, eschewing *The Jew of Venice*, an adaptation by George Granville that had held sway as "Shakespeare's" play since its appearance in 1701. Second, Macklin took it upon himself to painstakingly research what he believed to be Jewish costumes,

customs and mannerisms, appearing onstage in historical dress and attempting to "act" appropriately Jewish. Finally, he elected to portray Shylock as a
straight man, rejecting the overwhelming expectation of the character as a
laughable comedic figure.[5] Unwittingly giving keen insight into some of the
anxieties and solutions that he himself found when approaching Macklin's
life story as his third biographer, William Cooke writes of Macklin's strategic
approach to Shylock:

> He very properly considered he was then in a situation, which, by assi-
> duity and enterprize, [sic] might add something to his rising fame as an
> actor, which at no other time of his life before he had such an opportu-
> nity of attempting; and that "there was no lucky minute after the first
> opportunity." He therefore cast about in his mind what new part he
> should adopt, and to this purpose carefully looked over the stock list, as
> well as several obsolete plays, to find out one which he thought appropri-
> ate to his own powers and conception.[6]

Cooke depicts a very cunning approach to the selection of roles by an actor
who connected novelty with long-lasting appeal. Macklin's own writings
uphold Cooke's understanding of the actor's career strategy, revealing its ram-
ifications, with the actor writing pitifully on February 17, 1773, toward the
end of his time onstage, to Drury Lane manager George Colman that it was
imperative he not be featured too frequently in two of his main roles because
his success at that point primarily relied on novelty.[7] But in 1741, according
to Cooke, Macklin was simply looking for the right vehicle to stardom. This
approach seems to foreshadow that of the great biographer James Boswell,
whom Leo Braudy describes as having the revelation that he "had the desire
to write but no subject," and "he wanted to be recognized but wasn't sure
why or how."[8] Cooke writes, "Macklin saw this part [The Jew] with other
eyes; and, very much to the credit of his taste and understanding, as well as a
proper estimation of his own powers, he found he could build a reputation by
reviving the original of Shakespeare, and playing the character of Shylock in
a different manner."[9]

   Shylock, or the Granvillian adaptation that Macklin confronted, actually
formed an ideal entry point for an actor who was conscious of the existing
onstage pecking order. In reviving Shakespeare's "original" work, since it had
been unseen and unheard for four decades, he bypassed the threat of treading
on the toes of the more experienced thespians in his troupe, who had not had
the opportunity to play Shylock using Shakespeare's script. The existence of
the adaptation allowed Macklin to bypass the father (Granville) to confront the
grandfather (Shakespeare), without having to grapple with a developed oral or

written tradition about exactly how Burbage would have played the role under Shakespeare's direction (tragic or not). Furthermore, by performing the role in a tragic manner, he evaded the likelihood of merely replicating his immediate predecessor in the role. In his bid to secure fame as Shylock, Macklin not only dismissed the tired customary Shylock outfit, he tossed out the prompt-book of Granville's script that had been handed down through decades of Shylocks, and spurned the performance of traditional points and flourishes expected of a comedic Shylock. Thus, Macklin became both "original" in the sense of a novel take on an existing work, and "original" as indicative of a return to the character's roots.

Although writing the definitive biography of Charles Macklin might not seem to have notable parallels to acting the definitive portrayal of Shakespeare's Shylock, Cooke and his fellow Macklin biographers seem to have recognized a kindred spirit in their subject's drive for possession of a story already told. Macklin's story was an attractive one, both because of his strongly delineated characters (personal and onstage) and his immense longevity: his first and third biographers record him as living for 98 years, his second biographer 107. He had come to the theatre later in life, achieving prominence in his forties or fifties. This timing was ideal for a theatrical biographer because a work about Macklin could align perfectly as a companion piece and continuation of Colley Cibber's *Apology*, which had offered the history of the stage from the Restoration until 1740. Macklin's biographers could present Macklin as a second Cibber figure, with the history resuming neatly in 1741 (the year that Macklin achieved prominence as Shylock) and continuing up to the very end of the century.

Undoubtedly, this propitious timing occurred to Macklin, who had set about beginning his autobiography, outlining it in his Autograph Papers with the aid of materials about himself culled, possibly beginning as early as 1754. The autobiography was to call upon his commonplace books as well, in which he had written his observations on miscellaneous subjects of interest to himself and, presumably, to posterity. Numerous friends remarked that it would be a great project, but that Macklin lacked the temperament and discipline to complete such a ponderous task when there were innumerable projects among which he could flit until they no longer amused him.[10] Ultimately, the majority of the notes and outlines for that work were lost when a ship carrying Macklin's worldly effects from London to his native Ireland capsized; the remaining scraps suggest that a life of Macklin by Macklin might have consisted of many political digressions and moral lessons, hardly the tour de force that his third biographer, Cooke, imagined that such a work might have been.[11] And, as Cooke was well aware, Macklin left behind a field of opportunity for the biographer eager to weld his own name to Macklin's story.

Rising to the Biographical Occasion

The question must be asked: How could one capture a thespian's onstage antics in a book, given the different dynamics of each situation? Paying attention to how acting was evaluated at the time actually suggests biography's place as a useful representative art. Having indicated the potential obstacles to preserving onstage action (Cibber says it is impossible to preserve the electric fire of "harmonious elocution" and "elegant grace"), nearly all a function of the supposed poverty of memory and difficulty of intermedium translation, I turn specifically to three components of acting theory and pragmatics. These three components, while not solving the totality of problems arising from attempting to encapsulate a theatrical performance on paper, at least provide a poignant counterpoint to our assumption about the absolute inability of biography to capturing onstage antics.

Paradoxically, the obsession with time that characterizes Cibber's "Pity it is" comment actually touches on the period-specific principles used to critique acting, which both justify and disqualify biography and autobiography as suitable genres for the recording of performance. Palfrey and Stern note that pronuntiatio and actio—pronunciation, particularly as pertains to the delivery of a speech as outlined in the five canons of classical rhetoric, and movement/gesture—were considered, from the time of Shakespeare, to be measures of successful acting.[12] William Worthen, in *The Idea of the Actor* (1984), observes a desire in Renaissance, Restoration, and neoclassical acting to discover universal gestures; in *The Actor, or A Treatise on the Art of Playing* (1750), John Hill similarly emphasizes the yearning to standardize interpretation.[13] Joseph Roach identifies Gildon's 1710 biography of Betterton (which, lacking biographical detail per se, I prefer to classify as an acting treatise) as "modernizing *pronuntiatio* and *elocutio* of classical rhetoric" to provide for posterity a "monumental record of what eloquence meant to their forebears."[14]

The qualities of pronuntiatio could be demonstrated in brief snatches: for example, Sarah Siddons's biographer Thomas Campbell, writing in 1834, constantly praises the actress's remarkably clear and powerful elocution, but only specifically describes her initial difficulties in overcoming her unfortunate "provincial ti-tum-ti."[15] Campbell also records Garrick's obnoxious reliance on the verbal padding "eh, eh." Assessing his own performances, Cibber comments that he was hampered by his own voice quality—specifically, the thinness of it—but he cannot represent this thinness. Unhappily for Cibber, *The Laureat*, an anonymous response to the *Apology*, offers a singularly unflattering review of the actor's pronunciation as Richard III: "Our Comic-Tragedian came on the Stage, really breathless, and in a seeming Panick [sic], screaming out this Line thus—A Harse, a Harse, my Kingdom for a Harse."[16]

Generally, though, an unkind review or brief reference to vowels or errant breathing habits constitutes the recording of pronuntiatio available to biographers. (And autobiographies seem not to labor on elocution, perhaps because of the authors' perceived license to omit parts of their own life, especially shortcomings.)

Autobiography—and especially biography—excelled at describing actio. On its most basic level, actio can be described like pronuntiatio: Siddons is depicted by Campbell as "rolling [...] from side to side, swelling with the triumph of her son" as Coriolanus's mother, just as evocatively as Cibber was depicted as "screaming" his lines in Richard III. Both recountings provide sharp sensory impressions.[17] But an understanding of eighteenth- and nineteenth-century acting conventions again reclaims biography from the perceived futility of capturing onstage performance. Actio, besides being theorized in rigorous detail by actors like Heywood, Cibber, and Betterton, was also measured by the curious convention of theatrical pointing.

"Points," declares Worthen, "provided a structured moment of intense emotion,"[18] and in fact became the key marker of an actor's success or failure in a role during the majority of the eighteenth century. As "a device emphasizing technique more than meaning," pointing promoted comparisons between actors in the same role precisely because comparisons were possible when applied to isolated moments of a longer performance.[19] A steady theme of auto/biographies about actors in the long eighteenth-century is these "pointed" comparisons. The two most well-rehearsed moments occur in Hamlet, when Hamlet encounters his father's ghost for the first time, and in Macbeth, during Lady Macbeth's candlelight scene. Betterton's name is inevitably linked to the actor's innovation of falling over a chair upon seeing the ghost.[20] Biographers and critics delight in discussing Garrick's mechanized "shock" wig and horrible grimace, the latter of which is immortalized in a series of paintings.[21]

Sarah Siddons describes her decision to break with Mrs. Pritchard's traditional candlelight "point" as Macbeth's wife: it was "presumptuous innovation" to dispense with the candle, a hallmark expected by the audience; the candle's absence became one of her own signature moments.[22] Similarly, in taking over the part of Lady Randolph, Siddons omitted Crawford's signature scream, a gamble that incited audience approval.[23] In the earlier part of the century, Colley Cibber understood the theatrical economy of comparison, observing that an actor's deviations, perhaps even more than his successful replication, brought to mind that actor's predecessors. As anomalies were the heart of criticism, violating the established points was a sure way to differentiate oneself, receiving harsh censure or rapturous applause.

Points themselves emphasize the delicate balance actors faced: one might either be compared unfavorably to one's forbear in a role because of misguided innovation, or participate in what Joseph Roach calls "the doomed search for originals by continuously auditioning stand-ins."[24] Cibber, having been called as understudy to a character usually played by Doggett, assayed to be the best Cibber-as-Doggett-as-Old Batchelor (rather than the best Cibber-as-Old Batchelor); conversely, Siddons was known to gamble with innovation due to her "fear of being taxed with imitation."[25] Theatrical criticism and practice as mixed together in auto/biography reveal—and revel in—an inherent conflict: how should one treat the standard delivery that was handed down from player to player while hoping to make a name for oneself?[26]

As an actor does, the biographer receives some immutable facts, but he maintains the prerogative of presentation in the form of inclusion, emphasis, and interpretation. Although biography cannot entirely capture the anxieties of originality and precedence made manifest onstage, the genre productively enacts such anxieties of originality and competition in an unexpected way (especially for a genre that, some insist, does not partake in creativity). Theatrical biography's use of points to achieve the fundamentally stated goal of the genre reifies and amplifies the competitive element of ownership that might otherwise still be present, but less visible, in other forms of biographical writing.

Not only are points, fixed moments in an otherwise fluid performance, able to be conveyed by biographies, biographical art imitates theatrical art as these points in turn became expected in biographies, varying only by the biographer's arrangement of the point in relation to his larger narrative and his critique of the specific actor whose points were recounted. Thus, the point, which allowed the audience to evaluate an actor compared to his predecessors, mapped onto biography, with any biographer worth his salt seizing on predictable points of the actors and, as time went by, predictable points that stood out in other auto/biographies. These points translate quite wonderfully into the form of anecdotes: both are short and characteristic moments of significance that have been pared down for ease of memory. The effects of anecdotes as succor and threat to the success of the biographical project will receive extended consideration shortly, but for now I will stress their similarity to points in becoming expected moments rife for comparison between "performers"—actors, and then, biographers.

For example, Cibber's oft-repeated "Pity it is" comment, quoted at length earlier, achieves a similar shorthand status as the tale about Kemble's controversial substitution of an empty chair for Banquo's ghost, or Quin's comment upon finding out that he had acted in an adaptation rather than in Shakespeare's "original" Lear: "Have I not all this time been acting Shakespeare's play?"[27] Such points become expected in auto/biography; all three of these anecdotal moments appeared in Campbell's biography of

Siddons as a deliberate nod to expectations. Carlson's discussion of theatrical adaptation, a genre that gradually fell out of favor in the nineteenth century, praises the efficacy of allowing audiences to focus not on "what the plot is but how it's being presented, allowing an avenue of uniqueness without losing the benefit of familiarity—in effect, the author can stress his own originality by presenting a variation on a known story."[28] This relationship similarly allows the artist to make his own impression while telling an already-told life—the domain of history. Thoroughness and presentation are reinforced as means of originality, a characteristic generally (and unfairly) denied to biographers.

While stage biographers in the eighteenth and early nineteenth centuries theoretically attempted to capture the theatrical experience of their subject through conveying, with varying degrees of success, the actor's delivery and gestures in reference to specific roles, the very act of shaping the narrative results in a competing story focused on the biographer himself and his relationship to his competitors in terms of originality. In a sense, every biography becomes autobiography. Cibber recognizes the competitive aspects of autobiography, noting that he penned his own biography before anyone could "interrupt" or "contradict" him: he triumphs both as the chief authority on himself (the original performer of the "role" of Colley Cibber) and as the first to write about his subject extensively.[29] The authority for applying theatrical terminology to auto/biography is no less than Cibber himself, who wittily announces, "The Part I have acted in real Life, shall be all of a piece [...] I will not go out of my Character."[30]

With Macklin's failure to produce an autobiography, three competitors came to the fore: Congreve, Kirkman, and Cooke. Each of them brought his own character, as well as his interpretation of the role of the biographer and how his aim might be best achieved. The competitive spirit manifested itself in three discrete attempts at the hybridization of theatrical biography with other genres—literary biography, fictive biographical novel, and collections of anecdotes—innovations designed to snatch the laurels from the earlier biographer or biographers.

The part of the biographer

One need look no further than Macklin's first biographer, Congreve, to perceive a defensive, forward-looking attitude toward his task, presented as being steeped in comparison and competition. Notwithstanding that Congreve's biography is little more than a pamphlet some sixty pages in length, its author appears to have an esteemed opinion of what he is doing, not just because of the value of biography as a genre, but due to Macklin as a subject. He says, "Few characters, who have filled the circle of active or busy life, have more justly merited the recording hand of Biography, to perpetuate their names, than the late Father of the British Drama."[31] The impersonal unity implied by the hand of Biography simultaneously deflects and points attention to Congreve, who stresses his own honesty and attention to correcting false details and adding new, true ones. Again, we see the attention paid to Macklin based upon his relationship to time, as well as to Britain's history. Congreve notes, "His [Congreve's—not Macklin's] labours will meet with that reward, which a just and liberal nation is ever ready to bestow on productions of real worth."[32] Perhaps he protests too much: with his subject's worthiness and his own veracity balanced to correspond with Britain's maintenance of its reputation as "a just and liberal nation," Congreve's aggressive defense of his project points to a possible gap between author and audience in terms of the text's—and perhaps the genre's—perceived contributions.

Just as Thomas Davies grounds the legitimacy of his biography of Garrick in the urging of Samuel Johnson, Congreve hearkens back to Rome to establish his work's pedigree and, correspondingly, to demand respect from his fellow Britons. He contrasts the value of his work in present-day Britain with the equally meritorious biographies of Roman actors that Britain had once "consigned to oblivion" by "the spirit of contumely." He claims that such an attitude no longer prevails in Britain. Congreve has seized upon the competitive nature of his enterprise. Pitting present-day England against the England that failed to preserve Roman biography, he compares actors, "the children of the histrionic muse," to "the patriot or the hero" as equally deserving "a niche in the proud structure of Fame." For Congreve, his project's worth is inseparable from his subject's worth; the value of subject and iteration in turn grant him legitimacy as one who "perpetuate[s] the actions of men, eminent in their respective professions, [which] ought ever to be the theme of the impartial Biographer."[33]

Having ennobled his subject and his enterprise, he reveals a lofty intent to correct the existing factual inaccuracies to spare the embarrassment of "the future Biographer."[34] This is the prerogative of a man who is celebrating his luck at arriving first on a stage that will soon become crowded. While Congreve may merely intend to minimize the economic motive of making one shilling and sixpence per copy, his wording suggests that he anticipates further Macklin studies, and that he sees his role as not only gathering the facts of Macklin, but also as paying particular attention to correcting the untruths of illegitimate, less formal accounts in preparation for his successor. Congreve can afford to be generous, as he has not had to compete with other biographies of Macklin: he is, in effect, the originator of the role.

Congreve does, however, have his own model in mind, one that speaks to his view not only of his subject, but also of his genre and even of his own authorship. Congreve elects to end the character sketch, and indeed the entire biography, by comparing Macklin to Samuel Johnson, whose biography had appeared in 1791. Perhaps in a quest to look impartial, as he had sometimes indicated a fondness for Macklin, or with the goal of imitating Boswell imitating Johnson's love of balanced character assessments, Congreve first highlighted primarily unattractive qualities. Dr. Johnson and Macklin shared a "dictatorial style" of conversation, a pronounced dislike of Scottish people, and a resolute desire to obtain victory in arguments, "for if his pistol missed aim, he would knock a person down with the end but [sic] of it."[35] Nonetheless, Congreve says, adopting the traditional verdict of Samuel Johnson that Boswell also embraced, Macklin's failures were outmatched by his virtues, with abilities "few have equaled, still fewer excelled." By concluding his biography with the claim that Macklin was like Samuel Johnson, Congreve is according the comparison great importance. He was, additionally, attempting to harness some of the immense popularity of Boswell's biography, which Congreve and many of his intended audience had undoubtedly read.

It was, of course, common for the biographer to stress the exemplarity of his subject, especially at the end of a work. Boswell, for his part, concludes his biography of Johnson by professing to be so overcome by the death of Johnson that he requires the support of a friend's words:

> I shall, therefore, not say one word of my own, but adopt those of an eminent friend, which he uttered with an abrupt felicity, superior to all studied compositions: – "He has made a chasm, which not only nothing can fill up, but which nothing has a tendency to fill up. Johnson is dead. Let us go to the next best: – there is nobody; no man can be said to put you in mind of Johnson."[36]

Immodestly, Congreve makes the claim that, as early as 1798, someone, namely a cranky Irishman known for his terrible temper, tedious lectures, and flights of fancy, *could* put you in mind of Johnson, and he, Congreve, had taken the liberty of writing that very man's biography. Boswell's eminent friend, William Gerard Hamilton, had wished to stress the exceptionality of Johnson by suggesting not only that nothing could replace Johnson (a typical sentiment) but also that nothing would even make the attempt to fill his place. Hamilton's sentiment could hardly be applied to Macklin, whose roles were designed to be filled and had already been apportioned out to spryer actors, including Henderson, King, and Kemble, with the next big Shylock, Edmund Kean, debuting the role in 1814.[37] Possibly because he was all too aware of the onslaught of competition for Macklin's limited laurels, Congreve challenges Hamilton's assertion by positing Macklin as a surrogate Samuel

Johnson through his persona and cultural importance. Moreover, Congreve lays siege to the notion that authors are less easily replaced than actors: by aligning Macklin with Johnson, Congreve may even seek to suggest that there is not a natural tendency for something to "fill up" the space of Macklin, only the artificial demand made by his profession.

In addition to claiming a high cultural position for Macklin, Congreve's appropriation of Samuel Johnson as parallel to his subject implies a comparison between Congreve and Boswell as biographers. If comparing Macklin to Johnson might serve to revise Macklin's status as an inherently replaceable actor, aligning himself with Boswell catapults Congreve's biographical endeavor not only toward the more serious pursuit of literary biography, but also, indeed, aims at the apex of that genre. Finally, the implied similarity of Congreve to Boswell negates Congreve's earlier stated intention to provide a strong foundation for a future, and presumably superior, biographer. If Macklin, like Johnson, is not replaceable, and Boswell was invaluable in capturing Johnson's allure, so too Macklin's achievement would be inseparable from Congreve's telling of the story.

Congreve's monumental moment of hubris to invite comparison between his meager pamphlet-cum-biography and Boswell's voluminous story of Dr. Johnson was answered, poetically, only a year later by Thomas Kirkman, the second "player" to inherit the role of Macklin's biographer.[38] Congreve would have had the greatest advantage relative to time: not only would his memory of Macklin onstage be the freshest, but with the exception of a few long-circulated anecdotes, large parts of Macklin's story were virgin territory, becoming Congreve's to tell for the first time. However, Congreve's biography was in no way comprehensive, and Kirkman had two tactics with which he sought to supersede Congreve's work, beyond simply ignoring any references to Congreve as a stepping-stone for his own biography: a personal relationship and access to private documents.

Like Congreve before him, Kirkman grumbles nonspecifically about other sources that had polluted the truth of Macklin's life, but asserts his role as the first actual authority with the power to set the record straight. Undoubtedly aware of his secondary position, Kirkman additionally elects to claim precedent of knowledge over prior storytellers based on his unique position as Macklin's close relative who had lived with the actor for some number of years before his passing.[39] Curiously, the exact relation between Kirkman and Macklin is unspecified, leading scholars to suspect that Kirkman exaggerated the degree of closeness between himself and his subject. Kirkman claims that his subject specifically requested that he write the biography and furnished him with private memoranda.[40] Routinely, the reader is confronted with Kirkman's insistence on his literal ownership of the story: "We shall here present the reader with Mr. Macklin's own account [...] copied verbatim et literatim from his Memorandum book, now before us."[41] "We shall present the reader with the following specimens of the lectures [...] copied verbatim from the papers of Mr. Macklin."[42] Congreve could not have hoped to compete with Kirkman, who, scholars have confirmed, did in fact have access to a veritable treasure-trove of Mackliana with which to set his account apart. Kirkman parlayed his familial connection to Macklin and the access to Macklin's notes into a rollicking multivolume farce that more closely resembled a Fielding novel than the sober biographical efforts of his predecessor.

Faced with challenging the precedent set by Kirkman, William Cooke, Macklin's third biographer, would seem to come up woefully short. He could not benefit from the clean slate that Congreve had, or follow in Kirkman's footsteps by denying his predecessors, because Cooke needed to mine much of his material from Kirkman, who had enjoyed superior access to documentation. But his reliance on anecdotes and bons mots provided by Kirkman placed Cooke in the delicate position of avoiding merely duplicating his immediate predecessor's work. Looking farther back, Cooke takes a cue from Congreve's obsession with objective fact, contrasting his own objectivity with the whimsical Kirkman, whose conception of anecdote may be more in line with Jacky Bratton's: an anecdote about actors contains "a kernel of factuality [... and] expresses [...] truth to some ineffable 'essence,' rather than to proven facts, is what matters most—hence [anecdote's] mythmaking dimension."[43] Cooke does not compete with Kirkman's mythic image of Macklin, and by presenting his account as unvarnished truth, he needed to establish his supremacy over Congreve. He accomplishes this by showcasing his superior access to Mackliana—which of course was largely made possible through Kirkman. While Kirkman already began the cycle of balancing time elapsed from the events with the possibility for further research or documentation to be discovered, Cooke seeks novelty in the other gift provided by the passage of time: perspective on the significance of his subject's life. However, Cooke was only writing seven years after Macklin's death, so benefits of retrospection were minimal. The other intervention that Cooke made was altering the emphasis of his biography from a focused, narrative-driven life featuring anecdotes to a book built around anecdotes featuring a loosely narrative-driven life.

In 1891, eighty-seven years after the first appearance of Cooke's biography, a new biographer, Edward Abbott Parry, would openly mine all three preceding biographies for choice anecdotes. He claims ascendance based on his ability to glean insight from almost a century of time elapsed, which, as suggested, gave Parry an advantage in assessing Macklin's importance to theatre beyond his immediate time period but correspondingly set him at a disadvantage for any personal connection to his long-deceased subject. As a biographer, Parry is emblematic of John A. Garraty's (1957) claims that all biography is doomed to fall short of perfection: retrospective biographers excel at discussing trajectories, including career and reputation, but contemporary biographers paint superior pictures of character. When assessing his limitations, Parry must have realized that anecdote provided the best means of evading criticism about the divisive lines drawn between character and narrative by some biographers, as was later described by Donald Stauffer (1941). Unabashedly collecting the most questionable anecdotes from every source possible, Parry thrives on sensationalism, but also pays considerable lip service to the duties of a biographer. Mindful of the extent to which he relied on the earlier biographies for his information, Parry preemptively strikes out at critics who might discount his biography as being "a work of paste and scissors, to which a kindly critic would perhaps add—and research."[44] His plan to mine large swaths of the previous biographies using "their own language and without paraphrase" is justified, he says, by his presumably self-effacing belief that "the research, the scissors, and the paste, in that order, are of greater value to the reader than the biographer's pen. And it is for this reason that I have endeavored, wherever possible, to find and use the words of others instead of my own." Parry, then, navigates the continuum between Garraty's theory of time elapsed and corresponding strength of perspective (contemporary biographers excel at character, distant ones at assessing the life's meaning and subject's reputation) by choosing to add his viewpoint in between the earlier biographers' stories— unchanged—that readers had come to anticipate.

Finally, in 1960, the first "scholarly" biography of Macklin appeared, titled *Charles Macklin: An Actor's Life*. This fifth, and as of this writing, final, competitor for the definitive Macklin biography, William Worthen Appleton, chastises Parry for being a "mere compiler" of the other men's works and important documents, faults Cooke for similar but less flagrant misconduct, faults Kirkman for unhinging the narrative from reality, and awards the palm to Congreve with the qualification that he had lacked the scholarly apparatus now offered by Appleton's own biography.[45] Luckily for Appleton, but perhaps not for those interested in longitudinal studies of Macklin biographies and the people who write them, Appleton's biography has held stage uncontested for the past five decades. It is doubtful that Appleton could have anticipated such success, as the vogue for scholarly lives of other eighteenth-century and early nineteenth-century actors has produced over a dozen biographies of Garrick and at least four of Siddons, depending on how one delineates a "full" biography.

Even this brief survey of the five extant full-length biographies of Macklin demonstrates that in each case, it was imperative for the biographer to justify why his retelling of Macklin was necessary. Along the way, not only did the view of how the biographer should approach his task seem to shift, but also the understanding of exactly what that task included seemed to expand or contract with each successive iteration.

Perhaps not surprisingly, the quest to originate the role of Macklin's biographer is reified most prominently by the comments of his fourth biographer, the unapologetically cutting-and-pasting Parry, who traces the lineage of prior Macklin biographers until himself, capitalizing, I believe, on the trend of retiring players to pass down their part-books—and, in effect, the sanctification of legitimacy—to select newer actors. Unembarrassed in his obvious reliance on those who came before him, Parry limns the stories offered by his predecessors, introducing the three largest ghosts that he must overcome in his quest for originality as, similarly to the anxieties expressed by generations of Shakespeare editors, there is no need for a new edition unless it provides further insight. This truth speaks to a key difference between the anxieties of an actor and a biographer: because the earlier player dies, the new player could have a reasonably successful career impersonating the lost player, but since the biographer leaves his "performance" intact, the urge for originality is even stronger for biographers, translators, and other practitioners of what were heretofore considered the less-creative/historical/reference genres.

This fourth biographer is perhaps unusually opinionated: he excoriates the last of three key predecessors, Cooke, as "not [...] more trustworthy than his fellow-biographer" Kirkman, who was widely known to be a teller of tales. Parry also condemns much of the speculative interpretation involved in filling in gaps in Macklin's history as "wretched heresy."[46] Nonetheless, Parry explains that he will quote these other faulty biographers at length "in order that every one may form his own opinion," which allows him to gather the best fruits of the earlier laborers while marking his own interventions and improvements.[47] What is perhaps most important to the encapsulation of theatrical experience is the strong sense of ownership over a "part"—in this case, the right to tell a life's story and the theatrical measures taken to secure the laurel over other potential interpreters. To look at a more in-depth case, let us turn to the ways in which these first three men actually represented Charles Macklin, as the most-contested "site" or subject of theatrical biography at the cusp of the eighteenth and nineteenth centuries.

First Fruits: Congreve's *Authentic Memoirs of the Late Mr. Charles Macklin* (1798)

For all of his efforts to assert the importance of his project, Congreve seems to fail at actually representing Macklin as an actor. As mentioned earlier, of Macklin's biographers, Congreve had the great fortune of writing in the closest proximity to the actor's death. Ironically, while Congreve should have excelled at giving concrete detail about Macklin's character and characters, he might not have felt a need to describe Macklin's acting style in great detail since it should have been etched in his readers' recent memory. A second probable explanation is Congreve's rigorous upholding of a traditional generic feature of early theatrical biography: the separation of narrative and character.

It seems that, particularly among less sophisticated biographies, the author tended to remove characterization, or the focused description of an individual's traits, from the chronological, plot-based narrative, saving the description of the subject's physical appearance and moral fiber until after the subject had died and the narrative section of the memoir had closed, perhaps in a distortion of Solon the Athenian's warning not to judge a man happy until he has met his end.[48] Stauffer argues that the division of character (a purposeful depiction of the person as he "was" through appearance, thought or deed) from narrative (a chronology of happenstances or social events) weakens biography, for "an impersonal chronicle" and a "static character" remain "two incompatible fragments" that do not replicate "the unity in which it [the subject's life] was lived."[49] Stauffer is highlighting a problem of motion: biography, as a narrative, demands movement, while character becomes not unlike a portrait, fixed in a moment in time and often abstracted from context.

The best biography, then, would find a means of fusing character development with the action of the narrative, a requirement that frequently evaded Congreve. This difficulty is doubly present for the theatrical biographer, who is beholden to supply the actor's character offstage as well as his characters onstage. The two responsibilities twinned each other in later biographical practice: I believe that anecdote, like "pointing" on the stage, was the tool of choice for fusing offstage action and character together, as anecdote highlighted some aspect of a character's personality, often in the context of a discussion with some physical action, even if it didn't necessarily advance the plot. Biographical authors came to understand the power of anecdote as part of characterization, and also eventually to remove anecdote from larger narrative substance—a move that, while providing bursts of unity between narrative and characterization that had defied Congreve, still tended to stick out awkwardly from the plot or background narrative.[50]

When assessing the successes and failures tied to the character sketch at the end of Macklin's biography, it is important to remember that it was an expected feature of the genre, even as it seemed to have impeded other biographical goals when it dealt with theatrical subjects. During the course of his narrative, Congreve does make a token effort at assessing Macklin's acting. When writing about Macklin's historically disastrous portrayal of Macbeth,

Congreve says that although the aged thespian lacked the memory, utterance, elegance, flexibility of face, and dignity of Garrick, who usually played the role:

> He [Macklin] shewed so complete a knowledge of the character, so just a conception of the manner, in which it should be personified, so accurate an attention to the propriety in the scenes, dresses, decorations, and other incidental parts of the performance, as afforded a very general satisfaction, and produced universal applause; of his own representation of Macbeth, there was not so much unanimity of opinion.[51]

How Macklin could have "shewed so complete a knowledge" of Macbeth and yet fail to deliver a convincing representation does not appear to trouble Congreve. The best indication of precisely how Macklin portrayed the king is given in a popular poem contained within a footnote, which goes through a pithy assessment of the eight most notable actors to assay the role: Macklin's only victory is that he "falls the last," likely a reference to his age rather than to any spectacular acting skill.[52] In both instances of assessment, Congreve pits Macklin against his competitors, first the much younger Garrick, and then a succession of Macbeths, simultaneously suggesting a never-ending supply of Joseph Roach's "doomed surrogates."

Although some critics might argue that Congreve, writing a simple pamphlet about Macklin a few months after the man's death, might not deserve the title of biographer, Congreve's persona was determined to stand on generic ceremony (i.e., the character sketch) as a means of asserting his skill in the chosen role: "Having now brought this Memoir to its concluding period [Macklin's death], it remains alone to give a sketch of Mr. Macklin's manners and temper, such as may claim a just right to that impartiality which ought ever to preside over the pen of a Biographer."[53] Congreve simultaneously reminds the reader of his role as a biographer, calling attention to his own character as an "impartial" and dutiful biographer even as he ostensibly intends to unveil Macklin's character.

Those hungry for a glimpse of Macklin as a man might be surprised to note that within the realm of his character sketch, Congreve commented on Macklin's movements and speech rather generally, revealing more about Congreve's biases than about Macklin's perambulations or locutions:

> He was remarkably upright in his stature, both off and on the stage, and disdained all that "twining of arms and tripping of legs, &c.:" which modern actors make use of to aid their delivery. His mode of acting was

certainly peculiar, and if it was not altogether pleasing to the "common eye," it always gave satisfaction to the connoisseur.[54]

Congreve, then, is a connoisseur, one with the requisite judgment to write a biography of this actor, and a traditional man, suspicious of "modern" fads. It is difficult for Congreve, who announces himself as impartial, to avoid giving as many hints about his own character as about Macklin's, even though in comparison to later Macklin biographies, Congreve's pamphlet is notably more fact-based than anecdotal, speculative, or philosophical. Although commendable for its factual approach to Macklin's life events and for its own vast claim to generic importance, Congreve's work does not uphold the Cibberian intent of the genre: Congreve does not capture even a glimmer of Macklin's genius.

Lines of Competition Embellished: Kirkman's *Memoirs of the Life of Charles Macklin* (1799)

Congreve's slender volume made little claim to the biographical field beyond arriving first to the task and limning the verifiable facts of Macklin's life. James Thomas Kirkman, second in line, appears to have written his biography with the intent of countering Congreve by providing two sizeable volumes of massively exaggerated, and in some cases, rather transparently imaginative, adventures of Macklin. Just as Congreve claimed affiliation with Boswell at the end of his character sketch, so too did Kirkman have to make his claim to legitimacy. He does so implicitly by the scope of his story and his investment in providing Macklin's own written pieces, and explicitly in his claim to personal knowledge and kinship with his subject. However, his thousand-page narrative frequently reads like a novel rather than like a trustworthy biography, and otherwise like a cobbled-together collection of litigation and other undigested documentary remnants of his subject, the effect of which could easily be confused for the work of the notorious bookseller and pseudoliterary shill Edmund Curll. Kirkman's biography, while not a reliable source of information about Macklin, is useful for investigating the ways in which Kirkman responded to Congreve's biography. Far from being completely superficial in his undertaking of Macklin's story, Kirkman shows awareness of the difficulty and importance of his job, ultimately attempting to work through his own theories of how best to preserve the British stage in print.

Kirkman's title, *Memoirs of the Life of Charles Macklin, Esq.*, not only makes that explicit claim for the increased authenticity of his provenance, "principally compiled from his own papers and memorandums," but also goes on to note that those papers—and by extension, the memoir—"contain [Macklin's] criticisms on and characters and anecdotes of Betterton, Booth, Wilks, Cibber, Garrick, Barry, Mossop, Sheridan, Foote, and most of his contemporaries." Already, Kirkman has made a much greater claim for Macklin's status ("Mr." has become "Esquire"), added "compiler" to the task of the biographer, and enlarged the scope of the biography to not only include Macklin but a veritable roll call of the actor's famous colleagues.[55] Immediately following this on the title page is the offer of "[Macklin's] Valuable observations on the Drama, on the Science of Acting, and on various other Subjects, The Whole forming A Comprehensive but succinct HISTORY OF THE STAGE; which includes a period of one hundred years." Kirkman's claim to provide a history of the stage as well as a few acting treatises threatens to catapult his biography into the broader disciplines of history and philosophy, while still maintaining the titillation of "anecdotes" and "criticism," both agreeable currency for the gossip market.

Congreve had suggested that his motive for writing was to enhance the veracity of materials available to future biographers, but Kirkman immediately envisions his project in a way that strongly suggests a direct reaction to Congreve's project. Kirkman critiques a pair of biographers whose work was "very dull and uninteresting memoirs," which were "universally read" by readers who were "only astonished, that so much time should have produced so very little incident."[56] It is hard to imagine that Kirkman was not intentionally taking cues from Fielding in promoting what he saw to be a more exciting, vital type of biography. After all, Fielding had lashed out against Colley Cibber's *Apology* and its subsequent popularity, parodying them in a number of his books. In *Tom Jones* particularly, the narrator charges Cibber's work with dullness due to its relentless obedience to strict chronology.[57] Moreover, the narrator describes his own present approach as "a new province of writing."[58] Similarly, Kirkman reveals his intention to create a gripping narrative designed to amuse, perhaps in a bid to encourage his readers to perceive his work as something to be read and reread, rather than thrown aside after consumption.

Kirkman was utterly obsessed with the concept of time, and within that, how to ensure one's own continued existence in the face of newer attractions. This preoccupation with time may have caused a particular affinity to Macklin. Because Macklin was so old, Kirkman writes, "His biographer considers himself, therefore, as discharged from the necessity of apologizing for the subject he has undertaken."[59] Kirkman's interest in time permeates his writing, most frequently appearing in his excuses or justifications for his project and its shape.

Rather than expending energy on the odious task of making lists or dwelling on less fertile ground anecdotally, Kirkman pleads the excuse of time—his desire not to waste time, that is: "It would be an uninteresting and tiresome task to the reader to go through, if it were possible to give a detail of, the various characters he played, or the variety of offices he executed."[60] It should be noted that Fielding had already played this narrative card in Book 2 of *Tom Jones*, on the page following his attack on Cibber's *Apology*:

> When any extraordinary Scene presents itself, (as we trust will often be the Case) we shall spare no Pains nor Paper to open it at large to our Reader; but if whole Years should pass without producing any Thing worthy his Notice, we shall not be afraid of a Chasm in our History; but shall hasten on to Matters of Consequence and leave such Periods of Time totally unobserved. These are indeed to be considered as Blanks in the grand Lottery of Time.[61]

In the context of Kirkman's memoir, this strategy allows him to indulge his novelistic impulses both in ignoring the demands of chronology and in filling in gaps according to his own whimsy:

> Sometimes he [Macklin] was an architect, and knocked up the stage and seats in a barn; sometimes he wrote an opening Prologue, or a parting Epilogue, for the company: at others, he wrote a song, complimentary and adulatory to the village they happened to play in, which he always adapted to some sprightly popular air, and sung himself: and he often was champion, and stood forward to repress the persons who were accustomed to intrude upon, and be rude to the actors.[62]

However, if Kirkman does not have time for the basic chronology of characters and other "offices" filled by Macklin beyond describing him in terms meant to promote Macklin as the very reincarnation of the jack-of-all-trades titular hero in *Tom Jones* (and perhaps Kirkman as the reincarnation of Fielding), he nonetheless finds time to provide a voluminous "history of the theatres." Kirkman employs the clash between actors and managers for control of Theatre Royal, Drury Lane, in 1733 as a framing device; the well-established Drury Lane saw an exodus of dissatisfied actors to the lesser Little Theatre, Haymarket, directly leading to new actors like Macklin catapulting onto the mainstream British stage at Drury Lane. Thus, Macklin's ascent is situated within a historical framework, as a means to tell "the following history of the theatres, which we have faithfully compiled from Mr. Macklin's memorandums on the subject."[63] Beginning with the reign of Elizabeth I, Kirkman quickly lays out the two rival patentees in the Restoration and the subsequent unification and eventual fracture of 1733. Linking the narrative of Macklin to a larger, more universally significant strand of history, is a transparent bid to fulfill one of the more difficult generic desires of his audience, one that would be more likely to secure the longevity of the biography. In the process of offering political history, however, Kirkman begins to consider what is innately required of his genre. He gravitates toward comparisons of the actors as performers rather than toward comparisons of the managerial systems or the actors' deportment during the revolution. Kirkman names seven great actors and six great actresses of the Restoration through eighteenth century, and pontificates on the progressive loss of ability to sharply recollect each specific performer over time:

> And here, thinking of the mighty dead in that line, recollecting, as we do, Garrick, Barry, Mossop, and many others, whose exquisite performances have so often thrilled to our marrow, and almost suspended life, we cannot help lamenting the fate of such great men, and regretting that their labours, like those of the poet or the painter, cannot go down to after ages, as a testimony of their excellence, and a record of the delight and improvement they afforded. We know, and our children's children will know hereafter, how a Shakespeare, an Otway, a Congreve, or a Sheridan WROTE – but how shall we be able to conceive how a Betterton, or a Nokes ACTED? – or how shall those, who are to come after us, be able to form any adequate idea how SHAKESPEARE's Lear, and OTWAY's Jaffier, were improved by the inimitable performances of BARRY? – how Shylock was identified, and CONGREVE's Sir Paul Pliant supported, by MACKLIN – or how SHERIDAN's Sir Fretful Plagiary could receive as much support from an actor's merit, as it does from the author's wit, when they will not be able to conceive how it was performed by a PARSONS?[64]

Kirkman seems overwhelmed at the difficulty, but also the necessity, of fulfilling this specific demand of theatrical biography. When given the chance to perform his office, however, Kirkman defers to a literary source rather than attempting to describe "how a Betterton, or a Nokes ACTED."

Much as Boswell snatches a particularly poetic sentiment from a friend when faced with trying to express the significance of the dead Johnson, Kirkman appropriates Thomas Sheridan's lengthy poem written two months after the actor's death and originally delivered as a monody in the theatre under the title *Verses to the Memory of Garrick*. The most significant point based on Kirkman's lead-in seems to be the series of lines on the nature of the poet's fame in comparison to the actor's; the author's fame, the comparison implies, is safe because his monument is secure. Sheridan's actor "only shrinks from

Time's award;/ Feeble tradition is his memory's guard," and "E'en matchless Garrick's art, to heaven resigned,/ No fix'd effect, no model leaves behind."[65] Sheridan refers to action, expression, gesture, silence, speech, and finally passion as integral to forming Garrick's success, but he spends little time developing or describing the "grace of action," instead focusing on the audience's supposed response to Garrick's performance. The "gesture that marks" and the "sense in silence" are described as forcefully, conveying Garrick's "feeling fraught" and "will in thought," respectively; his speech "gives verse a music" due to its "pure and liquid tone." Provincial or foreign speech might perhaps be easiest to encapsulate or preserve through time, but Sheridan dismisses the characteristics of Garrick's acting as "all perishable! like the electric fire, But strike the frame—and as they strike, expire."[66]

Sheridan claims that the "blest memorial [... of] Our Garrick's fame" is best understood as residing within the reader, who has presumably seen Garrick on stage and now has a responsibility to convey to others. Yet Sheridan, in providing a pathos-driven model of what it might look like to repay Garrick for his final onstage tears (as he claims readers should, too), sets Garrick's boisterous memory to poor advantage by refusing even to attempt a description of how Garrick's acting works. Just as Garrick is "a martyr" to the fancy and superstition that will obscure his memory, Sheridan—and Kirkman—willfully, even gladly, adopt the role of "martyrs" in taking on a task that both poet and biographer had declared to be impossible: translating the fluidity of Garrick (or Macklin) onstage into the static medium of written remembrance. Kirkman's failure to provide descriptions of those actors may have to do with a strange philosophy centering on the relation of events in time.

As has been expressed by nearly all subsequent writers on Macklin, Kirkman was a capricious but voluminous writer, so any omission on the part of Kirkman thus seems more significant than for a concise writer like Congreve. Congreve gives a handful of basic details of Macklin's life before he came into prominence on the English stage, but Kirkman is an opportunist when it comes to the intersection of time and historical fact. He creates stories when the record is meager (in this case, forty or fifty years of Macklin's life before he came to the British stage),[67] and he reverses his own biographical prerogative about the extent to which some details could be known, and how. In the midst of his citations of the great famous actresses and actors leading into the time of Macklin, Kirkman notes that the actor Edwin Booth refused comparisons to other actors, especially if they were in his favor, as a mark of respect towards his predecessors. Kirkman does not hesitate to cite Cibber's opinion that Betterton was superior to Garrick and Barry in a number of roles, but notes that Booth (who, Kirkman reminds us, Cibber did not like) approached Betterton as a worthy rival. Having engaged in relaying Cibber's comparison, followed by Booth's dislike of comparisons, Kirkman superciliously adds that Booth was right to decline comparison, "which it is impossible at this day to make."[68] Kirkman's rationale for the limitation of comparisons appears to be temporal, thus leaving room for Cibber's comparisons to be legitimate, since he had personally witnessed all actors involved in the comparison.

Kirkman's premise that comparisons including long-dead actors are less valid sets serious limitations on the biographer if comparison is, as I argue, the primary currency of the evaluations that frequently form the best attempts at preserving an actor's memory. Advantage then rests with the most long-lived biographer, or with biographers who had the fortune to live during a period with a large cluster of talent, for each biography would, at best case, likely be limited to sixty or seventy years' worth of comparisons. This contradicts Kirkman's avowal of comprehensiveness, or at least his title-page claim to present one hundred years of the English stage. Nonetheless, Kirkman, for whom seeing Betterton onstage was distinctly improbable, feels comfortable relying on Cibber's comparisons, and generating his own just one page after his temporally circumscribed premise. The Restoration actor Montford becomes "the Barry of his day"—though whether Montford was the Barry of his day based on shared good looks, proper enunciation, or ability to move a crowd is left unspecified.[69]

It appears that Kirkman is working his way through a philosophy of preservation comprising memory, homage, comparison, time, and propriety. He writes, "To convey a just idea of the excellence of deceased actors, is, *as before lamented*, impossible. The best mode of giving a notion of their style and merits, is *by a scale of comparison with some actors in remembrance*."[70] Kirkman simultaneously raises the stakes from long-dead actors to all deceased actors, and denies his premise by saying that comparisons are not a necessary evil based on convention, as implied by his use of Cibber's judgments, but that they are the only means of resuscitating a deceased actor's merits. More important than Kirkman's inability to maintain a consistently principled approach to the problem of writing about deceased actors is his obvious awareness of the problem, and the easily shaken veneer of comfort with his task that his original premise is meant to suggest. Having abandoned the premise, Kirkman fills the next pages by justifying a stream of comparisons between Montford and Barry (who would almost have exactly answered one another's descriptions); between Kynaston and Mossop (allowing Kynaston to have "more grace and dignity"); and between Underhill and Lee (who were seemingly interchangeable as second-rate versions of Nokes but who specialized in the roles Nokes couldn't quite pull off).

Discreetly acknowledging his own temporal limitations based on not being directly familiar with the work of many leading thespians to whom he made reference, Kirkman notes that "we have no one to compare [Nokes] with." He thus obliquely makes the argument that his wholesale incorporation of swaths of Cibber's autobiography would be justified, and that Kirkman himself could not join the conversation if a comparison to a modern actor could not be made.[71] Kirkman has also highlighted the tremendous temporal advantage of Colley Cibber's biography, which had become the supreme thespian autobiography and a main autobiographical source of theatre history. With each passing year, Cibber's written legacy became more valuable because first-hand accounts of Betterton ceased to be possible once Betterton and all of his audience had ceased to exist. Other actors could perhaps seek to recreate Betterton based on collective memory passed down from other actors, but no biographer born after Betterton's death could claim the cultural capital of having seen Betterton act.

Kirkman's direct competition as the biographer of Charles Macklin came from other Macklin biographers, past and future, particularly given the temporal proximity of the three accounts by people who had lived contemporaneously to their subject. Nonetheless, Kirkman's decision to mine material from Colley Cibber's account, and to a lesser extent, from Benjamin Victor's *The History of the Theatres of London and Dublin from the Year 1730 to the Present Time* and Davies's *Memoirs of the Life of David Garrick*, among other texts, emphasized Kirkman's inability to successfully challenge earlier biographers' advantages, which included witnessing their subjects in action and approaching the field uncluttered by predecessors.

Despite the lamentations about Macklin's fleeting stage life and the impossibility of preserving his legacy, the onus fell to the biographer rather than on Macklin, as the actor could no longer speak on his own behalf. In life, of course, Macklin, as Shylock, was able to circumvent the temporal obstacle Kirkman faced relative to past intercessors of a role. We recall that even though Macklin did not have the advantage of Burbage, who was likely trained by Shakespeare in the art of playing Shylock, or the ability to have seen Burbage in action, Macklin was nonetheless heralded as having produced, in 1741, "the Jew that Shakespeare drew." Departing from the past precedents of playing Shylock as a comedic character, Macklin did not need to consult with Shakespeare or witness Burbage to offer what audiences deemed to be a "correct" or "true" interpretation of Shylock, even after well over one hundred years. Conversely, a removal of one hundred years between Kirkman and the subjects that he wanted to talk about who had been working at the beginning of the eighteenth century understandably proved problematic.

Macklin as an actor was only in thrall to time when it came to the preservation of his memory. His ability to do his job was not dependent on the distance between his subject (Shylock via Shakespeare's text) and himself as the player. In fact, that Macklin was supposed to have been able to divine Shakespeare's intent for Shylock from Shakespeare's writing suggests that eighteenth-century folks were less interested in a multiplicity of interpretations than in finding one canonical interpretation, and moreover indicates that the audience felt they would know "Shakespeare" when they saw his intent laid out by a player onstage—even if that new canonical interpretation wildly deviated from the long-standing canonical understanding of the role. This trend of "resurrecting" Shakespeare from text alone speaks to the growing preference for and belief in the infallibility of the archive, an attitude that is at odds with modern critics.

In writing a biography of Macklin, Kirkman would constantly be reminded of his limitations as he attempted to tackle a lengthy life that had been lived, for the most part, before Kirkman was born—the life of a man who became famous, at least initially, for unseating the prevailing interpretation of Shylock. Macklin served as a deterrent to anyone who hoped to write a "definitive" biography of the actor; his restoration of Shakespeare over Granville profoundly shifted both script and onstage character, signaling that definitive status (which Granville was long assumed to have achieved) could be reversed in a single blow. Kirkman no doubt could imagine the sting of a rival biography of Macklin outselling and replacing his story—this is, I contend, why he went to such lengths to conjure up such a boisterous and seemingly unsurpassable monument to Macklin. However, considering that Congreve's biography had only been available for a year before Kirkman attempted to unseat his fellow biographer, it would seem logical that time should weigh so heavily on Kirkman's mind as he anticipated the approaching specter of Macklin's next biographer. As it turns out, that biographer would not challenge Kirkman on grounds of fact versus imaginative fiction, but on the centrality of Macklin's role in the narrative.

An Impressionistic Memoir: Cooke's "New Species" of Biography (1804)

In an effort to foreground narrative while delivering character, Kirkman frequently chose to stretch anecdotes and basic facts into multi-page diversions, torturing what appears to be a rather spotty archive into a continuous master version of Macklin's life. Although Kirkman's tale is more entertaining than that of the drier chronology of Congreve, he sacrifices the honor of a biographer to attempt to tell the truth. Of course, biography is the attempt to provide a reasonably cohesive understanding of a life in full, and as Stacy Schiff (2012) suggests, even the honorable biographer realizes that she must operate within gaps and introduce some speculative interpretation not only to move the narrative along, but also to endow the life with some purpose.

Cooke's *Memoirs of Charles Macklin, Comedian* finds its own purpose not *in* Charles Macklin's life, but *around* it. The author introduces his book by expressing regret that Macklin did not leave behind a finished autobiography.[72] However, the value that Cooke assigns to Macklin's life is less about Macklin himself as actor and more about Macklin as observer of the world around him. Cooke notes that Macklin's autobiography would have been valuable due to his ability to provide "a regular history of the stage," rather than for facts or perspective specifically about his own life, as in a true biography. Timing is everything:

> His acquaintance with the stage had just preceded the retirement of Cibber, he could have, from tradition, informed us of its usages and customs since the beginning of the last century; the professional and private characters of the principal performers; the talents and estimation in which the dramatic writers were held, with their characters, &c. the number, temper, and acumen, of the several audiences; together with the progressive manners of the age operating on the whole.[73]

Macklin's autobiography would actually have been more of a history, in any case, closer to Kirkman's vision rather than Congreve's, but ultimately closest to Cibber's and Davies's work. It may be that Cooke not only had a grasp on what his readers wanted—theatre history loosely woven around the unifying strand of a central figure—but moreover that he had taken his cues from Macklin's notes for his own memoirs, either from reading Kirkman or from gaining access to some of Macklin's outlines for the autobiography.[74] It seems to me that Cooke was responding to readers' tastes—Cibber had popularized the notion that the most useful biographies should also include smaller embedded biographies of other leading thespians and commentary on the manners and conduct of the times—but he also was narrowing the field of research and subject matter by centering his subject on Macklin. Finally, the spottiness of documentation about parts of Macklin's life, and the man's tempestuous character, led to very vivid stories floating to the top of a murky background. Macklin's obscure origins, numerous interactions with curious characters, and strange behavior suited a narrative design that merged the late eighteenth-century love of capsule biographies (ones in which an outline of a life is compressed into a paragraph or a page) and anecdotal collections with the interest in full-length biography. For example, the first few chapters of Cooke's biography feature a number of capsule biographies of actors who would have been at the end of their careers when Macklin's began, in place of Macklin's early life, since not much was able to be said about that.

Cooke's impressionistic technique was not appreciated by all readers. An anonymous critic, writing in 1805 on behalf of the London Philological Society for its publication, *The European Magazine and London Review*, commented in a section of reviews preceding the second edition of Cooke's work that the book was "not, correctly speaking, biographical" because "it seems to us, from its detached parts, consisting of characters, anecdotes, notices of manners, &c. a new species of composition, in which a *Life* is rather *indicated*, or involved, than given."[75] This review, as damning as it may appear to Cooke's sporadic claims to be a biographer (rather than a compiler), was included in the front matter of the second edition of Cooke's *Memoirs of Charles Macklin*, most probably because of the reviewer's claim that Cooke may have created "a new species of composition." I share in the impression that, in comparison to other biographies prior to and contemporary to it, Cooke's was unusually liberal in stringing chunks of narrative together. This technique sacrificed the periodic smoothness of Kirkman's approach to anecdotal interpolation but created a greater impression of trustworthiness on the part of Cooke, since he was not willing to create elaborate flights of fancy to connect disparate sections or use the sleight-of-hand fiction techniques employed by Kirkman.

Cooke recognized the potential downside of his approach. Adopting the defensive posturing we have seen in both of Macklin's earlier biographers, he attempts to justify *how* he approached his craft, just as he had felt the need initially to justify the subject matter itself. Curiously, Cooke's thesis statement for his text arrives somewhat unexpectedly, mid-narrative. "It is not within the province of these anecdotes to relate a regular life of Macklin, which has been already done in various forms, but to touch upon points of his long intercourse with the stage not generally known, and which might best elucidate the manners and characters of the times in which he lived."[76] Cooke is writing not a "regular life"—a memoir or a biography—but a collection of anecdotes loosely gathered around the twin points of novelty and education. The emphasis on things "not generally known," coupled with the observation that "various forms" of Macklin's memoirs have already filled the need for traditional biography, suggests Cooke's profound interest in placing his own spin on Macklin.

But while Cooke was attuned to trends, he saw his work as occupying a timeless place of value. When inserting a very long digression about *The Beggar's Opera*—because, Cooke notes, everyone loves that play and has come to expect a section on it (an observation borne up by the content of both preceding Macklin biographies), he not only appeals to current taste but to posterity:[77]

As such, we insert the following; well knowing how perishable the anecdotes of modern tomes are, which, from being too often only committed to memory, die within their present possessors, and are lost to posterity. How little, for instance, do we know of the familiar life and habits of Shakespeare, who lived in an age when history began to assume a creditable shape, and whose high and transcendant [sic] talents should have commanded the attentions of the whole literary world! yet that little would have been less, were it not for the researches of Rowe, who, perhaps, just in time, snatched those materials from perishing, and left them as a basis for his succeeding biographers to build upon.[78]

Cooke's point about the slipperiness of memory is applicable to any art form or past happening, but it is no coincidence that he should appeal to Shakespeare—an actor and author—as his example of a life that merited detailed preservation. To make the judgment that the actor/playwright "should have commanded the attentions of the whole literary world" carves out a privileged space not only for biography, but specifically for thespian or stage-related biography.

It is my contention that anecdote in theatrical biography has two specific roles: first, anecdote is a tool to "preserve" a person, as frequently anecdotes speak not only to the presumed mind-set of a character, but may also describe his motions and speech patterns. Anecdote seems particularly suited to seeking to encapsulate the goings-on of the theatre because of the shared precision of spatiotemporal limits involved in recollection. One can only recall an encounter in detail for so long, and the expense of print and the necessity of portability place spatial limitations on any one remembrance in a larger work. Cooke appears to have used his anecdotal tissue life of Macklin as a catchall memorial for numerous thespians. He sees it as his duty not only to rescue the comedic actress Peggy Woffington from the incomplete accounts provided by her biographers (who often focused on her personal life, especially her relationship with David Garrick),[79] but also to assist Spranger Barry in achieving the proper posterity-directed fame that the actor himself had not been forward-thinking enough to secure during his lifetime.[80] In each case, Cooke provides a wealth of admittedly tired anecdotes about the character in question, sometimes featuring a cameo role for Macklin, and then he shifts his tone from the jocundity of anecdote to the serious pronouncements of a character sketch. Thus, an anecdote becomes a gateway to a character sketch that includes a chronological timeline and some characterization.

Spranger Barry's approaching obscurity raises a philosophical edge to Cooke, who figures the poet and the historian as dually yoked in creating a memorial of the thespian's art. He also uses the sketch to argue for the theatre's contribution to moral education and social manners before turning to the formal character sketch, showing his continued awareness that his text should act as a constant but gentle defense of the theatre just as much as a defense of the larger applicability of his own project. As part of a capsule biography, character sketches, for Cooke, illustrate a man's worthiness, and thus serve as a moral example in the midst of the amusements provided by anecdote.[81]

With respect to his treatment of the actor Spranger Barry, Cooke follows the model supplied by Garrick's biographer, Thomas Davies, singling out specific lines and attempting to relay how Barry delivered them.[82] For example, Cooke transcribes two lines of the "tender ejaculations" of Othello in reference to Desdemona, inserting the comment that Barry's "voice was so melodiously harmonized to the expression, that the sigh of pity communicated itself to the whole house, and all were advocates for the sufferings of the fair heroine."[83] In such a moment, the success or failure of Cooke's description stands to impact not only Cooke's reputation as a believable, knowledgeable guide, but also Barry's reputation as an actor. If Cooke's description leads the reader to determine that such a sigh of pity as described would be appropriate to the situation, he will not only think well of Barry, but also think well of Cooke for his accurate description. Alternatively, Cooke might describe the actor's action or speech and then frame it disapprovingly, as in the case with his assessment of Macklin's failure to merge the theoretical and the representational as Macbeth. The burden is on Cooke to do a good job of portraying acting poorly, for his description must not only seem to convey the objective facts of what the actor was doing but also introduce the subjective elements of taste that suggest the critic-biographer's superior knowledge. Cooke records:

His [Macklin's] figure (even from his boyish days) was never calculated to impress the character of a dignified warrior; and in his first scene, when the audience saw a clumsy old man, who looked more like a Scotch Piper than a General and Prince of the Blood, stumping down the Stage, at the head of a supposed conquering army, "commanding a halt upon the heath," they felt it under an impression of absurdity and ridicule. His address to the witches, and his reflections on their prophecies, however, were given with such a knowledge of the character as to redeem the first impression; and his subsequent interview with Lady Macbeth was very much in the spirit of the author; but when he came to the dagger scene, which requires both a marking eye, as well as grace of action, he failed, at least in representation.[84]

As we see, the biographer has the onus of describing the acting in such a way that the reader vividly understands why that approach was not effective—in this case, the description of Macklin "stumping down the Stage" accomplishes that both clearly and pithily. The biographer must also clearly iterate why the particular performance of a scene merited retelling, since scenes that were most useful for such purposes were usually very well known. In the instance above, Cooke takes it upon himself to anticipate that the audience will summon to mind a successful example of a "marking eye"—quite probably Garrick's—with which to contrast Macklin's.

But if Cooke strove for novelty, or a new spin on the same old story, and certainly we can see that he was aware of the need for his own interpretation, he was sometimes too focused on his interest in educating his readers philosophically to rise to the occasion of providing all parts of his own interpretation, including description and significance. Cooke relies on Thomas Davies's excellent descriptions of Spranger Barry onstage initially, gradually emulating Davies's technique of focusing a pinpoint of light on particular lines of the play rather than falling prey to the usual vagueness that haunts descriptions of actors' crafts. However, when Cooke writes about Macklin's turn as Shylock, arguably the most important individual task of providing a snapshot of Macklin as a man of theatrical significance, rather than attempting to describe what Macklin's success consisted of, he elects to present the critique as Macklin's own recitation of what happened on opening night. Macklin describes a slow start and a gradual warming of tone and temper until he notes, "[I] threw out all my fire" and finally, returning to the green room amid applause from the audience and praise from his fellow performers, Macklin recalls:

> My brethren in the greenroom joined in his [the manager's] eulogium, but with different views – He was thinking of the increase of his treasury – they only for saving appearances – wishing at the same time that I had broke my neck in the attempt [...] By G-d, Sir, though I was not worth fifty pounds in the world at that time, yet, let me tell you, I was Charles the Great for that night.[85]

Allowing Macklin to speak for himself illustrates the starts and stops in Macklin's natural speaking voice, and his ability to tell an engaging narrative. However, in deferring to the proud thespian, Cooke does not bother to describe what Macklin actually did on stage to deserve such applause; rather understandably, following Macklin's lead, his focus is on the generalized positive reaction of the audience. He can isolate specific scenes (the trial scene and the denunciation of Jessica by Macklin as Shylock), which provoked the greatest audience reaction.

This account is entertaining and educational, but Cooke neglects the duty of replicating Macklin's performance even though he clearly understands and is capable of glimmers of performance when discussing the highlights

of Spranger Barry's onstage success. It is almost as if, in his incredible awareness of the popular audience's desire for amusing anecdotes and the genre's
requirement for philosophical teachings if it hopes to be "legitimate," Cooke
rather carelessly uses Macklin as a magnet for anecdotes, saving his superior philosophical musings and sensitive reiterations for other characters and
events. Macklin becomes a prop for Cooke's larger history, rather than the
history being a stage for Macklin's art.

Macklin, Interrupted: Multiple Threats of Displacement

Perhaps the most startling aspect of Macklin biographies is the extent to which
anecdote sometimes obscures Macklin as a subject. I have suggested that in
a number of theatrical biographies, anecdote is used to describe the onstage
behaviors of an actor, as in the case of Booth's famous felt-lined socks, which
allowed him to present a particularly convincing ghost in *Hamlet*.[86] Anecdote
can also be used to capture the reaction of the audience, as in the delightful
tale that Parry relates surrounding the rivalry of Spranger Barry and David
Garrick as Romeo: "When I saw Garrick, if I had been his Juliet," quipped one
woman, "I should have wished him to leap up into the balcony to me; but when
I saw Barry, I should have been inclined to jump down to him."[87] One does not
have to read particularly widely to gather a considerable store of disconnected
but lovely anecdotes about various thespians, particularly since theatrical biographers rarely constrain their storytelling to the immediate subject at hand.

   In the previous sections, I have demonstrated that each biographer has
manifested significant anxiety about his project in relation to other biographical enterprises that centered around Macklin, and that each has made an
effort to carve out a particular niche for his work. I have shown the limitations of separating characterization and narrative, highlighted the misdirec-
tion of Kirkman's treatment of biography as novelistic fiction, and suggested
that anecdote provides a great parallel to the onstage pointing technique that
allows critics to compare and encapsulate the work of their favorite thespians.
In the process, I have provided a number of instances in which theatrical
biographers freeze moments of performance. Kirkman, Cooke, and Parry all
partake in this tradition to varying degrees—but primarily do so when discussing other actors besides Macklin. Macklin's biggest anecdotal moments take
place offstage, rather than onstage, in these biographies. This can perhaps be
explained by Macklin's bigger-than-life flair for offstage dramatics, or by the
trend of theatrical biographers to want to cover new, undiscovered territory
for their readers.

   I have suggested that, in the case of Cooke's anecdotal approach, the stories threaten to displace Macklin himself. Similarly, one printing of the book

Joe Miller's Jests, or the Wits Vade-Mecum (1744) was dedicated to a handful of distinguished persons, including Macklin. The book promised to tell anecdotes about numerous colorful characters. Yet for all of the anecdotes numbered therein, Macklin only had a part in one: the quip about the Jew that Shakespeare drew.

In fact, the "Jew that Shakespeare drew" appears to be the only Macklin anecdote that is universally required among Macklin biographers. It is pithy, to its great advantage, and it rhymes, which sets it apart from the great bulk of Macklin anecdotes. Nonetheless, one would assume that there were certain episodes that must be covered in any respectable biography of a life—for instance, Macklin's murder of fellow actor Hallam in 1735; the first meeting of Macklin's lecture series, "The British Inquisition," in 1753; and Macklin's much-advertised and advised-against portrayal of Macbeth in 1773. Although two of these stories do not, per se, reveal Macklin onstage, I join Jeffrey Kahan in believing that sometimes real-life anecdotes can be useful for assessing onstage behaviors.[88]

The first event under consideration, the death of Hallam, took place in the green room at Drury Lane. Accounts seem to concur that the conflict arose over a specific wig that Macklin wished to wear onstage, but which Hallam claimed for his own. The two men verbally sparred, and Macklin appeared to relent, ignoring Hallam for about fifteen minutes before lunging at him and skewering his eye out with a stick or cane, depending on the version told. It is a graphic event, and rather heavy for an amusing anecdote, but it is an unexpected turn of events that is important enough to attach itself in capsule biographies of Macklin within larger biographies about other thespians.

Congreve does not make use of the theatrical possibility of making us see the attack. He merely reports its happening and claims that the act was not premeditated: Macklin "drove at him with a stick which he had in his hand, without any aim it is supposed, but unhappily with too fatal effect, as it entered the right eye of his opponent, penetrated the brain, and caused his death the next day."[89] Congreve notes that the action transpired in "a hasty fit of passion [...] repented of as soon as done." With the degree of Macklin's culpability clearly iterated (manslaughter), Congreve returns Macklin to the stage in the next sentence.

Kirkman, however, supplies an incredibly long-winded narrative from the trial itself in order to be beyond reproach as an honest biographer in his own right and in deference to "the memory of Mr. Macklin."[90] Thus, Congreve's paragraph-long account becomes a sixteen-page interpolated trial record, unmediated, Kirkman says, so that the reader might make up his own mind as to Macklin's guilt. He quotes Thomas Arne, who describes himself as the "numberer of boxes" at Drury Lane and, more importantly, an eyewitness.

Arne recalls Macklin yelling at Hallam, "Damn you for a rogue, what business have you with my wig." Having described an interval of cooling after the initial skirmish, Arne continues:

> Upon which the prisoner started up out of his chair, and, with a stick in his hand, made a longe [*sic*] at the deceased, and thrust the stick into his left eye; and, pulling it back again, looked pale, turned on his heel, and, in a passion, threw the stick into the fire – 'G-d d-n it,' says he; and, turning about again on his heel, he sat down.[91]

Arne goes on to describe how Macklin goes to Hallam and cradles the eye, reassuring the man that it hasn't fallen out because he can feel it under his hand. Arne reads Macklin's actions sympathetically: when Macklin (acting as his own lawyer) asks Arne whether he showed concern to Hallam, Arne replies: "I believe he was under the utmost surprise, by his turning about, and throwing the stick into the fire: and he shewed a further concern when he felt the eye-ball."[92] Kirkman adds, in Macklin's own words, as taken from the published account of the trial proceedings, that Macklin urinated in Hallam's eye, supposedly at the request of his victim, and supplied a guinea—"all the money I had about me"—to the cause of Hallam's surgeon's bill.[93] It is interesting, and troubling, to see how Kirkman relies almost entirely on the words of Arne and, by extension, on the court proceedings, to describe the murder, when generally Kirkman liberally adds his own voice and framing.

Perhaps more surprising, Macklin's third biographer, Cooke, ignores the Hallam episode entirely. It may be that Cooke recognized that such a gruesome murder did not lend itself to a pithy anecdote, and thus he made use of his prerogative as a collector of a constellation of anecdotes loosely orbiting Macklin to skip this one very unappealing, but nonetheless revealing, happenstance.[94]

The Hallam episode is a particularly unsatisfying but representative example of those times in which Macklin's biographers appear to abdicate really representing him, receding behind other men's words on one hand but trying to interject their own details to justify their expertise. Of course, the lack of effort in recreating the scene may stem from the impossibility of any of the biographers having witnessed the slaying: the time of the event, sixty years prior to the first biography, and the place, the private green room, makes the staging of this particular scene only accessible by secondhand knowledge.

The second isolated event that I wish to focus upon, Macklin's founding of "The British Inquisition," a dinner and lecture series foray designed to give him a captive audience for pontificating at large upon philosophical questions and dramatic matters, gives a better scope of the possible reactions of each biographer in attempting to make the story at hand his own. Congreve, whose Boswellian ambitions, alluded to in the closing paragraphs of his biography, are barely detectable in his stripped-down retelling, reproduces the advertisement for Macklin's first meeting. The "Inquisition" is "upon the plan of the ancient Greek, Roman, and Modern French and Italian Societies of liberal investigation," writes Macklin loftily.[95] He details his plan to "lecture upon the Comedy of the Ancients, the use of their masks and flutes, their mimes and pantomimes, and the use and abuse of the Stage." The list of potential topics continues, establishing an ongoing trajectory for these lectures, the first of which was to be on *Hamlet* and was to feature a post-lecture debate over "whether the people of Great Britain have profited by their intercourse with or their Imitation of the French nation." Each biographer replicates the notice in full, because the amount of hubris required for one man to undertake such an effort demands documentation.[96]

Congreve displays little incredulity at Macklin's plan, noting that it was ill-advised, that "a cotemporary [*sic*] diurnal writer" affirmed an attendance of over eight hundred people at the first lecture, and that the venture was not helped by the antagonistic raillery of Samuel Foote. He provides no example of Foote's needling, although Foote was a noted wit with a sharp sense of humor. Kirkman, whom one might expect to reproduce Foote's many witticisms at Macklin's expense, blames the failure of "The Inquisition" on Foote's nastiness, but yields no sampling of the caustic barbing. Kirkman does augment Congreve's account by providing several excerpts that he claims were abridged notes from Macklin's intended lectures, including *The Art and Duty of an Actor, On Acting, On Newspapers*, and *Garrick-Bane*. Congreve was not one for anecdote, which explains his silence about Foote's quips; Kirkman's love of anecdotes could only be stifled by his transparent reluctance to make Macklin, a "close relative," the butt of the joke. This is even seen, in one instance, where Kirkman takes an insidiously rude quip about Macklin at the hands of his sometimes-rival, James Quin, and turns it into an opportunity to laud Macklin's patience in enduring such rudeness.[97]

Under no compunction of allegiance to Macklin, Cooke makes the best of Macklin's foolhardy plan. He critiques Macklin's intended regimen of lectures by pointing out the chasm between Macklin's enthusiasm and his ability to fulfill his scheme. Cooke offers the account of an anonymous "literary gentleman" who attended the initial meeting of "The Inquisition" and witnessed the "dumb show" that Macklin puts on as head waiter and proprietor:

Macklin himself always brought in the first dish, dressed in a full suit of clothes, &c., with a napkin slung across his left arm. When he placed the dish on the table, he made a low bow, and retired a few paces back towards the sideboard [...] He had trained up all his servants [...] and one principal rule [...] was, that not one single word was to be spoken by them whilst in the room [...] The ordinary, therefore, was carried on by signs previously agreed upon.[98]

Cooke describes Macklin's highly theatrical transition from headwaiter to lecturer, wherein he would break from character: "Macklin, quitting his former situation, walked gravely up to the front of the table, and hoped 'that all things were found agreeable.'" He then bowed and retired, only to return in character for the lecture. "Of the other part of his plan [the lectures] [...] it is impossible to think, without ascribing to the author a degree of vanity almost bordering on madness," begins Cooke, who tells four anecdotes resulting from "The Inquisition," all of which reflect poorly on Macklin. The first shows Macklin expounding to Garrick about his plan to contrast Garrick's Romeo to Spranger Barry's. Macklin describes Spranger's cocky swaggering as enough to wake the Capulets up, in contrast to Garrick's muted approach, which he describes as being "like a thief in the night." Garrick begs him not to continue, implying that Macklin's plaudits, while well-intended, were not desirable. Macklin remains delightfully oblivious.[99]

It turns out that the majority of catchy anecdotes in the memoirs of Macklin pertain to other characters entirely, or to situations in which Macklin is the butt. I have already remarked upon the strange reticence of our biographers to take it upon themselves to describe Macklin's debut as Shylock. It remains to be seen, then, whether they are more willing to rise to the occasion with Macklin's much-discussed decision to assay a series of three tragic roles in his dotage. He had an ambitious plan to play Macbeth, Richard III, and Lear as he felt they should have been played, an extension of the plan iterated in "The Inquisition," which called for his opinions on what Shakespeare intended his famous characters to be like. Years earlier, Macklin had tried to convince Spranger Barry to lend him the right to perform some of the more substantial tragic characters alternately with Barry, to no avail. So when Macklin took the stage as Macbeth, disrupting the understood pecking order of the theatre in which certain actors "owned" particular roles, not everyone was pleased. I have earlier discussed Congreve's opinion that although Macklin showed a good understanding of the role, his portrayal was not entirely successful. Congreve includes an apparently popular poem that compares several actors' Macbeths by figuring them as the eight kings that appear in parade, noting that the descriptions "are so happily characteristic of the manners of the different performers, that it is needless to make any apology for inserting them":

"Eight Kings appear and pass in order, and Banquo the last,"
  Old Quin, ere fate suppress'd his lab'ring breath,
In studied accents grumbled out Macbeth.
Next Garrick came, whose utterance truth imprest,
While every look the tyrant's guilt confest.
Then the cold Sheridan half froze the part,
Yet what he lost by nature, sav'd by art.
Tall Barry now advanced tow'rd Birnam Wood,
Nor ill performed the scenes he understood.
Grave Mossop next to Fores shap'd his march,
His words were minute guns, his action starch.
Rough Holland too—but pass his errors o'er,
Nor blame the actor, when the man's no more.
Then heavy Ross essay'd the tragic frown,
But beef and pudding kept all meaning down.
Next careless Smith try'd on the murd'rous mask,
While o'er his tongue light tripp'd the hurried task.
Hard Macklin late guilt's feelings strove to speak
While sweats infernal drenched his iron cheek.
Like Fielding's kings he fancied triumph's past,
And all he boasts is that he falls the last.[100]

This droll poem clearly indicates the desire to crystallize performers in a compact and comparable way: each Macbeth receives a couplet that describes his weakness, with the exception of Holland, whose failure is alluded to by the descriptor "rough" and the horrifyingly endless possibilities left open by the author's refusal to specify his precise "errors," and Garrick, who appears to have been a Macbeth beyond reproach. Moreover, Macklin's claim to fame, "fall[ing] the last," points to a desire to not be replaced or replaceable, but also indicates that simply being the most recent, or having the last word, does not automatically equal success.

It was, after all, Garrick's excellence in the role that led his supporters to take their place in the audience in order to heckle and hiss at Macklin. Congreve merely says that Macklin received "repeated marks of approbation" before the smaller number of critics began hissing. Nonetheless, the hissing turned to rioting and eventually to Macklin's removal from the stage "by order of the public." Understandably incensed, Macklin filed a lawsuit against the principal hissers for loss of livelihood. Kirkman devotes two hundred pages (roughly one-fifth of his *Memoirs of the Life of Charles Macklin*) to the trial, yet seems to have deemed a description of Macklin's performance unnecessary.[101]

To Cooke go the representative laurels: in an inverse of Kirkman, he devotes a few sentences to the hissing and subsequent trials, but several pages to critiquing Macklin's Macbeth, scene by scene—a treatment which, unfortunately, he does not give Macklin's Shylock earlier. Cooke notes the moments at which Macklin soared highest and sunk lowest. Most notably, Cooke highlights a known point for actors playing Macbeth—the moment in which Macbeth replies to the messenger who reports the movement of Birnam Wood. Cooke gives the four lines, in which Macbeth threatens the messenger with hanging if he is lying and tells the messenger that, if the report is true, he wouldn't mind if the messenger hung him. Cooke writes:

> The first part of this speech was delivered in a tone and look of such terrible menace as almost petrified the audience; while in the last line he fell into such an air of despondency, as shewed the effect of contrast in a most masterly manner. In short, this little speech might be classed amongst the chef d'oevres of general acting, and as such was applauded by the whole of the audience.[102]

It seems that we get a much better idea of how Macklin acted, or at least the high and low points of his skill set, from his assaying the role of Macbeth than we get from his Shylock. Perhaps this can be explained, as Cooke notes, by the uniqueness of Shylock: "If he could not play Richard or Macbeth to any advantage, Shylock was exclusively his own, beside a number of other characters, where he had few competitors, and no superior."[103] Perhaps Macklin's first three biographers had difficulty discussing Shylock because descriptions were based around contrasts, and no strong competitor had emerged with which to juxtapose Macklin. We can recall Kirkman opting out of trying to discuss Nokes as an actor because there was no present-day actor who roughly corresponded with him in terms of skill set.

Perhaps we can excuse the lack of description about Shylock, but the fact remains that the choicest anecdotes in Kirkman's work pertain to Macklin's childhood and early years, a time that remains contested and cloudy. Cooke's most memorable anecdotes focus on other characters in the Macklin universe.

Extending the *Memoirs of Charles Macklin*: J. J. Cossart and the Act of Annotating

The motivation of anecdote, like the one for all storytelling, is to amuse or to educate, often some combination of the two. For a biography to shun anecdote was to deny readers a fundamental joy of the medium. Seizing upon and trading anecdotes was a celebrated and stigmatized pastime, as evidenced

by the reactions of some publications to rival journals or books that ped-
dled anecdotal extracts from cohesive narratives. This section focuses on the
accretive efforts of J. J. Cossart, an annotator whose quest for the most comprehensive set of anecdotes compelled him to spill into the margins of the
sanctioned text, radically reinvisioning biography as a shared treasure-trove
of anecdotes pertaining to all characters, rather than as a narrative focusing
on a main character. In short, Cossart sees in the ongoing battle between characterization and narrative a license to act as unsanctioned biographer–editor,
expanding Macklin's world and reaching even further, through Cossart's own
knowledge and reading.

Cossart's approach was not without precedent. In fact, anecdotes often
formed the first grains around which a larger narrative of a theatrical life
developed into a publishable work. It is no coincidence that Macklin's second and third biographers, Kirkman and Cooke, serialized their memoirs of
Macklin for newspaper print before presenting their work whole as freestand-
ing volumes. However, while Cooke's narrative ran unmolested by abridgement, Kirkman's more fanciful and novelistic rendering of his protagonist's
life was reduced from a tissue of anecdote-driven narrative to a collection of
anecdotes without the gathering membrane of a larger story. For example, one
installation of Kirkman's memoirs appears in *Edinburgh Magazine, or Literary
Miscellany* in June 1799, under the heading "Anecdotes of Charles Macklin."
It was indicated that it came "from his *Life*, in 2 vols., by Kirkman." Like the
collections of primarily unrelated anecdotes to which the *Theatrical Monitor,
or the Green Room* belonged, *Edinburgh Magazine*'s presentation of Kirkman
cherry-picked anecdotes from the narrative. One characteristic example is
an anecdote centered on the manager of Covent Garden, Rich, who, upon
witnessing a patron tumble from the upper galley of Covent Garden, "very
generously ordered that he should have every possible assistance [...] at Mr.
Rich's expence [*sic*] [...] Mr. Rich told him that he should be welcome to
the freedoms of the pit, provided he would never think of coming onto it in
that manner again!"[104] In the context of the magazine, the anecdotes were
not used for the sake of illustrating anything particular about Macklin. They
stripped Kirkman's attempts at philosophical or moral framing and frequently
focused on secondary characters in Kirkman's narratives who tangentially
suggested something about the subject of the anecdote and his relationship
with Macklin, if indeed Macklin appeared at all.

In the dismembering of Kirkman's volumes, the newspaper editors made
headings of character names, for example, "Macklin" or "Anecdote of Rich,
the Manager," to force crude divisions between anecdotes that, in Kirkman's
work, appear many pages apart and thus are not intended to be seen as
immediately connected. The anecdote of Rich as manager, stripped of its

embedded meaning in the narrative, stands out in a smattering of anecdotes about Macklin, suggesting both a disinterest in restricting the subject matter to the supposed subject, Macklin, and a desire to maximize Kirkman's writing as a source of brief, catchy stories at the expense of subordination to a greater purpose.[105]

Although eighteenth-century biographies bore little resemblance to today's heavily researched and properly cited scholarly works, and much of the genre was populated by hack authors committing cut-and-paste assaults on existing documents, a certain type of reader took particular biographies reasonably seriously. In Chapter 1, we saw Queen Charlotte's painstaking extra-illustrations to Davies's *Memoirs of the Life of David Garrick*, as well as the work of the anonymous collector who patched together Davies's and Arthur Murphy's biographies of David Garrick, along with Garrick's funerary register. The anecdotal approach of Cooke's *Memoirs of Charles Macklin* attracted the attention of J. J. Cossart, a collector who took pains to annotate his copy.[106]

Like Cooke, Cossart's main interest seems not to have been Macklin, but the collection of anecdotes pertaining to the stage and to its key figures.[107] Cossart demonstrates a commitment both to the gathering of anecdote and to the verification of such stories, demonstrating a growing preference for archiving a primarily oral tradition. Providing a mark of respectability to Cossart's anecdotal annotations is a very lengthy letter from the actor William Ballantyne, designed to buoy the possibly apocryphal story of Macklin incurring some trouble with a landlady over his name change.[108]

Cooke's work comes significantly nearer to our present understanding of the requirements of biography than the prior two works about Macklin do, in terms of content, organization, verifiability, and a glimmer of engaged skepticism. The bridge between florid exaggeration and cautious restraint was indicated in Cossart's many annotations, a number of which augmented Cooke's more reasonable account with some of the wild anecdotes generated in Kirkman's novelistic rendering and in the gossip-heavy *Gentleman's Magazine*, even as other notes seemed to demand a higher standard of scholarship by indicating the weakness of Cooke's understanding of his subject. For example, Cossart takes umbrage at Kirkman's earlier classification of Thomas Doggett as a "low" comedian, and says, "Vide Tatler No. 122/120 with respect to this performer.—A low Comedian is a technical term applicable to the most excellent in that walk. A very low Comedian implies very little merit."[109]

At another point, Cossart refers the reader to a playbill from a play featuring Peg Woffington, latching onto the trend of supplementing biographies with the type of documentation one can paste into the biography, as evidence of one's proximity to the subjects discussed. Another note indicates that a letter that Cooke identified as from Swift to Gay was actually to Swift from Gay.

Cossart writes in all caps "ERROR" before correcting the record.[110] Later, Cossart inserts an anecdote that he identifies as coming from a different letter written by Gay to Swift, not only inserting a pleasing side note, but also indicating his familiarity with a corpus of Gay's letters. Emending Cooke not only created a more accurate biography, but also allowed Cossart to show off his knowledge as a scholar and as an interlocutor familiar with the stage.

Cossart is not only a historian; he is also a critic. Like Kirkman and, to a lesser degree, Cooke, Cossart points to his qualifications by noting his connections to the stage. His defense of Garrick as "the most sober man I ever knew," not only indicated Cossart's proximity to big names, but also formed the backbone of Cossart's handwritten contention that Garrick did not make a mistake when he slept onstage in the characters of John Brute and King Lear. Cossart, who explicitly claims knowledge of Macklin's opinions in one note and of theatrical practice and criticism in several notes, adds that not only was it Shakespeare's original intention for all Lears to sleep onstage as Garrick had, but that all previous Lears had done so as well.[111] (Macklin, however, we learn, rails in his own notes about Garrick's ridiculous and novel notion of sleeping onstage as a means of avoiding the challenge of delivering a believable representation of Lear's emotions in that scene.)

In the same passage in which he chastises Cooke on the proper term for "low comedian," Cossart asserts that Macklin "not only exceeded the Shylock immeasurably of all other performers but was equal to any of Garrick's best performances."[112] Later, he writes, presumably from direct experience of seeing both actors, that while Barry was inferior to Garrick as Lear, he made "a very fine" Othello.[113] Cossart compares Arthur, Yates, and Shuter on two separate occasions, finding all of them inferior as Shylock to the actor Cooke, who was widely estimated to be equal to or a bit below Macklin in that role.[114] Cossart finds Shuter, Yates, and Arthur all superior to Macklin in the role of Sir Francis Wronghead, since "I have seen them all play it."[115] This latter criticism contradicted Cooke's assertion that Macklin's Sir Francis "was by far the best of modern times, because Macklin could remember the manners from which the original was composed."[116]

In emending Cooke's work, Cossart had three primary advantages. As mentioned above, he was not beholden to other critics or scholars, but moreover, he was not obligated to follow a reasonably firm structure of narrative, and he was writing his notes several years after the biography had been published, giving him the advantage of adding significant incidents that happened after 1804. These last two advantages allow Cossart to circumvent some of the temporal or spatial boundaries that Cooke experienced.

By literally transcending the space of the formal narrative—Cossart wrote his notes in the margins, with one note spilling across several subsequent pages—Cossart could afford to offer information such as how Hyppesly, an actor famous for his role in the *Beggar's Opera*, "kept a Coffee-house" and died in 1748. Hyppesly is surely only incidental to the narrative, and one could easily imagine that Cooke felt strange enough dwelling so long on the *Beggar's Opera* (in which Macklin and his wife portrayed Mr. and Mrs. Peachum), but as many biographers noted, readers loved the *Beggar's Opera* and were always delighted by diversions, digressions, and tangents. Cossart's addition of the nickname story and Hyppesly's fate after the heyday of his fame actually serve as commentary on Cooke's composition: Cooke did not judge correctly what would interest the audience.

Such instances, when Cossart inserts information that Cooke should have known, based on chronology, stand in contrast to the points where Cossart updates the biography to include events that had yet to happen at the time of publication. Strangely, he adds a note nominating a new actor for Macklin's vacated title of "Father of the Stage," and then notes that that actor died in 1807. But Cossart marks the task of finding a new Father of the Stage as significant by devoting a note to it; moreover, he indicates that not even a position that we might think of as static can go for long without being filled when it comes to the theatre.

It is easier, of course, to annotate an existing biography than to create an entirely new version. Because he can cherry-pick the sections or tidbits to which he has something intelligent to add, Cossart's notes exhibit none of the defensive posturing that haunts the full-length biographer.[117] Cossart's form of biography is additive, accreting around a larger work. Furthermore, because his copy is presumably private, Cossart can afford to simply write a correction with himself as the implied source, or, when providing the source for a presumed correction or extension, can frequently instruct the reader to "*Vide Victor*," without specifying the reason to refer to the recommended text.[118] Cossart's comments were not rushed, and indeed they show evidence of revision: in one instance he corrected his own correction. Frequently, he directs readers to see one of his earlier notes, and sometimes even directs attention to notes occurring over a hundred pages later.

That Cossart should be so diligent in adding anecdotes and facts from other theatrical biographies and stage histories while serving as a belated editor suggests not only his own fairly pedestrian attempts to navigate truth and fiction, but also that setting a correct and comprehensive account of Macklin and his world was of value to him, instead of accepting the mythic possibilities of anecdote suggested by Jacky Bratton.[119] Thus Cossart became both a collector and a scholar, or an anecdote-monger and quibbler over small details, depending upon the value assigned to the particular theatrical biography in question and the veracity of the anecdotes and emendations offered.

Cooke's 1804 biography of Macklin did, in fact, fulfill the terms of Cibber's biographical charge most closely, despite the text participating in "a new form of [purely anecdotally based] biography." It therefore may be surprising to discover that only five years later, changes to the construction of London's only functional theatre would vastly alter the way the way that actors acted, and in turn, the way biographers rose to the challenge of onstage and off-stage representation. In the case of James Boaden, the subject of the following chapter, this would mean a severe restriction of the points and anecdotes that had formed the main tools of competition and success for Macklin's first three biographies. Boaden's vision of theatrical biography proposed yet more adjustments to the proper province of the genre, as well as to the role of the author in mediating his subject's story.

Chapter 3

EPISTOLARY RESURRECTIONS: JAMES BOADEN AND THE RISE OF THE PROFESSIONAL THESPIAN BIOGRAPHER

James Boaden as "Goodman Delver"

In *The Life of Mrs. Jordan* (1831), James Boaden describes himself as "the modern patron" of ghosts. A playwright as well as a biographer, he is discussing his plan to stage a deceased character in M. G. Lewis's play *The The Castle Spectre*, which Boaden calls *The Spirit in the Castle*. "I had no intention to give up the ghost," he quips, describing how he was able to rig an apparatus that allowed the "maternal shade" to levitate rather than shuffle across the stage. "But enough of such spectacles," he says abruptly, by which he means stage machinery rather than supernatural intervention.[1]

Today, James Boaden maintains a niche following among theatrical historians based on his delightful descriptions of staging ghosts in several of his own plays, and his recurring analysis of how Hamlet should have responded to his father's ghost in the pivotal drawbridge scene. In his auspices as a biographer, Boaden himself was the stage machinery that figuratively resurrected the dead, seeking, just as he had with the ghosts in his plays, to animate lost players, albeit by different techniques.[2] His first biography was motivated, he says, by his immediate and immense sorrow at the passing of his "excellent friend" John Philip Kemble, renowned Shakespearean actor. Appropriately, Boaden originally announces this plan in his *An Inquiry into the Authenticity of Various Pictures and Prints [...] Offered to the Public as Portraits of Shakespeare* (1824).[3] *The Life of John Philip Kemble* accordingly appeared in 1825, one year after Kemble's death. Next came the *Memoirs of Mrs. Siddons* (1827), followed by the *Life of Mrs. Jordan* (1831), the *Private Correspondence of David Garrick* (1831–32), and finally the *Memoirs of Mrs. Inchbald* (1833).[4]

Boaden is unique among early thespian biographers for the unprecedented fecundity of his biographical muse: he is, in a sense, the first professional theatrical biographer, based on output. His temporally brief but topically broad career offers a rare glimpse into the trajectory of an artist seeking to reevaluate not only his own work, but also the underpinnings of the genre in which he continually participates. His first statement on the task of theatrical biography, in the *Memoirs of the Life of John Philip Kemble,* is at once remarkably predictable and unusually self-assured: "The biography of an actor is the record of his art." This statement in support of the power held by theatrical biography seems to refute Colley Cibber's oft-evoked pessimism (or acknowledgment) of the pragmatic limitations of theatrical biography as a genre seeking to capture the actor; on its surface Boaden's claim would seem to collapse the distinction between the archive and the repertoire, but ultimately, as Diana Taylor would predict, it exults in the superiority of the archive as being able to contain the repertoire. Like Davies before him, Boaden quotes Cibber's "Pity it is" rallying call, and like Macklin's second biographer, James Thomas Kirkman, he includes Sheridan's verses expanding on Cibber's sentiment about the actor's art "unvouch'd by proof, to substance unallied!" As other biographers before him and after did, Boaden draws a melancholy comparison between an author who leaves "immortal writings to bear his name" and the actor, who cannot leave behind "the living organ of his success."[5] This chapter will show that Boaden struggled to address the task of preservation that he was heir to through Cibber, and that in the process of seeking out the appropriate tools, Boaden reinvisioned the basis of a successful thespian biography.

Boaden's struggles—and growth—as a biographer are less apparent in his first two biographies. Acknowledging the difficulties facing him as a theatrical biographer rather than as a literary biographer in the *Memoirs of Mrs. Siddons* (as a literary biographer could easily enfold the subject's works into his own work), Boaden nonetheless cheekily refers the reader to the *Memoirs of the Life of John Philip Kemble,* released two years prior, as a specimen of generic success. His work was well received by a wide range of readers who "placed it, where it was my ambition it should be, next to the delightful 'Apology' of Colley Cibber"; then Boaden offers *Memoirs of Mrs. Siddons* as "a suitable companion" to the excellence of his own portrait of Kemble.[6] As early as 1825, Boaden declared the act of preservation as a moral imperative:

> I cannot expect to have many readers, who remember these exhibitions of talent;– nearly forty years have passed away, since they delighted and instructed us: all, therefore, that I can hope to do, is to keep the memory of them alive, till some great and original master of the art arise among us; that he may catch, from what has been done [...] [and redeem us from stage antics] which degrade at once our morals and our taste.[7]

Having introduced the continued goal of preserving the actor as Boaden expresses it in the first half of his biographical career, this chapter continues the prior chapters' efforts to show how the biographer understood his own plight alongside the actor's in terms of confronting time and the threat of obsolescence. Using Boaden as a case study and leading figure in 1820s to 1830s theatrical biography, I hope to demonstrate how his specific preoccupations changed the contours—and to some extent, the very intention—of theatrical biography. Boaden, as I suggested earlier, strongly supports my contention that, at its root, theatrical biography is conservative in its tendencies, especially in opposition to autobiography: the increased emphasis on the actor's or actress's own voice sets Boaden's principles in conflict with the practices his autobiography-reading audience was growing to expect, even in biography.

Notwithstanding Boaden's initial bravado, by the 1820s, biographers appeared to be less sure of the feasibility of their enterprise than their predecessors had been. In earlier chapters, I have suggested that the most successful way of describing an actor's onstage presence during the late eighteenth century was through the use of points, brief physical pauses that supposedly encapsulate a character's essence during a particularly significant moment in time. I have also argued that the anecdote in written or spoken narrative mirrored the stage-bound tradition of "pointing." Even biographers who declaimed against anecdote as immoral saw the onstage anecdote—the point—as a useful rhetorical device for presenting and critiquing a palatable fragment that could stand in for the whole, the closest approximation to a collectable, tangible, artifact of the actor.[8]

Anecdote, as we have seen, is a staple of theatrical biography, a practice that I suggest is symbiotic with theatrical points. Anecdote and pointing attempt to concretize events that were originally oral with kinetic elements—anecdote offstage and pointing onstage. As we will see, there are precious few anecdotes in Boaden's work and a corresponding lack of expected theatrical points. The first such exclusion reveals one of his underlying principles of biography, namely that he does not report what he himself did not see or could not reasonably verify.[9] This heightened interest in material proof is linked to Boaden's rather conservative pre-Victorian moral viewpoint that the biographer is a reporter and interpreter, but not a rumor-monger. While Boaden seems to see anecdote as a means of conveying "essences," he does not embrace the mythic possibilities of anecdote unless that "essence" is factually supported.

Boaden's reticence toward anecdote also reflects a change in theatrical practice. Rather lambasted for his failure to participate in the anecdotal tradition expected of his genre, Boaden had the ill fortune to write about the eighteenth century from an early nineteenth-century vantage point in which several fundamental factors of the theatre had shifted in the first decade of the century. The destruction and rebuilding of the two main theatres, Covent Garden and Drury Lane, both of which had suffered from fires, had led to the construction of much larger, deeper theatres. Boaden records with disdain, "The gallery called the first, or two shilling gallery, had been hoisted up to the mansions of the gods; and those turbulent deities were indiscreetly banished [from] the house altogether."[10] The acting styles had changed to suit the setting, with much more interest in words and delivery than onstage movement, for theatregoers could "scarcely [...] see the actors, or what alone was of much moment, their faces." In other words, the power of representation seemed to have moved to pronunciation and verbal timing rather than physical embodiment. Unlike visual or kinetic components, scripts and, to a lesser extent, delivery, might be more accurately recorded.[11] For example, in his 1775 book *An Essay Towards Establishing the Melody and Measure of Speech, to be Expressed and Perpetuated by Peculiar Symbols,* Joshua Steele developed a specific set of symbols to represent pronunciation, which he applied to Garrick's delivery of the "To be or not to be" soliloquy of *Hamlet.*[12]

Steele's transcription is thought to be "the most faithful record of any human voice that had ever been made before the invention of the gramophone."[13] Such interest in material documentation, coupled with significant attention to making that documentation legible to posterity, allows authors to confront Sheridan's fears about actors being "to substance unallied." Theatrical biographies provided the best gathering place for those scraps of immortality.

Generally rejecting anecdote offstage for moral and professional reasons, and with pointing becoming a less appropriate means of onstage representation, Boaden had to find a way to capture his protagonists in brief moments of time. Boaden thus turns to scripts onstage and letters offstage, simultaneously realizing his own desire for material documentation as superior both as proof and as true representation. His own career as a playwright and Shakespearean critic greatly influence his approach: he believes that scripts accurately describe what a thespian should be doing onstage. Moreover, he holds a conviction about the power of letters to encapsulate a thespian subject's personality and acting style. Thus, Boaden seeks to overcome Sheridan's concern about material proof even as he overturns the expected conventions of pointing and anecdote so prized by his genre's earlier practitioners.

This alienation from accepted tradition did not come without consequences. As he cemented the supremacy of personal correspondence in his final three biographical writings, Boaden increasingly meditated on what space might be left for a biographer beyond the role of editor or letter curator. The use of actors' epistolary archives helped him bolster the legitimacy of his writings (which anecdote wouldn't have done), but it also shifted authority from the biographer to the letter writers themselves. Boaden therefore had to balance what he believed to be the best method of preserving the linguistic presence of the actor in a time where speech was increasingly considered superior to gesture: he also had to guard his own authoritative role in presenting the lives of his subjects. Thus, the biographer searches in each biography for new ways to assert his presence in the story: for Boaden, that means presiding over the narrative as a moral arbiter as well as an editor.[14]

More globally, the changes we see in Boaden's understanding of the task of biography and the relation of the biographer to his work highlights the shift in emphasis from kinetic motion to aural speech to letters. Thinking about the theatre becomes more literary with the passage of time, resulting in a more textual, concrete product that more closely resembles "professional" biography today in both aim and methods.[15] His efforts are hotly contested by a rival biographer, Thomas Campbell, and obliquely by Boaden's own son, John, a painter and champion of that art's superior ability to capture the actor.

Professional Approaches: Privileging Aural/Textual and Documented Sources

Throughout the present work, I have suggested that authors of theatrical biography seek to work out their own anxieties about time and memory through their writing. The act of biography is often reflexive as well as subject-focused, as the author must confront suggestions of his own mortality as he performs an extended eulogy of a fallen thespian. Perhaps nowhere is this more clearly iterated in Boaden's writings than in his defense of having written and published the *Memoirs of Mrs. Siddons* in 1827.

The introduction to the *Memoirs of Mrs. Siddons* is very concerned with justifying the decisions to write Siddons's life and to present the memoirs before the actress was dead, two different decisions, one of which was mildly contrary to established conventions of full-length thespian biographies, which almost uniformly appeared after their subject's passing. Mrs. Siddons lived until 1831, four years after Boaden's biography was published, during which time she managed to bequeath her memoranda to Thomas Campbell, who produced Siddons's authorized biography in 1834.[16]

Although not satisfactory to Siddons, Boaden's rationale can be seen as a defense not only of his own authorship, but also of theatrical biography as an enterprise, demonstrating the tight intertwining of himself and his works in his own mind. He lists five reasons in support of his decision, only two of which indicate any legitimate urgency to publish: he wants to reinvigorate the theatre by providing his memoir for educational purposes, and he wishes to have the volumes examined and corroborated by people who would have seen Mrs. Siddons and her counterparts in their prime. Boaden stakes his claim as providing moral or artistic benefit to England, and stakes his ethos on seeking out knowledgeable critiques of his work. Additionally, he argues that Siddons will not be embarrassed about her "unblemished personal life." The marked absence of any activity offstage should be an honor, he suggests, to the morally upright actress; this is the only consideration for Siddons's own perspective that he offers. The remaining two reasons justify his authorship but not his publication timeline: Boaden cites his own dwindling life expectancy as a source of immediacy (and, indeed, he only lived for six years after its publication), as well as his conviction that Siddons's biographer should not be someone who has only seen Siddons in her twilight years.[17]

This specific rationale was vindicated in 1834, when Campbell, Siddons's chosen biographer, admitted that he was not equipped to carry out the charge without considerable assistance from Boaden and several other sources.[18] Although some of his rationale proved valid, Boaden's decision to publish was primarily self-focused as a means of garnering some combination of money and fame, capitalizing on the interest that his *Memoirs of the Life of John Philip Kemble* had generated. Conversely, a pure desire to immortalize Siddons might have resulted in a book written in 1827 but published in the year of her decease. Matthew Toothill, in a thesis entitled *The Stages of Celebrity* (2013), opines that Boaden's choice highlighted the perception that for Mrs. Siddons, who formally retired in 1812, "her career was over and [...] [she was already living] an afterlife of sorts."[19] This sense of suspended living, or death-in-life, infiltrated Boaden as well. Preparing to commemorate yet another death in *The Life of Mrs. Jordan*, the elderly author quips: "I feel myself becoming like 'goodman delver' in 'Hamlet,' a recorder of the dead, and my place among the living somewhat coloured by my intimacy with the departed."[20]

Toothill, as well as a number of then-contemporary reviewers, attributes Boaden's twilight interest in thespian biography to the precedent set by Thomas Davies, who made a considerable profit from his *Memoirs of the Life of David Garrick*. (Davies's career as a thespian biographer is discussed in Chapter 1 of the present work.) Like Davies, Boaden experienced significant financial upset that seemed to precipitate his arrival into the field of biography; Boaden's fourth work, the *Private Correspondence of David Garrick*, was offered by subscription, a measure often meant to secure a sure income. Toothill suggests that the two-volume edition was released to coincide closely with Siddons's death, as Siddons and Garrick were often linked as Shakespeare's most accurate representatives. Having already produced a biography of Siddons before her death, Boaden's turn to Garrick at that time seems inevitable if, after anticipating success with the epistolary *Life of Mrs. Jordan*, he was looking for a similar project and an opportune time to present it. In 1831, the same year as the first installment of Garrick's correspondence, Boaden released his biography of Dorothy Jordan, famous for her dual roles as an actress and as mistress of the recently crowned King William IV back when he was still the Duke of Clarence.[21] A contemporary review of the *Life of Mrs. Jordan* in the January 1831 edition of *Fraser's Magazine for Town and Country* offers strenuous, damning criticism, asserting that the nature of the memoir, with its private letters detailing Jordan's well-known affair, indicated Boaden's attempt to shame the royal family into giving him money to remove the more damaging letters from circulation.[22] This seems a far cry from the Boaden who had delighted in his king's special encouragement at the beginning of his biographical career.

It is easy to sketch a picture of Boaden's last ten years that is marked by opportunism, a scavenger among the relics of the turn of the century English stage. However, Boaden's choice of Kemble as his first subject makes sense not only pragmatically, as his recent death created a void to be filled by monuments of all types, but also idealistically: Kemble was above all a Shakespearean actor, and Boaden was a Shakespearean critic. Both were demonstrably pedantic and formed what Boaden shows to be a most convivial friendship based around pronounced views of correct stage representation. Furthermore, the book had been supported by no less than George IV, to whom Boaden dedicates the biography. The biographer thanks "Your Majesty [who] has deigned to express your royal satisfaction, 'that a permanent record of that life was in contemplation.'"[23] The project was to be not only a "faithful" portrait of Kemble, but also a "not uninteresting" history of the stage in the tradition of Colley Cibber (acknowledged) and Thomas Davies (unacknowledged)—no light undertaking.[24] Boaden's first two biographies were histories of the stage, the last three epistolary based.

But what was the impetus for the shift between the two periods of Boaden's theatrical biography style? Fundamental to understanding the changes in Boaden's biographical practice is his initial conception of the role of the biographer and the techniques appropriate to his station. Although the primary tools of the trade may shift, the evidence is overwhelming that Boaden believed that delineating onstage characters was part of a biographer's task, at least in the first two biographies. In *Memoirs of Mrs. Siddons*, he writes:

> However imperfect the attestation of the surviving spectator, [a particularly stunning moment will] be remembered [...] some art is, moreover, acquired in the practice of painting our impressions, and we shall always communicate by our touch some of the electric fire which we have received. It is, therefore, gratitude to the actor and duty to the public to perpetuate the character of excellence, and afford models for imitation to future artists.[25]

The task of theatrical biography, he announces, "is not, however, a task for every hand nor for all periods," implying that he is in possession of the appropriate talents at the best time for such a composition; this perspective mirrors his contention that Siddons, having been born "in the exact position of life, and at the precise time she was," was particularly suited for the stage from birth.[26] Boaden's aggrandizing sense of destiny aside, he vacillates greatly about how to capture actors in action, primarily because he has a moral and aesthetic opposition to theatrical pointing.

Just as Boaden rejects anecdotes as not conforming to the proper ethos of a biographer, so he rejects points as inappropriate for stage criticism. In the *Memoirs of Mrs. Siddons*, Boaden explains that points are morally damaging to the stage, as they "produce a ludicrous effect," whereby the audience, specifically the uneducated, hangs on the points at the expense of the rest of the play. The audience, according to Boaden, "is attentive to what it best knows, the fine things extracted. A slight whisper is heard in the house just before the admired passage is delivered, followed by an immense applause when it is concluded. The actor [...] learns to humour the audience by an awful preparation and more sonorous declamation.[27]

In actuality, Boaden is not the first to suggest that points encourage untutored and inappropriate clapping, or unwanted audience participation, as audiences were prone to begin reciting the choicest lines in anticipation of the "point." Instead of focusing on the audience, however, Boaden's ire is for the actor whose interest in points prohibits him or her from performing a role appropriately—specifically, as the playwright's text would indicate. He offers the example of the maid Emilia in *Othello*. That character attends to Desdemona, having no meaningful lines or actions, and "does but one thing of any consequence" by stealing the handkerchief that forms a central plot point. The actress playing Emilia, Boaden notes wryly, "entertains a very different notion of [her role's] importance [than the playwright had]. Kept unwillingly in the back, longing to break forth and show the wonders of her voice and the energy of her action, she contrives by outdressing her lady [...] a rich plume of feathers [...] waves her promise to the spectators that, at last, their patience shall be repaid." Othello berates Desdemona, Iago comes to comfort her, and then Emilia has her moment, "and forth she rushes to pronounce the following morceau." Boaden quotes the lines at length, a dialogue in which Emilia rails against Othello's cruelty: "The actress becomes a perfect fury; and as if she waved the brand of Tisiphone [...] parades herself to the lamps in a semicircle, and speaks thunder to the gods themselves." The audience, in turn, "send[s] down a roar to 'tell hell's concave,'" which leads the actress later to brag about having received more applause than that night's Desdemona "(perhaps Mrs. Siddons)," adds Boaden slyly in order to truly convey the insult to good judgment and theatrical decency.[28] Boaden's own interest in play texts and playwrights as the ultimate sources of authority on the stage manifests in his emphasis on considering the author's intent, rather than simply the believability of a given actor's representation.

To a great extent, the contents of his biographies were driven by Boaden's own beliefs and interests, but he still bows to readerly expectations by including some points.[29] Merging established conventions with his own style, it is from *Hamlet* that Boaden offers his most sustained look at recognized theatrical points. He does so primarily in the *Memoirs of the Life of John Philip Kemble* and *The Life of Mrs. Jordan*, which are yoked together as being more lively and more derived from personal observation than the remote *Memoirs of Mrs. Siddons*, and more theatre-focused than the delightfully literary *Memoirs of Mrs. Inchbald*. In both *Memoirs of the Life of John Philip Kemble* and *The Life of Mrs. Jordan*, the points are evaluated from an aural rather than the expected gestural emphasis, having been filtered through Boaden's own sensibilities.[30] As Boaden interprets them, points provide the occasion for textual criticism; they allow a discussion of how to interpret Shakespeare's own words, rather than simply evaluating correct emotion.

Shearer West argues that the era of Garrick privileged feeling over judgment; Kemble's era reversed the equation.[31] Boaden, firmly straddling both eras, recognizes the utility of points, but takes his cues from the increasingly "judgmental" turn of the century. "A pretty extensive list of such points is before me, noticed by myself and others, where Mr. Kemble differed from Garrick or Henderson, or both," he offers, keenly aware of the competitive nature of points, wherein audiences would critique various actors in the same role based on their performance in the most popular "moments" of the role rather than holistically.[32] "The points too are curious in themselves, and merit to be here preserved; besides, that criticism unexemplified is as fruitless as metaphysics where the terms are not defined," notes Boaden, giving insight into how he perceives his obligation.[33]

In this instance of sustained comparison, he provides relevant lines and shows, with italics, how Kemble's pronunciation differed, and how that difference altered the meaning: in Horatio's line "Sir, my good friend! I'll change that name with you," Kemble emphasizes "that" rather than "change," which Boaden believes to be the better emphasis to suggest that Hamlet will be Horatio's servant, rather than Hamlet and Horatio being equally friends. "Henderson, evidently so understood it," observes Boaden, for Henderson delivered the line as Boaden would. Similarly, Kemble directs Hamlet's "Good even, sir," to Bernardo, even though "the commentators were too busy in debating whether it should be evening or morning, to bestow a thought as to the *direction* of this gentle salutation."[34] Contrasting the "melting softness of

Kemble" to the "almost stoical firmness" of other Hamlets in scenes involving Hamlet Sr., Boaden invokes the power of Kemble's emotional pauses at the first meeting: "My father,—methinks I see my father"—and Hamlet's "pan-egyric" on his father's memory. Boaden quotes and characterizes Kemble's tribute: "'He was a man, take him for all in all' [said Kemble, and] a flood of tenderness came over him, and it was with tears he uttered, —'I shall not look upon his like again.'"[35]

It is in this contemplation, so hinged on voice delivery, that Boaden battles with himself about whether the authentic words of Shakespeare should be subject to interpretation for added effect. Thus, points become a moment to consider textual authority rather than to marvel at kinetic representation—for Boaden, points are no longer about the audience feeling the depth of emotion conveyed onstage, but whether the actor conveys the precise emotion that Boaden believes Shakespeare "intended" the audience to see based on the text.[36]

Fiercely protective of words, Boaden rails against common omissions of those who do not pay proper attention to the author's intention as laid out in a script, especially if that author was the immortal Shakespeare. In a rare instance of tolerating points, during *The Life of Mrs. Jordan*, Boaden nevertheless tightly bounds their use: "The only question [about whether the staging is just] is what Shakespeare himself intended," blusters Boaden, aggrieved over the ongoing conflict about whether to stage Banquo's ghost or to have it appear as a figment of Macbeth's imagination. "The imagination here is in the poet, not in the character," snaps Boaden, drawing attention to the stage direction "Enter Ghost," which he feels is rather self-explanatory.[37] Boaden opposes the omission of stage directions in collected works as well as abridged performances onstage because they leave out important information planted by the author to bring his characters to life.[38] Earlier, in the *Memoirs of the Life of John Philip Kemble*, having acquired a copy of *Hamlet* with Garrick's alterations, Boaden notes with indignation: "There are upon this copy of *Hamlet* evidences of some unpardonable liberties taken by another great actor, Mr. Betterton," Boaden notes, as the copy, from 1703, indicated which lines had been cut from production:

"Angels and ministers of grace defend us!
What may this mean,
That thou dead corse [sic] again in complete steel," &c.

Boaden declares, "All the solemn gradation by which Hamlet adjures the spirit (so dear to an actor, who can discriminate,) were omitted."[39] This explains why Cibber said that the Hamlets of his recollection "absolutely *bullied the ghost.*"

Having employed an adaptation of the text, those actors did not have the lines "that would have *taught* them how to approach so awful and mysterious a being."

In the canon of Boaden, a discussion of *Hamlet* is never just a discussion of *Hamlet*, but the touchstone for many of his personal views on theories of theatrical performance and preservation that in turn deeply affect the very way that he approaches the task of a biographer. Boaden's theory of lines as providing clear evidence of *how* to act (which arguably has some merit) in turn endows the written word with particular preservative properties. If a dramatic author's words should make it clear to readers how something is to be acted, then it should be sufficient for a theatrical biographer, seeking to preserve the best of the stage representation of his own time, to merely include the sections of the script that are most elucidating.

To follow this theory to its most extreme conclusion, there should be no need for anyone to preserve the individual performances of an actor, unless it is to record incorrect interpretations as a caution to later thespians: otherwise, the mere existence of the script negates the need for the theatrical biographer, unless he supplies notes on the physical appearance and personal life of the actor.

Of course, Boaden doesn't actually believe that the script reveals, at all times, how it is to be acted: he seems to suggest that Shakespeare's plays in particular have that quality. This is why he feels that quoting two lines from *Macbeth* should suitably illustrate Siddons's portrayal of Lady Randolph in John Home's *Douglas*. In his selection of the finest moments of Mrs. Siddons in that character, Boaden declares, "The utmost anxiety was felt around me, as to the mode in which she would deliver the famous 'Was he alive?' Shakespeare shall say how. As one, then—'Who almost dead for breath, had scarcely more/Than would make up the question.'"[40] This reference to Act 5, Scene 2 of Macbeth—the messenger arriving to tell Lady Macbeth of the king's approach—not only alludes to Siddons's most famous role, but also exemplifies Boaden's theory that the lines themselves can encapsulate an actor's representation, a rather backward notion for most people.

Moreover, Boaden contradicts himself on his own principles. In *The Life of Mrs. Jordan*, he claims that one can simply read the lines of Shakespeare's Falstaff and thus be able to know how to play it, describing the fat knight as "a part so made out, that every speech is a lesson as to the mode of its delivery."[41] This comment seems paradoxical since Boaden himself rather frequently makes distinctions between Falstaffs who have graced the stage in his own lifetime. If his claim is simply that there is a "right" way to act Falstaff (and therefore, that many of the actors misread it), then his premise—that everyone can understand what Shakespeare means—is demonstrably incorrect. Nonetheless,

Boaden maintains that scripts could easily stand in for the actor: more likely, the actor stood in for the script, as the emphasis to Boaden was on author first, and then actor. This unusual viewpoint may account, at least partially, for the mixed success of Boaden's theatrical biography in "capturing" the actor.

It is, however, important to remember that mixed success in representation was a feature of the genre well before Boaden. In earlier chapters, I have suggested that biographers claim to represent actors' onstage antics, but actually fail to deliver through limited use of points or emphasis on actors other than the subject thespian. Certainly, biographers were expected to describe the pantheon of actors who worked beside their specific actor, and even those long gone, as a recitation of the history of the stage since the Restoration had become ingrained as an expected feature of most large-scale biographies.

Preserving actors who might otherwise go unheralded was also part of the task. Boaden caters to these expectations accordingly: "To those who have never heard Miss Catley [a contemporary of Garrick], I must, as my manner is, try to give some notion of what was peculiar to her," he writes.[42] Boaden marks the fulfillment of his readers' expectation but emphasizes that he will represent her as "my manner" dictates. He therefore highlights the *hearing* rather than the *seeing* of Mrs. Catley as worthy of preservation. This is not to say that Boaden could not create traditional points. After describing the voice and verbal emphases of Henderson, a particularly phenomenal Falstaff, Boaden acknowledges, "He would sometimes delight to show, without language, the rapid and opposite emotions, as they rise and chace [*sic*] each other in the mind."[43] The example given is Falstaff's reading of Mrs. Ford's letter in the presence of Mrs. Quickly. Note that the crucial point is Shakespearean, and also involves an actual letter—Boaden is rarely subtle in his opinion of what constitutes good theatre. Falstaff manifests detestation of the messenger, "pished at [the letter's] apologies" and then transforms accordingly as he continues reading:

> The Cudgell [*sic*] of Ford then seemed to fall upon his shoulders, and he shrunk from the enterprise. He read a sentence or two of the letter, – a spark of lechery twinkled in his eye, which turned for confirmation of his hopes upon love's ambassadress – and thus the images of suffering and desire, of alarm and enjoyment, succeeded one another, until at last the oil of incontinency in him settled above the water of the Thames, and the "divinity of odd numbers determined him to risk the *third* adventure."[44]

Thus, Boaden describes a significant moment in the development of Falstaff's character, one that was so powerful that it did not require an aural element, and yet was cherished among its audiences.

While Boaden could, and occasionally did, indulge the reader with an old-fashioned theatrical point, much more frequently he *tells* rather than *shows* what an actor does. To modern readers, this shortcoming would seem to be the bane of all descriptive writers who have an implicit obligation to encapsulate an actor onstage for his readers. However, as suggested, Boaden believed that one best displayed an actor through supplying the script. This could be taken to extremes, however, when Boaden pursued textual criticism of specific lines in place of an actor's delivery. Boaden writes that Robert Bensley's voice "had something super-human in its tone, and his cadence was lofty and imposing. If I had been suddenly asked what Bensley was most like, I should have said, a creature of our poet's fancy, Prospero." Instead of attempting to describe the voice, Boaden defers to Shakespeare.[45]

In the above example of Bensley, the implied dialogue by a hypothetical reader who is curious about Boaden's opinions is a recurring feature that goes hand-in-hand with Boaden's view of himself as a critic-biographer. In this instance, Boaden follows the specific flight of fancy to its most likely conclusion, given his own proclivities: "I avail myself of the present opportunity to say [on the topic of Prospero] that, much has been done in the way of scenic allusion, [and] much is to be done" for Prospero as well as for "the royal shade of Denmark" in terms of costuming to prolong the illusion.[46] It is not unusual for Boaden to describe the actor's portrayal in rather vague terms and summarily shift emphasis into how a particular role or play should be staged—usually roles or plays pertaining to ghostly apparitions. The irony of Boaden's being sidetracked by literal theatrical ghosts while pursuing figurative ones continues to be a source of entertaining metacommentary in the narrative as Boaden offers it.

It seems to be even harder to "stage" these figurative ghosts in biography than their counterparts in the theatre. The evidence against (or rather, lack of evidence for) theatrical biography's ability to live up to its generic impetus is formidable in Boaden's biographies, to the extent that he makes the effort to do so. Shortly after Boaden declares his need to preserve actors as a moral imperative in the *Memoirs of the Life of John Philip Kemble*, he backs away from describing Mrs. Pope in the character of Abigail, saying that "it was too much like the lightning" to be captured.[47] Similarly, the preservation of Mrs. Abington cannot be guaranteed by Boaden, as she "is not so easily described [...] Mrs. Abington remains in memory as a thing for chance to restore us, rather than design."[48] Such moments undercut Boaden's claim to intentionality (the prowess of Boaden as a theatrical necromancer rather than a meandering old chap with occasional bursts of luck and inspiration). Furthermore, his assertion that describing long-lost but good actors will cause reader-actors to reform their styles (a greatly emphasized moral-educational component and justification of the genre) hinges on the biographer's ability to purposefully and usefully transcribe the actor's art so that another generation can glean enough to fully embody the actor in question.

If we accept Boaden's contention that theatrical biography has a moral imperative to revive a fallen actor's style for the betterment of future generations of actors, but find that Boaden fails to capture the actors' moves enough for other actors to imitate them, then Boaden must then fail as a biographer. Should Boaden not provide detailed enough descriptions for contemporary actors to imitate, the desired resurrection of past genius stops at the level of page and never (re)manifests on stage, rather like a script that, having been written, is never read for performance.[49]

Using textual materials to fill in gaps in all the wrong places, Boaden makes a valiant effort to capture Thomas King playing Lord Ogelby.[50] "I yet seem to hear him in that delirium of ecstacy [sic] to Lovewell in the fourth act," he writes, and accordingly, provides the lines of dialogue between the two characters, with only the stage directions for Lovewell: "Where are they, my lord? (*Looking about*) [...] [Ogelby's line] [...] What company have you there, my lord? (*Smiling*)."[51] Boaden clings to scripts, offering hints on specific actors' delivery by way of capitalization and italics: for example, he offers "the sullen aversion of her look—the 'I a'n't *deaf*'" of Mrs. Jordan in the character of Mrs. Prue—and indeed, Mrs. Jordan presents a distinct obstacle to her biographer, as her chief recommendations appear to have been her smile and her laugh, rather than any easily demonstrable physical tic or speech pattern.[52] Boaden seems to "give up the ghost" almost entirely at times, citing a line from "The Soldier's Daughter" and laconically noting, "Mrs. Jordan spoke this address beautifully."[53] While Boaden's textual emphasis aided him in representing the actors' personal or offstage lives, it seems to have hampered him in the original task of preserving the onstage actor.

The failure is almost inevitable for Boaden not only because of his textual proclivities, but also because of his preference for hearing over seeing. These two characteristics combine most unproductively with regard to Siddons as Lady Randolph in the play *Douglas*. Boaden writes: "I have thus attempted to mark the most striking, or most applauded passages of [those] performance[s]; but I am sensible that the great charm of all, which may be admired, but produces no applause, is that unity of character, that absence of self, that fixed attention to the whole business of a scene."[54] Thus, Boaden seems to imply, theatrical biography is a doomed enterprise, despite his earlier boast about theatrical biography as the record of an actor's art.

In this instance, Boaden has, in fact, run through the most significant lines in each scene: "In the following scene with Glenalvon, the amazing intelligence of her look, and the action of her right arm, when she uttered 'I have not *found* so: thou art KNOWN to me.'" Boaden describes that at another high point, "she pierced every bosom with the tones in which she exclaimed, 'Inhuman that thou art!/How could'st THOU kill, what waves and tempests spar'd?' The triumphant burst at last; 'Tis he! 'Tis he himself! It is my son!' only her own organ could convey."[55] Boaden has both rushed to fulfill and exonerated himself from the expectation that he would deliver the exact specifics of Siddonian excellence: a few motions are thrown in, giving new meaning to "going through the motions," but Boaden insists that hearing the words, through Siddons's "own organ," would do the experience justice, and only then in the context of the "full business of a scene."[56]

If one could agree that the voice was impossible to preserve in its entirety— a reasonable belief reached by Judith Pascoe in *The Sarah Siddons Audio File* and myself, among others—this left the script as the supreme artifact. (This conclusion is debatable, with clothing, playbills, descriptions of gestures, paintings, or other memorabilia jockeying for position.) Boaden never seems to have reflected on the potential for scripts, based on the power that Boaden assigned to them, to overtake theatrical biographies as the record of choice. This may be because he recognized that neither pointing nor scripts could stand in for the other main component of theatrical biography: the coveted insight into the thespian's offstage character.

If points onstage represented a moral lassitude, traditional anecdotes to represent offstage antics were similarly antithetical to Boaden's conception of himself as an author and of theatrical biography as a genre. While a number of biographers added the expected protests against the illicitness of unfathered anecdotes, Boaden takes a stronger stance than most by almost entirely excluding anecdote as readers had come to anticipate. His opposition to anecdote rests on the twin motivations of morality (frequently, the ones that caught on were scurrilous in nature) and also on authenticity (as befits a man whose career included an inquiry into the legitimacy of portraits said to be of Shakespeare, Boaden wished to indicate his sources in order to be perceived as reliable). Correspondingly, Boaden's anecdotes generally fall into one of two categories: part of an existing narrative tissue as told through letters or writings that are reproduced in context by Boaden, or consisting of an oral transaction in which one of the involved parties was Boaden himself (thus, resting on the letter writer's, or Boaden's own, word as a gentleman). This latter move was a particularly effective method to accomplish Boaden's less explicit goal of proving himself indispensible to the narrative while still gesturing toward readers' expectations, an extension of the personalized participation explored in Chapter 1 with Thomas Davies.

Boaden simultaneously claims higher moral ground and unlimited license to center anecdotes around himself in the name of avoiding the hearsay commonly associated with the expected anecdote formula. In this way, he can "relate a simple fact to which I was a witness" and be safely beyond reproach.[57] Generally, though, Boaden mentions the existence of an anecdote with only enough detail to make it clear that he knows the story but not enough to indulge anyone who has not heard it. This is only done in service of correcting rumors about Kemble or another thespian subject. For example, when Kemble's book of "fugitive poems" was published without permission, Kemble supposedly sought to repress all evidence by purchasing and destroying 250 copies. "I have read a ridiculous story," huffs Boaden, outlining only the broadest facts of the accusation without any of the characteristic colorful details of the actual anecdote to which he refers.[58] He cites only to refute, thus furthering his own image as a gentleman and also suggesting that he, among the available sources of Kemble lore, is to be trusted, in contrast with the leagues of scalawag would-be colleagues. Anecdote-mongering, says Boaden, is not the province of a biographer: such writers "seem to have borrowed their notion of biography" from an unscrupulous theatre character.[59] He was explicit about his careful cultivation of a professional ethos since The Life of Kemble: "I have not ventured to record, what I had not every opportunity to know, to see, and to examine," declares Boaden as evidence of his trustworthiness.[60]

An unsatisfied critic in the National Magazine, and General Review says of Boaden's Memoirs of Mrs. Siddons that Boaden "contrives to omit all the information that people expect to find in books of this description"—namely, anecdotes.[61] But according to the OED, "anecdote" in that era had two meanings: the more popular "narrative of a detached incident [...] told as being in itself interesting or striking (at first, an item of gossip)," and the broader "secret, private, or hitherto unpublished narratives or details of history." The latter definition more precisely encapsulates Boaden's conception of anecdote, which was obviously at odds with his readers' expectations. In Boaden's increasingly epistolary conception of biography, the novelty and presumed secrecy of a "hitherto unpublished narrative" would pique his interest. Having precious few letters to call upon for the memoirs of Kemble and Siddons, and eschewing regular anecdote, Boaden heartily inserts himself as the hub of information in the Kemble memoir.

For example, rather than telling his readers that Kemble was fond of a particular poem by George Steevens, Boaden frames the information as a discussion between Kemble and himself in which Boaden "expressed some surprise" at Kemble's preference, leading the thespian to "recite in his silver voice" the disputed passage.[62] In another instance, Kemble expresses admiration for an epitaph for the deceased actress Mrs. Crouch, apparently rhapsodizing to Boaden, "Boaden, I have just read an inscription upon Mrs. Crouch's monument. As I feel every word of it, and know that I did not write it myself, I know

only one other man from whom it could proceed, and you are he."[63] The latter
anecdote best captures Boaden capturing Kemble: he seizes upon those parts
of Kemble that best reflect Boaden. Thus, Kemble as portrayed by Boaden
is a consummate Shakespearean critic and, based on the emphasis provided
by Boaden's text, a frequent sidekick to our biographer. In both the Steevens
and Crouch instances, not only is Kemble's range of motion centered around
responding to Boaden, but in both cases, Boaden supplies a piece of textual
evidence (lines from the play and lines from the epitaph, respectively). With
the assurance of his own experiences as represented in his own words, Boaden
can feel secure in his professionalism as a biographer, even as he threatens to
edge out his subject.

Boaden's almost obsessive need to insert himself speaks to the duality of the
biographical urge: the aging writer builds a monument not only to a beloved
deceased thespian, but also to himself. Thus, a description of Kemble's parents is prefaced with Boaden's announcement: "The reader who loved Kemble
may thank me here for the impression made by the persons and minds of
those from whom he sprung."[64] The parents merit inclusion in the narrative
because it is an opportunity for Boaden, who was in fact recording his own
meeting with them upon Kemble's introduction, to indicate one of many tangible marks of favor from Kemble and to imprint himself on the reader as part
of the cosmopolitan theatrical "backstage," if not a veritable social hub unto
himself like Cibber or Garrick's biographer Davies.

As with Kemble, whom Boaden knew, the biographer inserts himself into
The Life of Mrs. Jordan wherever he can avoid using the epistolary evidence
that would attest to his comparative unimportance in her life. Boaden records
an instance when he was asked about Jordan's beauty by someone who was,
presumably, too young to remember the actress: " 'Pray, sir,' said a young lady
to me, 'was Mrs. Jordan critically handsome?' My answer was the absolute
truth—'Dear madam, had you seen her as I did, the question would never
have occurred to you!' "[65] Boaden builds a significant amount of his ethos
on distinguishing between his directly witnessing his subject versus having
recourse to secondary sources. This authority is temporal—a privilege available only to the contemporary historian—and social, emphasizing the distinction between traditional orally transmitted anecdote and Boaden's more
refined unveiling of proprietary information.

Not only are Boaden's "anecdotes" not pithy; but they are also not humorous, and not entirely about the thespian because the stories' existence and
inclusion are conditional upon Boaden's participation. While earlier anecdotes were parallel to theatrical points, quick and essential moments of characterization, Boaden's anecdotes were parallel to personal letters, irrevocably
bound to the narrator's own frame of reference and—at times—of dubious

interest. Most important, directly witnessed anecdotes and personal correspondence both stake higher claims to authenticity by seeming to have, or
actually possessing, concrete materiality.

Caring less about reliability, some critics were mightily displeased by
Boaden's straightlaced approach of leaving anecdotes out entirely, and the
simultaneous bait-and-switch method of reframing anecdotes to suit his ambition of showing his own wealth of private knowledge. A reviewer from *Robins's
London and Dublin Magazine* hotly declared of the *Memoirs of Mrs. Siddons,*
"Mrs. Siddons's fame will most certainly not owe its perpetuation to her self-
satisfied biographer" since the volumes barely addressed her private life, and
the worthwhile parts of the memoir, by and large, were pillaged from newspaper and magazine articles already made available to the public.[66] The reviewer
tasks himself with excerpting all the "readable" parts (a fairly common practice in reviews). However, he finds himself unable to recommend anything but
a few facts in relation to Siddons's childhood and one delightful, shining, *almost*
traditional anecdote in all its great glory (to be reproduced in full, momentar-
ily). For the rest, the reviewer declares, "Mr. Boaden's work has been rather
improperly entitled 'Memoirs of Mrs. Siddons,' for nine-tenths of it consists
of stupid criticism on damned plays and digressions."[67] Like the playwright-
biographer Arthur Murphy before him, Boaden's own interest in plays, above
and beyond the players, manifests in the magnified spatial presence granted to
plays and criticism.

Digressions, unlike anecdotes, served Boaden's purpose of self-
immortalization without the potential moral downside of anecdote.[68] If theatrical biography is an exercise in suspended animation, the digression is a
way of preserving the very movement of thought. To a greater extent than
for earlier authors who partook in digressions, it seems that Boaden's brand
of anecdote-into-criticism digression is a self-affirming exercise meant in part
to ensure preservation of Boaden himself: his ideas, passions, understanding.

Unfortunately, the Kemble and Siddons biographies suffer from their split
subjects of actor/author. The general impression is of a talented author whose
work is overrun by self-promotion. The reviewer from the *National Magazine*
quipped that, in his earlier memoir on Kemble, Boaden already revealed all
he knew "not only upon subjects connected with the stage, but upon almost
every other subject." Since Boaden doesn't feel obligated to confine himself
to the subject indicated on his title page, "the reader cannot therefore by any
stretch of foresight imagine what delectable matters he may meet with in one of
Mr. B's volumes—'perhaps it may turn out a song, perhaps turn out a sermon.'"[69]

Given Boaden's desire to mediate the experience of Kemble and Siddons
through himself, it should be less surprising to find that the single key anecdote in each of these narratives has not to do with either main subject, but

rather centers on the performative pragmatics of how Hamlet should properly behave when faced with his father beyond the grave. In other words, the anecdotes that merited inclusion were suggested by Boaden's own hobbyhorse rather than by any direct relation to the subject of his memoir. Moreover, on both occasions, the anecdote is properly situated in relation to Boaden, either as evidence of his self-importance or of his trustworthiness in only including verified anecdotes. The first anecdote, which appears as the veritable crown jewel in the *Memoirs of the Life of Philip Kemble*, was spurred on by Boaden's task of recording Macklin's death.[70] True anecdotes in Boaden's accounts come rarely, and, as I suggested, the story he tells is less of an anecdote and more of a revelation that emphasizes his own indispensability to the narrative.[71] Boaden frames the anecdote as a discussion about whether Garrick really invented the new stage delivery, calling upon a cherished memory of a conversation between Charles Macklin and himself.

In the story, Macklin is presumably railing about Garrick's exaggerated gestures, "by which, he said, rather than by the fair business of character, he [Garrick] caught and attained all attention to himself." Boaden broaches the endless inventiveness that Hamlets bring to their confrontation of the Ghost, which inflames Macklin and leads Boaden, like the second coming of Boswell, to bait Macklin into showing how he might play Hamlet in the scene: "He [Macklin] said, 'Remember, sir, to give me the cues.'" Thus, Boaden becomes Horatio to Macklin's Hamlet. Macklin-as-Hamlet begins his part "with indifference, a little sarcastical." In keeping with his commitment to the words of Shakespeare as speaking for themselves, Boaden faithfully transcribes, sans commentary, the exact lines of back-and-forth leading up to Horatio's gasp upon seeing the Ghost, finally getting to what long eighteenth-century, point-loving readers might consider the "meat" of the encounter:

> "Look, my Lord, it comes!" Macklin, here, with a sudden spring of the shoulders, and a slight throwing back of the body, the arms pointing downwards, and the fingers flying open, – in a breathless, scarcely audible tone, pronounced the ejaculation – "Angels and ministers of grace, defend us! From ALL surprise, it is not to be expected, that even Hamlet should be guarded; but always recollect, sir, that he *came* there, sir, to see his father's spirit."[72]

Boaden records Macklin as seamlessly transitioning from the vivid cry in the persona of Hamlet back to his more natural role as forceful preceptor— evidence of Macklin's skill as well as his rather abrasive, blustering personality.

To my knowledge, Boaden's is the only account of Macklin's brief turn as the Dane; thus, it is an instance traditional theatrical anecdote so prized by readers that, having happened to Boaden directly, does not compromise his authorial ethos. Furthermore, as in the examples involving Kemble and Boaden embarking on a shared Shakespearean critical question, Boaden's superior understanding draws his immediate subject—in this case, Macklin—into an interesting discussion that, in turn, furnishes material for the biography.[73] This anecdote travels far, as we recall its being one of only several key points (literally and figuratively), consistently offered up by reviewers seeking to isolate the best kernels of Kemble's lengthy biography.

The Life of Mrs. Jordan, which is allied to the biography of Kemble by bent of Boaden's personal relationship with his chosen subject, is much chattier in tone, its subject markedly less lofty. Surprisingly short of the gossip-based stories for a book that claims "anecdotes" as an essential component on the title page, an instance of Boaden attempting to correct, somewhat, for the critics' complaints in his subsequent works, *The Life of Mrs. Jordan* offers a brief anecdote about Garrick. Boaden records that whenever some new person told the renowned actor that he was attempting Hamlet, Garrick's most famous role, the veteran "used to turn his piercing eyes quickly upon the candidate, and favour him with a question of surprise. 'Eh!—how!—what! Hamlet the Dane?' Now what Garrick meant, is clear enough," concludes Boaden primly, suggesting that even when trying to appease critical demand for anecdote, the author's commitment to his own sense of morality was more important than delivering the entire transaction.[74]

Earlier, however, Boaden shared a much longer variation of this story in the *Memoirs of Mrs. Siddons*, which, like the example of Macklin as Hamlet in the *Memoirs of the Life of John Philip Kemble*, is the sole great anecdote recorded by the otherwise irritated reviewers. This anecdote is an excellent example of the Boadonian anecdote—one in which Boaden inserts himself and verifies the story's provenance—on exactly the same topic as the great *Kemble* anecdote—Hamlet's ghost—and once again, not involving the biography's titular subject. In this case, the story is authorized by Boaden's participation not as a key player, but as the direct audience of the actor and anecdotal foil, John Bannister. Boaden repeats the following lengthy story about Garrick:

My friend, John Bannister, gave me the following accurate detail of his own reception by Garrick, and even in the narrative veneration of the actor, the reader may indulge a smile at the vanity of the manager.

"I was," says the admirable comedian, "a student of painting in the Royal Academy, when I was introduced to Mr. Garrick, – under whose superior genius the British stage then flourished beyond all former example.

"One morning I was shown into his dressing room, when he was before the glass preparing to shave. A white nightcap covered his forehead, his chin and cheeks were enveloped in soap-suds; a razor-cloth was placed upon his left shoulder, and he turned and smoothed the shining blade with so much dexterity, that I longed for a beard, to imitate his incomparable method of handling the razor.

"Eh! well – what, young man – so – eh! You are still for the stage? Well, now, what character do you, should you like to – eh?"

"I should like to attempt Hamlet, sir."

"Eh, what! Hamlet the Dane? Zounds! that's a bold – a – Have you studied the part?"

"I have, sir."

"Well, don't mind my shaving. Speak your speech, the speech to the Ghost – I can hear you. Come, let's have a roll and a tumble." (A phrase of his often used to express a probationary specimen.)

"After a few hums and haws, and a disposing of my hair, so that it might stand on end, 'like quills upon the fretful porcupine,' I supposed my father's ghost before me, 'aim'd cap-a-pie,' and off I started.

"Angels and ministers of grace defend us!

(He wiped the razor)

Be thou a spirit of health, or a goblin damn'd,

(He strapped it)

Bring with thee airs from heav'n, or blasts from hell!

(He shaved on)

Thou coms't in such a questionable shape,
That I would speak to thee. I'll call thee Hamlet!
King, Father, Royal Dane! – O, answer me!
Let me not burst in ignorance."   *(He lathered again)*

I concluded with the usual,

"Say, why is this? wherefore? what should I do?"

but still continued in my attitude, expecting the praise due to an exhibition which I was booby enough to fancy was only to be equaled by himself. But, to my eternal mortification, he turned quick upon me, brandished the razor in his hand, and thrusting his half-shaved face close up to mine, he made such horrible mouths at me, that I thought he was seized with insanity, and I showed more natural symptoms of being frightened at him than at my father's ghost. "Angels and ministers! yaw! whaw! maw!" However, I soon perceived my vanity by his ridicule. He finished shaving, put on his wig, and, with a smile of good nature, he took me by the hand. "Come," said he, "young gentleman – eh, let us see now what we can do." He spoke the speech – how he spoke it, those who heard him never can forget. "There," said he, "young gentleman; and when you try that speech again, give it more passion and less mouth."[75]

It would be almost impossible to excerpt such an anecdote without losing some of its flavor. Boaden begins by touting the accuracy of what he is about to share, the veracity of which depends on his having heard it from the mouth of a participant, and the value of which centers on Boaden's surrogation of the now-absent but twice unforgettable Bannister and Garrick. Boaden thus reenacts Bannister, who reenacts Garrick (and himself): Boaden is only once removed from the action, but (indirectly) related nonetheless. (To draw attention to himself as "broker" of the story, he also interrupts the narrative to slip in an explanatory note about Garrick's "probationary" phrase.) This is a true anecdote because we get the brusque rudeness of Garrick, the proprietary attitude toward his role, and the legendarily paradoxical willingness to tutor potential competitors (this latter impulse tinged with the arrogance of an actor whom Alexander Pope predicted would become spoiled from lack of a true rival).

Most important to Boaden's conception of the role of anecdote, this story offered the public preservation of Garrick's character onstage (Hamlet) and offstage (Garrick), which—to the best of the present writer's knowledge—had not appeared in papers or other memoirs, unlike more traditional anecdotes that, like theatrical points, could practically be recited by memory among their intended audience. Thus, in a rare moment of synthesis between new (sparsely used, often directly mediated) and old (liberally included, frequently unverified) anecdotal styles, Boaden offers a rare extended glimpse of Garrick that Boaden had not published for fifty years.[76] As a biographer, Boaden could conceivably singlehandedly preserve that memory for decades beyond his own life by virtue of its publication in the *Memoirs of Mrs. Siddons*. This moment, then, was particularly successful, as Boaden extends the life of his own specific recollection beyond the temporally bound event of an oral retelling. In other words, Boaden ensures that, whatever happened to his own mind after his death, the product of his memory, at least, would survive. And, ideally, the two "memories" of Boaden and of his tale would be linked.

The linkage between teller and tale would be more pronounced than in prior biographies or other media because of Boaden's steadfast association of himself as the broker and guarantor of all that he presented. Crafting an image of himself as an accurate, source-giving gentleman-biographer in his own lifetime, Boaden likely imagined that he would be remembered because of the means (the Boaden-style anecdote) and accuracy of his memory (the citations and gentlemanlike guarantees).[77] In fact, contemporary references to him, while admittedly few, inevitably include choice sound bites from the biographies that have become entangled with his own.[78]

Letters and Collected Personal Archives

The most powerful source of Boaden's success is his decision to peruse the collected personal archives of his latter three subjects. This was the same strategy Macklin's second biographer, Kirkman, used with less discretion. Fortuitously, Boaden recognized that the inclusion of letters required a deft touch, and wrote disdainfully in the *Memoirs of Mrs. Siddons* about the epistolary upswing:

> If the worst of all friendly letters be those written with a view to ultimate publication, the best may be those which, flowing spontaneously from the occasions of the parties, by their intelligence and nature merit such a public disclosure. I write at a period when a deluge of epistolary publications, of all times and from every sort of character, compels one to see the striking advantage of the great fire of London.[79]

One of his next major projects after *Memoirs of Mrs. Siddons* would be a collection of the correspondence of David Garrick, in which Boaden's biographical talents were subordinated to his editorial abilities. A reviewer in the *Metropolitan* is appreciative of Boaden's efforts, noting "The Editor of this volume has given us an elaborate memoir [...] If we are instructed rightly, Mr. Boaden fulfilled this office and has done it with as much solemn care as if the fate of empires hung upon his commentaries."[80] Boaden appears to have greatly revised his appreciation of letters in service of biography at that time, as his next two biographies were based, like the *Private Correspondence of David Garrick*, on personal letters.[81]

Boaden's biographical approach can profitably be considered to have two different phases: lightly epistolary and therefore primarily driven by Boaden's own recollection and participation in the stage (*Memoirs of the Life of John Philip Kemble, Memoirs of Mrs. Siddons*) and primarily epistolary, each biography having been written with access to the deceased thespian's personal correspondence (*The Life of Mrs. Jordan, Memoirs of Mrs. Inchbald*). Boaden appears to have sought to correct *Kemble*'s flaws in the later Siddons memoir by focusing his memoir more closely around a single subject. *The Life of Mrs. Jordan* and *Memoirs of Mrs. Inchbald* both strive to provide fresh material about the titular thespian, which had been lamented as absent by critics of *Memoirs of Mrs. Siddons*. The critics' preferences appear to have been microscoping, rather than telescoping; audiences wanted a focused, potentially psychological, deeply personal account of the actor's mind rather than an urbane, witty recounting of general stage life loosely gathered around a thespian.[82] Letters were the way to achieve this new goal, simultaneously reintroducing some gossipy elements under the authentic aegis of personal correspondence. However, as we will see, Boaden's relationship with letters was at times uneasy, and he appears to have felt compelled to use greater numbers of letters as his career went on. The incorporation of epistles meant that Boaden had to balance his own authorial persona as a biographer with the increasingly prominent tasks of an editor.

What is the value of letters to a biographer, and to his audience? Letters appear to have three main sources of value to both parties: new information, reliability, and evidence of presence. To many readers, and almost all biographers, letters are noteworthy for the new information they provide, be it a show of emotion, a record of where someone will be or has been, an indication of who was part of a given social circle, or a description of something the letter writer perceived. Moreover, an underlying assumption of letters as pure outpourings of the heart makes correspondence almost sacred, an unimpeachably authentic source.[83] At its most basic level, the letter is important because it is evidence of the writer's physical act of writing. More abstractly, the letter's importance in the context of *theatrical* biography is elevated further in contrast to the physical act of onstage performance, which leaves no physical memento beyond a playbill (and that, having been mass-produced, likely never came into contact with the thespian, and was not of her "making" anyway). Thus, Boaden preserves a number of letters that are brief, little more than receipts, frequently pertaining to the financial business of stage, perfectly bereft of emotion, color, or personality. This letter from Dorothy Jordan seems somewhat typical, a basic contractual agreement:

> Sir,
>
> I agree with pleasure to your proposal of giving you thirty pounds rather than ever perform in York. I shall return to-morrow and settle the balance of the account. I am, Sir,
>
> > Your obligated, humble servant,
> > D. Ford.[84]

"The signature causes me to preserve it," writes Boaden, acknowledging that this letter, out of context, might not provide much useful content to the reader about Jordan. Intriguingly, the real signature, so prized by Boaden, is not present, even in a printed representation. We know that the technology did exist for such operations: lithograph signatures had become de rigueur under the images of thespians that extra-illustrators pasted into biographies, if the collectors did not have the connections to acquire authentic signatures on the margin underneath their portraits, like Queen Charlotte did, or the questionable cunning of the gentleman who pasted together a death roster of mourners' signatures from Garrick's funeral. It does appear that Mrs. Jordan's business expense receipts were a hot commodity for extra-illustrators and scrapbookers alike, as a number of them surfaced in augmented works dedicated to Jordan and David Garrick. The written receipts' small size, relative abundance, and lack of "deep" content may have made them ideal for collectors whose main interest was the signature rather than the substance.

Signatures could be important for several reasons: evidence of the signatory's presence, certainly, as Pointon suggests, but also potentially for evaluative purposes—what does the handwriting look like? This latter interest could, theoretically, be satisfied by lithograph. In Inchbald's biography, Boaden writes, "We shall, in its proper place, give Mrs. Inchbald's own remarks [...] from an extract of her letter to Mr. Harris, in her own hand-writing."[85] Here, he is stressing the authenticity of the piece rather than promising to replicate the writing. However, Boaden must be aware of what is lost in translating handwritten letters into a mechanical typeface, as he both commends and laments efforts to train ladies into having neatly anonymous handwriting:

> As far as the eye is gratified by neatness, the penmanship is improved; but we have lost the indication of character, which existed when the *writing*, like the walk, the various action, the manner of doing every thing, was individual and peculiar; and to a very nice observer sometimes made the letter itself a refutation of its contents.[86]

Boaden's comments map onto printing nicely: the uniformity of David Garrick's printed correspondence *(Private Correspondence of David Garrick)* releases a reader from the burden of deciphering a range of different handwriting techniques, and indeed ensures, by reduction of time and effort, that more people will be able to access what was in the letters. What is lost, as Boaden notes, is the individual character of the writing itself, which often aids in interpretation. Handwritten letters thus clearly function as a surrogate presence for the absent actor.

The value of mass-reproducing Garrick's correspondence, or Inchbald's private letter to a friend, is complicated by the extent to which the desire for presence is hinged on exclusivity. If everyone has access to a tremendous supply of physical letters signed by Jordan, her signatures will proportionally decrease in economic value (but may yet be emotionally valuable to the individual collector). If instead, everyone (or a great number of people) has access to a sizeable compendium of her letters as typed, abridged and transcribed by Boaden, the signature or actual presence is still evasive, but the value of the contents will depreciate as the news becomes dispersed. Thus, just as letters themselves present a challenge for the biographer by supplying authentic evidence in which to ground his interpretation but also threatening to overtake his spot as the source of knowledge in the biographical transaction, so too the act of reproduction both ensures the actor's memory but also cheapens its value in a market driven by scarcity.

This latter relationship is the same one underlying Kirkman's resentment of Macklin's first biographer, Congreve, or Murphy's resentment of Davies, or Campbell's of Boaden—there is a sense in which the first biographer has an easier task because of the comparative wealth of information that has not yet been released. Both Kirkman and Campbell attempt to get around the challenge of being second in line by deploying the "official" private writings of their subjects to which the earlier biographers did not have access. These corpuses of unpublished letters meant that at any moment, conceivably years past a person's decease (seven in the case of Siddons, and fifteen for Mrs. Jordan), the epistolary body could arise, in a sense reanimating a body long assumed to have been at rest: at once a literary corps and a literary *corpse*.

Such resurrections could be unsettling, the biographer likened to a grave robber. In 1831, Boaden released his biography of Dorothy Jordan, famous for her dual roles as actress and as mistress of the recently crowned King William IV back when he was still the Duke of Clarence.[87] A contemporary review offers strenuous, damning criticism, asserting that the nature of the memoir, with its private letters detailing Jordan's well-known affair, indicated Boaden's attempt to shame the royal family into giving him money to remove the more damaging letters from circulation. While Boaden paints a sympathetic portrait of the new monarch in the biography, he certainly capitalizes on the British people's potential interest in their new king by publishing a biography of his mistress using her own letters.[88]

A biographical subject already somewhat fleshed out through written communications is a great advantage to the biographer seeking to provide some depth and authenticity; it is also an obstacle to one's own storytelling as the source of authenticity. Exponentially more challenging is the subject who has written her own autobiography, or fragments thereof. When Boaden approached Mrs. Inchbald, his final thespian subject, he inherited not only a large corpus of letters, but also fragments from a much-anticipated autobiography and the daily ledger that she kept through most of her life, as many of her contemporaries would have done.[89] Boaden belies his purely scholarly interest in Inchbald when he rails against an advertisement promoting a book pretending to be the genuine autobiography of Inchbald, which had not been consigned to the flames after her death, as her will dictated. He writes, "I consider it a trick to impose some pretended Memoirs on the world, or, if a copy has been taken of what she really wrote, to defraud her executors."[90] He himself served as an executor, both in deciding how to dispose of her papers, and in insisting on her double death: the death of

the actress and the death of her autobiography. Inchbald, twice silenced, must tell her story through her living interlocutor, James Boaden, should Inchbald spontaneously appear in the form of her autobiography, Boaden's biography would have to rely on the most basic form of originality: arriving at the scene first, rather than on superior presentation of ephemera or a closer relationship with the subject. It is in Boaden's best interest to insure that Inchbald's resuscitation is tied to his own artistry, even within the context of her own letters.

In resurrecting this specifically literary corpse, Boaden satisfies not only his audience's demand for new material, but also his own moral requirements while cementing the supremacy of textual artifacts in preserving a thespian's memory. Recall that Boaden's earlier-mentioned resistance to traditional anecdotes can be traced at least as much to his own moral scruples as to his belief in written documentation as a legitimizing process. It is thus understandable that a man who would replace descriptive kinetic, gestural points with direct quotations of the relevant lines in a script would also herald letters as an equally powerful means of preserving the actor. In my understanding, no prior thespian biographer had so strongly asserted the impact of letters as Boaden had done.

Beyond the usual appeals that letters preserve the essence of an actor's personality by providing her own diction, syntax, and emphases, and that original copies may also act as a physical record of momentary presence, Boaden makes one more crucial claim for the power of epistolary intercourse in *The Life of Mrs. Jordan*, the first of his heavily letter-based biographies. Elevating the role of letters significantly, Boaden portrays and describes written correspondence as representative of Jordan's presence onstage. Just as a few lines from the script of a specific play, unmediated by commentary about gesture or delivery, could represent a character onstage for Boaden, so too could the actress's own letters. Boaden explicitly claims that, just as Dorothy Jordan's acting as a "romp" character was marked by exuberant emphasis, "her letters are always careless, unstudied effusions, written as fast as the pen will cover the paper."[91] In his preface to her life, Boaden announces:

Permitted to use the *very* documents themselves, I have printed them exactly from the ORIGINALS in her *own* handwriting; they are unstudied compositions, but they all sprung warm from the heart, and, like her acting, speak its true and impassioned language. Her ACTING, indeed, was *heart* in action; and its pulsations vibrated to the extremities of its theatrical habitation.[92]

Onstage, Mrs. Jordan was often described as a child of nature and, in the memoir, Boaden objects to Sheridan's attempts to shoehorn Jordan into a Kemble-like style of "high" delivery at odds with her vaunted naturalness.[93] Indeed, Boaden strives to debunk any whiff of artifice or performativity about Mrs. Jordan onstage, and transfers the ethos of the public actress onstage to the private lady in the midst of epistolary correspondence. He triumphantly notes that since "Nature's child" only dated her letters according to the day of the week, she made "a modest presumption, unsustained by the fact, that they can be only of temporary interest."[94] This claim would seem to defray any concern on the reader's part about Mrs. Jordan's conscious cultivation of a rhetorical persona that was at odds with the everyday situational reality. Jordan's specific epistolary style not only justifies it as more trustworthy than, say, the image-conscious Garrick, but also introduces letters as further evidence of acting styles, promoting the written word as a superior lifeline for the memory of actors on multiple levels.

It thus appears that letters, for Boaden, serve for the stage performer a function similar to an anecdote about a noted wit. Letters and anecdotes crystallize performance or truth, depending on one's level of confidence in the ability to dispense with any self-conscious element of *performativity* in a performance. In some instances, firsthand letters contain anecdotes, a treasure trove of delivery and characterization reflecting on both author and subject. (In a similar way, points in theatrical biography, reproduced in biography, might be thought to represent a referendum on the performance abilities of actor and re-performing biographer.)

Boaden may have believed that letters were a better replacement for traditional anecdote, because epistolary correspondence dispensed with the mediating teller of an anecdote; however, Boaden must have recognized that he was required to mediate the narrative to some degree or forfeit his own stake in the story. Instead of self-centered anecdotes in which he plays a pivotal role, Boaden finds the balance between his ethical commitment to authenticity and his personal commitment to self-preservation in assuming the role of moral arbiter vis-à-vis the increasingly private content of his thespian subjects' letters.[95]

As I suggested earlier, a reader approaching each of Boaden's memoirs would rather quickly discover the schism between his first two and latter three biographical efforts. While I have noted that the change in epistolary emphasis can account for the different texture, one might imagine that Boaden intentionally chose a more conversational, author-directed method that spared his dramatic thespians, Kemble and Siddons, from any inquiry into their personal lives, while he allowed the lower-class comedians to speak for themselves, airing their intimate affairs. In other words, Boaden's biographies appear to propose a radically different treatment for great tragedians than for comedians. (Jordan was great in her admittedly limited roles, and Inchbald vastly less successful in her career as an actress.) Garrick, unsurprisingly, stands out because of Boaden's strict editorial approach, which was closer to the austerity of his Kemble family biographies than his epistolary ones.

There is an alternative explanation for the crisp bisection between publicly figured tragedians and privately figured comedians: the inclusion of greater numbers of private letters almost necessarily means that more of the subject's personal life will come to the forefront. Boaden's least private (or most publically focused) biography is that of Mrs. Siddons, which boasts a handful of letters that were presumably written by Mrs. Siddons and read or released as damage control for a perceived insult to a needy colleague. These letters, Boaden snipes, were of inferior mettle and obviously written by Siddons's husband—undoubtedly without her eagle-eyed consent.[96] The value of the letters thus is doubtful, both because they were publicly released and because they might be products of a lesser hand. Having neither the handwritten presence of the thespian (the contents not having flowed from her brain through her hand and onto the page) nor the thrill of something once private, the meager cache of Siddons's letters recycled from newspapers only excites in its final few installments, chiefly in one beautiful letter written shortly after the untimely deaths of two of Mrs. Siddons's daughters. Boaden writes, "The actor shares in the common sufferings of his kind, without the sacred indulgence of his grief, which decency commands in every other condition. But let us hear Mrs. Siddons herself":

> If Mr.– thinks himself unfortunate, let him look on *me*, and be silent. The inscrutable ways of Providence! Two lovely creatures *gone*; and another is just arrived from school, with all the dazzling, frightful sort of beauty, that irradiated the countenance of Maria, and makes me shudder when I look at her. I feel myself, like poor Niobe, grasping to her bosom the last and youngest of her children; and like her look every moment for the vengeful arrow of destruction.[97]

It may be that this epistolary anecdote attracted attention because it fit into the popular image of Siddons as a tragedian, allowing her to have a semblance of personal life that nonetheless did not undermine her reputation as a rather pious actress devoted to her family and the stage.[98] It is a stunning departure from the "professional" letters drafted by Mr. Siddons, where she sometimes appears rather petty, the abovementioned letter, by contrast, would have been convincing evidence to the Romantic reader of Siddons's sensibility, moral uprightness, and occasional vulnerability at the appropriate moments.

It should be acknowledged that Boaden did use letters even at the beginning of his biographical career, albeit sparingly. Siddons's brother Kemble had several personal letters appear in his biography, courtesy of his younger brother, Charles Kemble. In praise of his subject, Boaden appropriates Cicero's encomiastic statement about the then-contemporary actor Roscius: "While he made the first figure on the stage for his art, [he] was worthy of the senate for his virtue."[99] Boaden frequently links a lack of a personal life with the presence of virtue. With both Kemble and Siddons, he seems to link excellent acting skills with a highly private offstage life. By virtue of Boaden's biases alone, there is little of note in those letters; rather, the majority of interest is in Boaden's mediation of events. The biographer notes with pride that he has "ventured to baffle the search of the malignant" who anticipate negative stories about Kemble, and that he has stifled any letter or story in which Kemble appeared to express a spontaneous opinion that seemed out of keeping with more leisurely pronouncements.[100] Evidently, Boaden feels very possessive of his friend's life story, even taking it upon himself to respond to a letter received by Kemble as Boaden believes Kemble would have responded. Boaden makes a similarly presumptuous venture as to Siddons's opinion in her memoir as well, when the appropriate letter could not be found.[101]

In short, Boaden exercises a very heavy hand over the inclusion and significance of letters in his first two biographies, almost exclusively preferring to include his own encounters with Kemble on moral grounds. It is therefore rather shocking to see the austere, moralistic Boaden not only select Dorothy Jordan as his subject, rather than another Kemble sibling, but also release a large number of letters from an actress known not to have had much discretion. However, Boaden doesn't flatten Jordan out to the vice in a morality show; he commends her fellow actors for their defense of her character when she performed onstage while pregnant and unmarried, noting that the theatre should not be confused with a sound moral education.

Certainly, Boaden has more to say about morality in the reasonably epistolary Jordan. Ironically, he takes a heightened moral standpoint when addressing the vastly epistolary Inchbald, whose life seemed much less exceptionable. It is probable that Boaden felt less need to assert his moral judgment in order to be heard through Jordan's letters; additionally, as with Kemble, Boaden could claim a personal relationship with Jordan. While Boaden cannot, and does not, celebrate Jordan for great virtue, he takes a tone of indulgence about his subject, especially in relation to the role that he himself played in her life: "We shall treat the memory of Mrs. Jordan as we always did her person; when she had at all suffered [...] we were happy to restore the equilibrium of her mind, by telling her anything of a soothing and respectful nature."[102] He defends her right to privacy, approving of the public's détente on speculations about

Jordan's love life. Nonetheless, there is an element of hypocrisy to Boaden's declarations, since he has published a book containing his own friend's very private correspondence.[103]

The great triumph of Boaden's transition into epistolary biography is that letters supply gossip and titillation while leaving Boaden almost beyond reproach due to their authenticity, simultaneously positioning Boaden as moral arbiter. Boaden shifts from a stage critic to a social critic. Once Jordan retires, the text gets increasingly personal, in sharp contrast with Siddons's life after retirement, which was so irrelevant in Boaden's eyes that her biography could be written while Siddons still lived.[104] Boaden's eagerness to resurrect Jordan in the depths of her pain as an ousted mistress coping with illness and exile is rather terrible to witness, so intent is he on providing an in-depth view of her life: "A momentous point in her life is about to open to us, which we are happily enabled to illustrate by her own letters."[105] At the conclusion of the second volume, after Jordan has quit the stage, slipped off to France, and died, Boaden callously opines, "the woman, in her, was too powerful for the genius."[106] This sentiment conforms to his earlier iteration that a vibrant personal life was at odds with a strong professional acting career. Ironically, Jordan's personal life forms the basis of her biography and marks her as a much more vivid presence than Boaden's saintly Kemble or austere Siddons; Jordan's offstage availability challenges the vacuum that Boaden usually filled with himself. Unfortunately, correspondence also overtook direct reference to Jordan onstage—and indirect reference, if one does not buy into Boaden's theory about Jordan's letters as accurately representing her onstage style.[107]

In sharp contrast to the nonepistolary-centered lives of Kemble and Siddons, Elizabeth Inchbald, allied with Jordan as a comedienne to whose letters Boaden had access, appears remarkably infrequently as an actress in her memoirs. Jordan, whose private life was troublingly public, had left piles of effusive letters supposedly with little thought to her textual afterlife; Siddons, whose personal life was remarkably separate from her professional transactions, left a carefully orchestrated set of recollections for a handpicked biographer (Campbell, not Boaden). Inchbald, not nearly as spontaneous as Jordan nor as controlled as Siddons, neither devil nor angel, wrote her autobiography but could not bring herself to publish it. While Boaden presumably had less work to do in terms of atoning for a glaring moral error, as in the case of Jordan, and less of a personal attachment to Inchbald, he had use of her personal reflections, including a daily log of activity and emotion that revealed an unprecedented amount of detail.

Stripped of his usual ability to generate the momentum of the narration with letters as punctuation or illustration, Boaden flounders to assert control over Inchbald's voluminous archive. For example, in *The Life of Mrs. Jordan,*

Boaden makes a meal of the scandal of Jordan having to recite a line about hoydens chasing after princes: did she speak such a line? He writes his own dialogue in response to a fictionalized gossip:

> Pray, madam, pay a little regard to chronology, and suspect any thing rather than a want of good taste in the Jordan: I can assure you, on my personal knowledge, that I have no such instances to record, and that you will be convinced of my sincerity, if you will honour me with your company into Yorkshire this very summer [...] you will see [events happening outside of London] [...] you must wait a while [for the part about affairs with princes].[108]

Boaden writes as though he is a tour guide who will lead the woman through time. In reality, his approach is not out of keeping with the task of a biographer, if a bit too direct.

With Inchbald, Boaden fails to gain much ground as an author rather than an editor in terms of structure. He painfully follows her day-to-day accounts, omitting large swaths but also preserving such fascinating details such as Inchbald's departure for Edinburgh at precisely 2 a.m. on July 2, 1776, arriving in Valleri on the 23rd.[109] Then Inchbald commenced a trip to Abbeville to see all its convents the next day, followed by Mass on the 25th.[110] The painfully rigorous chronology appears rather amateurish for a biographer of Boaden's experience, and the reams of factual evidence underscore that he played no role in Inchbald's life. Boaden doesn't afford much opportunity for his self-insertions as a character in the narrative, therefore, he uses the chronology to doggedly pursue his commitment to morality and tracks every instance of Inchbald attending church, commenting disapprovingly when she fails to be regular in her observance.

In Volume 2, Boaden records that she made but one religious entry in her diary for the entirety of 1799.[111] In contrast, only a little later, she committed an act of great Christian charity in sitting up with an ill maid, thus showing herself a true Christian woman.[112] Inchbald later came back to religion full force, lived in a Catholics-only house for a brief spell,[113] and attended many masses and very little theatre.[114] The link that Boaden traces inversely between Mass and theatre is supported by his belief—well established in the *Life of Jordan*—that theatre is not intended as a moral enterprise, but he is on dangerous ground in terms of his own faith, one would think, as a theatrical biographer. From 1777 to 1810, Boaden records periods of stunning religious inactivity on the part of Mrs. Inchbald, noting that even terrible events did not drive her to the church as one might have expected. Redeemingly, for Boaden, "the year 1813 was [...] all but devoted to religious duties."[115] In effect,

Boaden intrudes much more heavily into the personal and political views of Inchbald, possibly for two reasons: her life did not provide a straightforward moral warning like Mrs. Jordan's short existence, and the depth of discussion in Inchbald's letters and diaries doubtless equipped Boaden with more material to showcase his armchair knowledge of Inchbald.

Inchbald's autobiography proves a boon as well as a burden to Boaden. While the biographical outlines and chronology require a biographer with more discernment to harvest useful details, the extra documentation also allowed Boaden to expose Inchbald's personal life without remorse, as she herself had planned to do at one time. The moral censure that surfaced in relation to Jordan's actions, rather than her person, is acutely present when Boaden assesses Inchbald in the concluding "character sketch" as both a threat to and scapegoat for his own biographical practice:

> The materials of this biography are entirely her own – the record she wrote was a daily duty which she performed: she could at all times review her life, with a certainty that was equally awful to herself and others. Had we been disposed to dress up a perfect model of woman, there are many decided follies that we should have suppressed in pure compassion [...] [except that] our portrait so far would have been unlike the original.[116]

Boaden thus justifies the equivocal attention paid to Inchbald's religious doubts as to her life as a leading playwright. Of her acting career, he writes simply that she wished to be an actress but had a stutter; subsequently, he reports, she met and became an acolyte of Mr. Inchbald, who was "a master in his profession; and he made her an actress." Thus, Boaden dispenses with her acting career in a single line.[117]

Ironically, Boaden's study of Inchbald brackets her acting, but Inchbald's preparations as her own biographer circumscribe Boaden's ability to thrive as a biographer. For example, a signature component of long eighteenth-century biography was that of the "character," an ending summation of the actor as a person. This prerogative was generally reserved for a biographer, but had already been supplied by a good friend of Inchbald's, Mr. Moore. This man had provided a character of her, which the actress had reviewed, found rather delightful, and preserved, likely as part of her planned autobiography:

> Inchbald, Mrs. – A very lively and ingenious English authoress, whom Fortune maliciously placed in a situation, and threw into a profession, beneath her merits, though her genius were to be left out of the account. Nature felt the affront, and was resolved to vindicate the claims of her

favourite. She inspired that energy which looks on difficulty as the natural element of superior minds. She remembered that Shakspeare as a player was only the tame and unskillful representative of his own apparition: as an author he had soared to the sublime enthusiasm of Hamlet and Othello. Our fair authoress thus instructed, but unsullied by her intercourse with the world both in her dramatic and other pieces, has displayed a quick intelligence of the foibles of our nature – an horror at vice yet pity for the vicious – and an assertion throughout of the native dignity of steady moral principles. Her conversation was easy and animated. Her curiosity was not such as is blasphemously imputed to her sex; yet she was inquisitive. Never did an antiquated matron trace a tale of scandal through all its meanders of authority, with more undeviating eagerness, than our heroine hunted out a new source of useful information. Her school was society; to which she gratefully returned, as an instructress, what she had gathered as a scholar. Her passion was the contemplation of superior excellence; and though her personal charms secured her admirers, which flattered her as a woman, she preferred the homage of the mind, in her higher character of a woman of genius. A little disposition to coquetry perhaps she had, but the frankness of her nature disdained it; and when necessity called for the choice of the one or the other, sincerity was sure to triumph. She was born in the year 1753, and passed to a better life (as one of her contemporaries predicted) in the THREE HUNDRED AND FIFTIETH year of her age.[118]

In a moment of clear concession to Moore's more privileged position, Boaden transcribed Moore's words seemingly exactly. It is a credit to Boaden that, in this instance, his desire to provide the clearest portrait of Inchbald overcame his renowned interest in self-promotion. Boaden would have been guilty of a grave omission had he not included Moore's sketch, which captures that man's affection for the author-actress and her apparently whimsical nature.

If Boaden suppresses the ability for Inchbald to fully reanimate herself (reiterating that the autobiography had been destroyed), he does recognize a kindred spirit. Inchbald's motivation to promote her own self-consciousness well beyond her time on Earth appears rather transparent throughout the memoir. Boaden records the proposed table of contents for her fractured autobiography, almost unintelligible in its vagueness and painfully similar to Charles Macklin's chicken-scratch sketches for the autobiography that never happened.[119] Such fragmentary autobiographies underscore the same menace of time that harrows the actor: memory runs out, whether it is collective memory of one's time on stage, or individual memory upon a prospective autobiographer's decease.

Although a rather widely applicable scourge, time is uniquely apparent in Inchbald's writings, as she writes a retrospective of herself entitled "Septembers Since I Married" which Boaden introduces and then replicates via chart. Boaden cutely speculates that she commemorates Septembers not for her birthday (in October) or wedding anniversary (in June), but for her debut as Cordelia to Mr. Inchbald's Lear, making Inchbald a kindred spirit to Boaden's own Shakespeare-centered interpretational lens. Inchbald ranks her overall mood for each year's September from 1773 to 1808 as "very happy" to "extremely unhappy."[120] The year 1791, designated as "after my novel, 'Simple Story,'" is the only year to receive the top designation without caveats, and 1808 represents her lowest recorded, year based on the continued backlash from the critical prefaces (discussed below) and her favorite sister's declining health. Boaden observes of these years, each of which receive a few highlights in clipped phrases, "In fact, as actress and authoress, hers is truly a stage existence. [...] [Her Retrospect is] bounded by her theatricals, though embracing other topics in subordination."[121]

The task of Inchbald's biography was certainly split between literary and theatrical biography, and this tension was exacerbated by Boaden's maturing preference for all things written, especially plays and letters. Inchbald's own correspondence and accounts, as offered through Boaden, at no time show much interest in how to act a character, or in preserving her own theatrical legacy as a thespian. Accordingly, Boaden lightly suggests that Inchbald could not have hoped to have secured immortality on acting alone, but that happily, her pen was a better bet.[122] Indeed, Inchbald's best performances were those that took place on paper, through plays and letters. Consequently, Boaden had a better corpus of Inchbald than in his other biographies; in many ways, Inchbald's was more of a literary biography than a theatrical biography.

Inchbald's unique positioning as someone who saw herself as both literary and theatrical, like Boaden, was furthered by her own forays into writing thespian biography. As referenced in her most melancholy entry for 1808 in "Septembers Since I Married," Inchbald had had a relatively successful career as a prefatory biographer, until one particularly disgruntled writer had criticized Inchbald for including criticism of plays in his biography; in this man's mind, the tasks of biographer and critic were mutually exclusive—a perspective anathema to Boaden.[123] Inchbald, therefore, in perceiving the critical part of her task as a biographer as particularly significant, and in writing so much material about herself, is almost as much a rival biographer to Boaden as Davies was to Murphy with regard to Garrick, or as Campbell was to Boaden himself when it came to Sarah Siddons.

Reviewers picked up on this unbalanced coauthorship of Boaden and Inchbald herself. A review from the *Athenaeum* on Saturday, May 18, 1833, shortly before the Inchbald memoir was made public, notes that the second volume, having a lot more of Inchbald's own voice in it, was markedly better than the first volume. Boaden can get bogged down in trifles, notes the reviewer, but his occasional lapses in judgment aside, "on the whole, Mrs. Inchbald's character comes out delightfully" in the biography.[124] It is Inchbald's character, rather than Boaden's character of Inchbald, that is commended. Tellingly, the review primarily quotes Inchbald's own materials rather than Boaden's additions. The chronicler is certainly a diminished attraction from his early days as a biographer playing multiple roles in the *Memoirs of the Life of John Philip Kemble*.

To briefly sum up several key relationships between the five Boaden biographies, the *character* of Boaden (that is, Boaden's reference to himself as part of the "action") seems to appear most strongly in inverse relation to his titular protagonist. More Boaden-as-key-player leaves less room for the actor or actress on whom he was supposedly focusing. This Boaden factor can be roughly assessed by the weight of personal correspondence in a given biography. The John Philip Kemble and Sarah Siddons biographies, gathered around two characters who should be larger than life, are also simultaneously acting as histories of the stage. There are few personal letters in either work. Neither thespian's private life is on the table for discussion, beyond Kemble's marriage and Siddons's children—more theatre at large and less private life equates to a rich stage for Boaden himself to caper about.

Jordan, as a stalking horse for a larger moral message (and possibly as an easy money-making enterprise) leaves room for a bit of Boaden because he knew her personally, but is heavier on her own correspondence. The narrative of Inchbald, whom Boaden did not know personally, is rather strongly gathered around her own correspondence and life offstage, so Boaden as a potential participant is severely limited. Finally, Boaden is most remotely related to David Garrick both in terms of their career periods and personal interactions; thus, Boaden almost entirely allows the letters to speak for themselves, formally accepting a position as an editor to the letters and demurring from the full biographical enterprise by providing a prefatory biography that he explicitly states will be a recapitulation of existing facts.

While Boaden attempts to control his own role in each biography as he modulates the balance of self-insertion to original correspondence, his struggle manifests itself clearly in what I would like to term the "Hamlet Index." I have earlier suggested that *Hamlet* provides a touchstone for Boaden, a means for him to discuss almost any issue, and a frequent resting place at the end of a train of thought. Intriguingly, when Boaden imagines or describes his titular thespians in the part of Hamlet, his level of eagerness appears to reflect the degree and nature of his personal involvement in the particular biography.

In the *Memoirs of the Life of John Philip Kemble*, his earliest effort, Boaden describes Kemble's Hamlet with significantly more relish than any other role: specifically, he compares the particular points where Kemble differed from Henderson and Betterton. For example, he writes, "It was observed how keenly Kemble inserted an insinuation of the King's intemperance, when he said to Horatio and the rest, 'We'll teach you to DRINK *deep*,—ere you depart.'"[125] This is one moment in which Boaden almost focuses on the Cibberean intent of the genre by describing what Kemble did to embody Hamlet. Ultimately, however, he is more interested in discussing how Kemble and he believed the ghost should be played, or how Kemble should interpret a line of Shakespeare. Such moments serve to emphasize his relationship with Kemble and his own skill as a Shakespearean scholar, as he justifies or censures Kemble's pronunciation choices. (The points that Boaden describes are primarily aural rather than gestural, again picking up on Boaden's sensitivity to changing theatrical conventions.)

Similarly, the strength (or weakness) of *Life of Siddons* is perfectly encapsulated in Boaden's decision to attempt to assess Mrs. Siddons's brief tenure as Hamlet in Manchester. He claims that he knew enough about Siddons's style to imagine how she played it—this ties into Boaden's earlier gambit of inserting himself into instances whether he was actually present originally. Moreover, he frames this speculative description of Siddons as Hamlet as "where and how she would differ from her brother" in the role.[126]

The Boaden who is participating in the Cibber/Davies tradition of "History of the Stage" is deeply aware of the competitive drive among biographers, and this manifests in his squaring off of the two siblings. Boaden relates that Siddons would show "more feminine alarm" when Horatio describes the ghost appearing: "As she heard a narrative at all times better than one was ever told, so I conceive her breathless attention to the spirit during his disclosure, again benefited by the sex itself, would, as before, be transcendent."[127] Her "To be" soliloquy would appear "like audible rumination" as compared to that of Kemble, who was overly declamatory in that scene. As to whether Siddons could transcend her brother, Boaden declares that, notwithstanding the inherit modesty of a female getting in the way of the manlier aspects of Hamlet (these he does not enumerate), "the conclusion at last might be, 'were she but man, she would exceed all that man has ever achieved in Hamlet.'"[128] In terms of the author's intimacy with his topic, Boaden's Siddons is primarily smoke and mirrors, a critic leveraging Shakespearean scholarship and speculation in lieu of an actual relationship with the object of interest.

Mrs. Jordan bears no relation to Hamlet, neither playing the character nor apparently producing any letters on it. The absence of Hamlet, however, heralds Boaden's inability to attend to theatrical details in lieu of the personal affairs of Jordan (and, indeed, Mrs. Jordan appears to have been an immensely personal choice, predicated on his relationship with her). Boaden still manages to indulge in some ghostly reminisces on Banquo's Ghost. These Macbethian musings are drastically removed from interest in Mrs. Jordan, per se; the further away from Hamlet-related thespians that Boaden gets, the less stage material appears, and the less opportunity for Boaden to unleash his torrent of personal knowledge while claiming to be on topic. Thus, the character in *The Life of Mrs. Jordan* who is described as playing a role in Hamlet is Boaden himself, as Goodman Delver: Boaden realizes that his own efficacy is drawing nigh and appropriately codes himself as a minor, albeit significant, character in charge of the twin paradoxes of burial and memory resurrection.

Continuing the downward slope of the immediacy of Boaden's pet projects and opinions in biography, Boaden merely mentions that Inchbald did in fact play Hamlet on a provincial stage at the beginning of her career.[129] Unlike Boaden's wildly enthusiastic speculations about the quality and nature of Siddons's Hamlet, Boaden discusses neither how Inchbald assayed the role of the Dane, nor how the production might have handled the intricacies involving the Ghost. How did Mrs. Inchbald react in that pivotal meeting scene? Boaden's estrangement from active theatrical involvement (rather than his moral quibbling about Inchbald's church-going activities) is most evident in this silence. Contrary to his claims in *The Life of Mrs. Jordan,* Boaden has, figuratively and literally, given up the Ghost. It is little wonder that Inchbald's is his final biography.

Time's Effects: Boaden between Davies and Campbell

We have seen that while letters underwrite the truth of the biographer's assertion, they also threaten his position as an artist. He may feel compelled to contort his preferred narrative around those instances for which he has epistolary evidence, or accord more weight to a relatively useless or bland letter for sake of the illustrious name or the fleeting grasp at the thespian's presumed presence. Moreover, he may need to look for new ways to assert his presence in the narrative and, for Boaden, that means turning more toward adding the character of a moral arbiter to the task of an editor.

The threat to biographers from letters has one more retrospective dimension. Not only could letters reanimate the dead; they could also, by virtue of an increased interest in evidence, call into question a biographer whose rendition had been celebrated or revivify a biographer's account that had been erroneously dismissed (not infrequently, by a rather biased author or acolyte of a new biography on the same subject). It seems that the treatment of letters constituted a particularly fertile battleground between rival biographers and biographies. The reviewer writing for the *Quarterly Review* in 1868 on the occasion of Percy Fitzgerald's new biography of David Garrick dismisses earliest biographer-competitors Davies and Murphy as having a negative agenda toward Garrick. "We should have had very different books from both, could they have dreamed that their own letters to Garrick, with the drafts of his replies, had been preserved," writes the reviewer. Those letters could "rise up in judgment" against the biographers as evidence contradicting their unprincipled representation of Garrick.[130]

Letters, then, continued to be seen as guarantors, taking precedence even over personal interaction with a thespian subject. Boaden, who received both correspondence and permission from the estate of Eva Marie Garrick almost a decade after her death, had not known Mr. or Mrs. Garrick professionally or publicly. Nevertheless, by means of the collected letters from the Garrick estate, Boaden attempted to overtake the prior two biographers as most trustworthy mediator. In effect, letters prolonged the potential field of competition and this, in turn, potentially made the reputation of any biographer who had been considered good in his own time subject to revision.

An interesting byproduct of Boaden's multiple biographies is a burgeoning regard for Thomas Davies, whose Garrick memoir had survived the slings and arrows of Murphy's criticism and stood up to Boaden's own primary-source investigations. Toothill has noted that Boaden imported the majority of facts in the prefatory biography from Davies's account, and that details in the correspondence itself corroborate Davies's account in those places that Murphy had erroneously challenged it.[131] Moreover, Boaden's forthright announcement that he intends to add no interpretation suggests a respect for Davies, as well as a reluctance to challenge him in the field of interpretational biography. However, Boaden fails to cite from Davies in this preface, as in other instances in his earlier biographies. Davies barely merits any mention in the *Memoirs of the Life of John Philip Kemble*, notwithstanding that the volume was a history from the time of Garrick to the midpoint of Kemble's career; he is cited only once, in reference to a story about Mrs. Cibber and Arthur Murphy deceiving Garrick by acting as though Mrs. Cibber was hopeless in a role from *The Orphan of China*, only to astound him by appearing to have improved so drastically in the span of a week or ten days. "The story is inconceivably foolish," says Boaden, which not coincidentally appears to be his general referendum on Davies's work.

In the *Memoirs of Mrs. Siddons*, Boaden mocks "my predecessor, as a historian of the stage," noting his failure as a bookseller and lukewarm acting career.[132] In the same volume, Boaden insults Murphy by opposing his indulgence in anecdotes, among other complaints. The disapproving biographer seems to consider the following insult to be particularly damning: "Murphy sadly disappointed the world by his 'Life of Garrick,' which in fact, however difficult such a process must have been, sunk below the level of Tom Davies."[133]

By time of *The Life of Mrs. Jordan*, as Boaden had begun working on his prefatory biography of Garrick, his perspective has softened toward Davies, but not toward Murphy. The latter culled from too many sources without purpose, and could not focus on sharing someone else's wit: he "would be too ambitious to display himself, to do complete justice to his friend."[134] These shortcomings, Boaden says, made Murphy's life stack up poorly compared to Davies's. He writes, "The bookseller [Davies] did not want vanity, but the actor reverenced the master of his craft. It was this feeling, added to a perfect memory, that made Boswell's record of Doctor Johnson the most striking achievement in biography."[135]

By the end of his biographical career, remarking on Inchbald's notation of having read Davies's biography of Garrick when it appeared in 1780, Boaden writes: "Garrick's *Life by Davies* was a professional lecture, which gave her both pleasure and profit."[136] In the next volume of Inchbald's memoir, Boaden declares, "Garrick's Life by Murphy, [is] the most incorrect of all lives, and wretchedly inferior to Tom Davies's, which he probably undervalued without reading it."[137] This latter comment offers some insight into Boaden as a seasoned practitioner of his craft, having sustained the barrage of criticism and fault-finding that inevitably accompanied the release of a thespian memoir, and suggests that the switch from a Cibber/Davies presentational mode to a more epistolary practice made Boaden nostalgic and also indicated the validity of what Garrick's earlier biographer had written.

This transformation did not, however, still the competitive spirit or Boaden's tendency to depict the project of biography as explicitly moral. Murphy's anecdote-heavy style, in Boaden's eyes, is immoral. Inchbald's declaration of the practical and moral applications of Davies's work seems to have urged Boaden to accept Davies as a fellow gentleman biographer, even as the tasks associated with writing the best type of biography appeared to be shifting.

In my earlier discussion of Charles Macklin's three biographers, I argued that the tension between the latter two came from a desire to put Macklin's work into the individual biographer's words. Notwithstanding that the second biographer, Kirkman, claimed to have access to Macklin's personal papers, the latter two biographies very much built an antagonistic relationship with those that came before it. One might be tempted to imagine that, in the instances where an actor has more agency in telling his own story (through the use of letters, commonplace books, memoranda, or previously collected essays), the author might feel less competition, as the weight of his own words decreases in value proportionally to the amount of previously unrevealed communication from the deceased actor to which the biographer has access. Isn't the biographer more of a skilled compiler, really—a literary scrapbooker, pasting together literary artifacts into a cohesive whole? In Boaden's case, his later-career technique of working off of thespian archives was somewhat successfully used against him.

As mentioned earlier, the resolutely alive Sarah Siddons had been unhappy with Boaden's nonposthumous biography of her in 1827. In 1834, the respected poet Thomas Campbell released a biography of Sarah Siddons with an immediate claim to preference over Boaden's: Campbell was Siddons's authorized biographer, having received a collection of "Memoranda" or "Reminiscences" from her several years prior to her death. Nina H. Kennard, who wrote a biography of Siddons in 1887, declared that Campbell struggled to do justice to Siddons's memory even with the substantial aid of the actress's memoranda, letters, and diary, which Siddons had requested that he "prepare for publication."[138] There is little doubt that Campbell interpreted Siddons's request as writing a *Life* rather than publishing her materials as an editor, and Kennard records that Campbell, as the chosen biographer, once remonstrated bitterly against one of Siddons's daughters for supporting a potential rival biographer.[139]

Having already bypassed Campbell in drawing a link from Cibber to Davies to Boaden, the *Quarterly Review* calls Campbell's status as a biographer into question: "We are much inclined to credit a prevailing rumor, that Mr. Campbell ought rather to be considered as the editor than as the substantial author of this book."[140] Whether there was a formal ghostwriter in place (entirely possible, given Elizabeth Inchbald's recollections of her own publisher authorizing her well-established name to be appended to biographies and critical editions by other hands), the reviewer stresses that of the parts of Campbell's biography not directly copying Siddons's notes, much was pirated, sometimes almost word for word, from Thomas Davies's *Dramatic Miscellanies*, as well as from the life and miscellany of the Scottish writer John Galt, "who himself professes to be only a compiler," and, of course, from James Boaden.[141] Campbell also had a third source for his account: theatre historian and Garrick Club secretary James Winston. Boaden, however, was Campbell's direct target.

The majority of references to Boaden in Campbell's *Life of Mrs. Siddons* are in the context of Boaden's mistakes.[142] The critic from the *Quarterly Review* rightfully notes Campbell's almost obsessive desire to show Boaden's imbecility "on what we think very inadequate grounds."[143] After a painful exposé that showed, line by line, how frequently Campbell pilfered material, uncredited, from Boaden, the reviewer justifies this approach as the appropriate response to Campbell: "We are obliged to dwell on these small matters by the tone of superior accuracy which Mr. Campbell so unmeritedly assumes."[144]

If Campbell rarely cited his sources, and frequently quoted them incorrectly, as claimed by the critic from the *Quarterly Review*, he also exercised remarkable freedom with excerpting Siddons's memoranda, leading the critic to complain that there was no sense of what percentage of Mrs. Siddons's own valuable materials were used, or what wealth of information Campbell might have neglected. Campbell doesn't supply enough Siddons: "A few pages of autobiographical memoranda, a couple of prosy dissertations on the characters of Constance and Lady Macbeth, and three or four very unimportant letters, are the only things that can in substance (if such trifles may, by any laxity of language, be called substantial) distinguish Mr. Campbell's *Life* from that of his predecessor."[145]

Indeed, it is likely—based upon the references to Siddons assigning Campbell the task of her biography with her collected papers—that Siddons was responding to Boaden's work: either the *Correspondence* model with David Garrick, which would have put Siddons in the position to speak for herself with Campbell as a facilitator, or the personal memorabilia–heavy memoirs of Jordan and Inchbald.[146]

Boaden's latter-day approach was not a sure hit, and a critic from the *New Monthly Magazine and Literary Journal* writing in praise of Campbell indicates both the promise and difficulty in working with so much documentation:

> With the exception of a few lively, fascinating, and interesting though, after all, not very instructive works of autobiography, we can not say that the English stage of modern date has afforded the elements, much less the fruition, of good works of the class of biographical literature. The memoranda, the diaries, and private letters of several actors and actresses of great merit would almost contradict one part of this position; but, unhappily, where we have been left in possession of these *disjecta* and *disjuncta membra*, they have fallen into the hands of book-makers, either of so little judgment that they knew not how to distinguish what was keen, *recherche*, new and interesting, from what was common-place, trivial and vulgar; or who have resolved to give a crude and undigested mass of the whole, in order to produce the dual number of ponderous volumes.[147]

By contrast, the reviewer claims, Campbell's work was rooted not only in correspondence, but also in personal friendship that helped to fill in a picture of Mrs. Siddons. "The very eminent poet to whom she had bequeathed the office of writing her life, knew her so intimately in all her domestic cares and private relations of friend, mother, wife, and wooer of the muse, that the chasms which he has filled up seem emanations from Mrs. Siddons herself."[148]

The reviewer declares that Campbell's book is intended "to raise our moral character by the freshness and cheerful vigour, with the healthy analysis of our passions and actions, which, to the author's honour, shine in every chapter." Thoroughly Romantic, the reviewer notes "many beautiful sentiments and fine discriminations, which may cleanse present society of the cant and morbid confusion with which it is so disordered."[149] Thus, Campbell appears to have taken the successful part of Boaden's approach to Kemble and Jordan (his personal friendship) and combined it with the epistolary parts of Garrick, Jordan, and Inchbald. He has also incorporated Boaden's pronounced call for theatrical biography as a redeeming moral force surrounding the otherwise immoral stage.

Based on the reviews of Campbell that refer to Boaden, the qualifications for doing the work of a theatrical biographer remain contentious. Campbell should excel because of personal knowledge of Siddons and access to her personal papers. Boaden, on the other hand, "has theatrical knowledge and personal recollections from the entirety of Siddons's career," as his advocate in the *New Monthly Magazine* argues.[150] The answer to which qualifications prevail depends on whether one wants a largely contextual history of theatres, or a narrow field of interest in great depth. In other words, do readers want the thespian as part of an ensemble cast, or solo, with frequent recourse to "soliloquy"? What role are readers willing to afford biographers?

As the nineteenth century began, theatrical biography continued to be challenged inwardly by biographers jostling for supremacy and by the generic changes arising from theatrical practices, audience demands, and biographers' innovations. As theatrical biography moved further away from preserving the actor onstage, painting, which lent itself to the convention of pointing, continued to focus on those moments of representation.

I have already suggested that audiences, through scrapbooking, had recognized the potential to yoke theatrical biography and painting together for maximum preservation; as mentioned earlier, Shearer West convincingly notes theatre audiences' appropriation of critical vocabulary from painting (undoubtedly spurred on by Joshua Reynolds's famous *Discourses* on painting; as Reynolds painted many famous thespians in character, he was very attuned to motion and theatrics). Unsurprisingly, biographers also acknowledged painting as providing a valuable facet—visibility—that their own genre could not. But with the seeming failure of theatrical biography's ability to represent the onstage actor, and its growing abandonment of that task, some painters asserted the superior power of their art to theatrical biography, challenging the need for written accompaniment when painting could take center stage, fulfilling the original demands of theatrical biography.

James and John Boaden, Father and Son, Clash over Sister Arts

Competition theory often holds that the son seeks to overtake the father in asserting his own way in the world. We have seen this in Boaden's disavowal and eventual acceptance of Davies, as well as in earlier chapters. Applying this theory more directly than it is usually intended, the business of preservation was, for Boaden, a family business. In 1826, one year after the *Memoirs of the Life of John Philip Kemble* and two years after Kemble's death, Boaden's son John published a book containing a series of eight portraits that the younger Boaden had painted of John Philip Kemble when he was alive. The published collection was dedicated to the actor's brother, Charles Kemble, "as a tribute of sincere respect."[151] We may recall that Charles Kemble had supplied the senior Boaden with a selection of John Philip Kemble's correspondence, supporting the biography of his brother with this epistolary vote of confidence. It is therefore particularly touching to see Boaden's son publicly acknowledge Charles's importance to those interested in preserving John Philip Kemble's memory.

Interestingly enough, the younger Boaden's painterly interest in recording Kemble evidently preceded the older Boaden's biographical impulse.[152] The sketches were on exhibit at the British Gallery during Kemble's lifetime, as the preface to the paintings records that the actor "spoke of it as an agreeable homage, and thought the whole of them was exceedingly like him."[153]

What the publisher refers to as a homage, or tribute, to Kemble, is also presented a bit grandiosely as "a rather comprehensive memorial" and "a faithful record of expression so varied." The latter claim may have emanated from the elder Boaden's pronouncement that "the biography of an actor is the record of his art," just one year earlier. The prefatory sentiments written on behalf of the younger Boaden suggest that the painter has a solemn duty to preserve Kemble's movement and visage: "'The animated graces of the Player (says Cibber) can live no longer than the instant breath and motion that presents them,'" he writes, showing his familiarity with Cibber's work and the primary challenge that Cibber perceived in writing a successful biography. Not only does John Boaden link his work with the genre of thespian biography based on purpose; he also asserts painting's supremacy over Cibber's (and, implicitly, his own father's) medium of the written word:

Painting, however, seizes a momentary and characteristic point of any performance, and can shew with some accuracy how the performer *looked*, whose eloquence must be mute forever. The representation of him during but a single moment will lead the imagination to complete our pleasure, and we trace him through the whole of a character, of which we possess but a single emanation.[154]

The certainty that "eloquence must be mute" rejects the power of the written word to transmit speech, the very pillar upon which Boaden the biographer based his work. The younger Boaden, likely less attuned to changes in the playhouse and more alert to the strengths of his own medium, wholeheartedly embraces physical points to the exclusion of the aural elements. We will recall that his father privileges speech over motion in his depictions. The struggle between the two Boadens reminds us that artists, like audiences, were not entirely unified in the best methods by which to preserve thespians, or even which aspects were most worthy of preservation. Painting's ability to capture movement is also not undisputed, as critics note that painting cannot adequately capture the charisma of the actor or the total effects of his or her physical presence.[155]

It may not escape the modern-day reader (nor that of the 1820s) that coupling descriptions of Kemble as Coriolanus with a painting of the actor in the role would be the best available method of accessing both pronuntiatio and actio, the criteria by which acting had been measured since the beginning of theatrical biography as a recognizable genre.[156] Additionally complicating the relationship between biography and illustration is the fact that paintings of theatrical subjects were often made to suit the prerogatives and priorities of the painter—a "mutual showcase" of painter and subject rather than a strict historical representation.[157] Of course, the latter objection might equally apply to Boaden, Sr., as critics frequently noted his intrusion upon the story of his subject. The fact remains that a strong relationship existed between biographers and illustrators of the same thespian subjects, a relationship fueled by a shared audience's interest in consumable products featuring their favorite actors.

Between the father biographer and the painter son, the Boadens could have been uniquely qualified to provide a document that featured a biographical narrative and a variety of paintings, with the potential benefit of intergenerational commentary about the actor. John Boaden's character portraits of Kemble showcase the actor in his eight greatest roles: Coriolanus, Hamlet, Hotspur, Macbeth, King John, Cato, The Stranger, and Penruddock. These works might have been inserted at the appropriate moments in his father's *Life of Kemble* (which is, undoubtedly, what some collectors did).

It seems strange, on grounds of familial ties (artistic and consanguine) that neither biographer nor artist mentions his relative's contribution to a collective art-based Kemble memorial effort. Certainly, Boaden should have mentioned his son's striking portraits during one of his laments on the difficulty of capturing an actor's actions by pen in his Kemble biography, or even when discussing the fine portraits of Siddons in his life of that lady two years later, or the fetching portraits of Dorothy Jordan in 1831. Alternatively, the son might have included a reference to his father's rather successful biography, which would have been fresh and timely, a textual portrait presumably of interest to those who wanted copies of eight painted portraits of Kemble. This latter transaction makes sense, particularly in light of the large demand for collections of actors' portraits designed to be pasted into scrapbooks. With John Boaden's reference to Cibber in his preface, it would seem likely that his prints were intended for that very purpose. However, his use of Cibber is less a declaration of intent to supplement theatrical biography and more of a threat against the theatrical biographer's claim to importance.

There appears to be a disconnect between painting and biography in this instance, at least on the part of the artists. At first glance, the elder Boaden seems more culpable for the omission of his son's painting talents, because he references and applauds a number of particularly impressive paintings of his thespian subjects. It is obvious that the biographer Boaden recognized that many actors lived out their "posthumous lives as occupants of a national portrait gallery," as Gillian Perry puts it, even more prominently than in biographies.[158]

Most likely, the younger Boaden's works on Kemble were not widely accessible at the time of his father's writings, and thus the reference would have been obscure. The younger Boaden's insistence on not linking his work's success to his father's memoir is ultimately more provocative, suggesting that painters—at least in the case of Boaden the younger—did not feel a need to ally their form of recorded memory to other forms of art.

Arguably, the eight portraits of Kemble by John Boaden do partake in some of the familiar tropes of scrapbooking. The portraits boast a detailed title page printed as to appear handwritten; similarly, the style and texture of the portraits replicate scrapbook margins and multidimensional insertions. Indeed, it is quite possible that the margins were widely spaced so that individual portraits could be easily inserted into a theatrical biography (most obviously, Boaden the elder's) at the proper intervals, based on the citation of Kemble in the specific role.

Although painting rather directly challenged theatrical biography's efficacy in its appropriation of Cibber's words, theatrical biography was beginning to recognize that an increasingly permeable genre membrane was the best strategy for continued relevance, especially in light of scrapbook tradition, which allowed readers to insert their own favorite portraits into biographies, along with a whole host of other multidimensional paraphernalia. Again, James Boaden would have been particularly attuned to the significance of portraiture in preserving the memory of a beloved thespian; his work on biography did begin with his project of cataloguing portraits of the elusive Shakespeare.

With his biography, Boaden sought to transcend the putative limits of his genre by achieving a visual realm in written medium: fans added the visual aids as a further completion of what the biographer began. John Boaden, however, since he did in fact pair his paintings with a written preface, seemed to understand that his artwork could not, alone, form an adequate memorial for Kemble. Considering the battle of genres depicted by the (written) introduction to John Boaden's paintings, some satisfaction comes in discovering copies of all eight paintings inserted into a particularly grandly extra-illustrated *Memoir of the Life of John Philip Kemble* at the Houghton Library: father and son are finally allied in their common goal of seeking to preserve Kemble for posterity. Still, as McPherson notes, the *"ut pictura poesis"* model is "doubly problematic because of its inherent literary bias"[159]; this can be seen even in the term "extra-illustration," which quite literally renders John Boaden's contribution as "extra," a delightful embellishment of the real focus, which is James Boaden's biography. The value of text compared to portrait may fluctuate as scholarly prerogatives shift, but the name and product of the biographer remains as part of the actor's legacy. Actor and biographer are joined in fame for as long as the monument—the biography—lasts, and, strictly speaking, it is the *biographer's* art, not his subject's, that lives on.

EPILOGUE: THE LIMITS OF MATERIALLY BOUND PERMANENCE

If the purpose of reading a theatrical biography is to feel more closely the presence of a particular actor, and if its authors in the eighteenth and early nineteenth century so frequently prove insufficient to the task, why should a contemporary audience continue to read these books? One answer is that they continue to retain relevance, in that, to the extent possible, the actor does live on in these works through anecdotes, descriptions of performance, comparisons, and facts that can help us to glimpse him as he might have appeared onstage. Of course, we know that scholars today read biographies quite often for characters on the periphery, and often for information about their private lives rather than public personae. Someone interested in Anne Catley might turn to Davies's *Memoirs of the Life of David Garrick*, and, using the ECCO (Eighteenth-Century Collections Online), might be able to use the keyword function to isolate all Catley references without further need for its focus on Garrick. Other readers come to the texts with the intent of finding a pithy anecdote or two that "captures" eighteenth-century theatre, society, or a notable individual. Additionally, of course, other readers tune in to these works with an eye to learning more about the biographer himself, or what was expected of the genre in that time.

One might then ask, how do our current theatrical biographies stack up to then-contemporary offerings? Throughout my survey of the genre, I have found a curious and delightful trend that would confound Boaden and delight Kirkman: in more recent biographies, it seems less imperative to know for certain whether something is or is not a fact, if it seems to lead to some truth. Jeffrey Kahan, writing in 2006 about Edmund Kean's appropriation of anecdotes and mythos about his personal and professional lives to gain the upper hand in both arenas, notes with a gleam in his eye that is almost visible through his jaunty prose that the book will cover "farfetched stories [...] which, if this were an orthodox biography of the actor, we might be forced by a lack of historical verification to disregard. But yarns have their value."[1] Ostensibly, Kahan's story is of the cult of Kean – how Kean acquired his reputation, but Kahan structures each chapter chronologically around an element of Kean's life, and thus there are, in a sense, several episodic biographies of Kean (or facets of Kean) that emerge from the study.

In a second entry in the catalogue of what one of this project's readers helpfully deemed "experimental biography," *Anecdotal Shakespeare: A New Performance History* (2015), Paul Menzer views the onstage history of Shakespearean plays through a screen of potentially spurious facts about props, people, and happenstances that cumulatively lead a careful reader to find often critical truths about individual plays. Menzer's work is not a biography of Shakespeare, nor a biography proper, except to the significant extent that "biography" gradually has been made to extend to material objects such as an actor's skull or a type of stage makeup.

These newer publications show a strong self-awareness about the biographer's style, namely his relation to a chosen subject and a rejection of purely "linear" biography about an individual to create something much more interpretative. In other words, we have come a long way since Congreve's fustian chronological narrative capped off by a careful character assessment at the end, but not, perhaps, so very far from more anecdotally led biographies. As predicted by the gradual increase in biographers' use of playbills, letters, and other paraphernalia, the fascination with material culture and the use of material culture to recapture something about an individual's life can be seen in these more recent biographical offerings, alongside anecdotes and objects that seem to manifest presence.[2] Consider, for example, Judith Pascoe's *The Audio Files of Sarah Siddons* (2011), which describes the author's trials in trying to hear the "essence" of what Siddons's audiences would have heard. As Pascoe predicts, she cannot reproduce Siddons's voice; however, appropriately enough, the subject's absent voice leaves a space that becomes filled with the author's voice. The result is a rather compelling blend of academic study and personal memoir about the research process that perhaps helps us to make some level of peace with the idea that the Siddonian essence is unrecoverable in its entirety. Colley Cibber would doubtless understand Pascoe's resignation in failing to capture the "glimmer of genius" that was the Siddonian voice, but at least we still have the consolation of written accounts, memorabilia, and even, in some cases, the highly schematized mathematical and musical efforts of then-contemporary auditors to capture specific gestures or cadences, all of which serve as limited bridges between time periods in the quest to recover an actor's presence.

Each of these more recent biographical offerings suggests a strong kinship to eighteenth-century theatrical biographies: the longing for presence, the desire to use material history to close the gap between reality and representation, and the shift, in some cases, from focusing on a person and instead tracing an aspect of a person, because a part seems more attainable than the whole. This is not so different, then, than the anecdotal *Memoirs of Charles Macklin, Comedian* favored by Cooke, or the insistence on capsule biographies, somehow more manageable, from Colley Cibber onwards. Finally, we see the gradual acceptance (even in "academic" biography) of a personal voice—the biographer's voice—as an enjoyable and almost necessary part of the process.

The biographies studied in the present work, then, are useful in understanding the precedent for a range of biographical approaches still seen in various combinations today, but also to remind ourselves that the culture of the eighteenth century, while it may seem very distant to the modern reader, partook of the same passion and frustration that we do in trying to preserve a beloved artist through biography. Removing video recording and audio recording, neither of which can be successfully incorporated into a paper book at this time, we haven't significantly improved on our ability to capture a voice in text alone, and even still illustrations or photographs of a modern performer like Madonna cannot really show you the extent of her stage persona or activities in the context of a written biography. Thus, to study eighteenth-century biography is to go back to the genre's origins and find that, in the grand scheme, not much has changed (but, I should hasten to mention, there are innumerable smaller features that will seem comparatively foreign). Perhaps, however, you already feel that the eighteenth century and the present day are not so far apart, in which case, the fuzzy feelings of universal frustration over evanescence aren't enough. What I do hope to have established is that theatrical biography, like all biography, does capture *an* artist—namely, the biographer himself or herself. Moreover, luckily enough for those who remain convinced that with just a bit more effort, we can resurrect a more concrete vestige of a past presence, biographers increasingly have turned to material and semi-material culture in order to stake their own claims on the subject.

NOTES

Introduction: Competition and Legitimacy

1   Kelly, *Mr. Foote's Other Leg*, 9.
2   Colley Cibber was, by all contemporary accounts, already assured a place in the historical record through his roles as poet laureate, character actor (most famous for embodying a character called Lord Foppington), and playwright before he took up the autobiographical pen. Cibber's other main source of fame—or, at this historical juncture, primary source of fame—is as the titular dunce in Pope's *Dunciad*: Cibber, as Laureat, displaced Lewis Theobald, or Tibbald, in 1742, just two years after the *Apology*.
3   Cheryl Wanko shows in *Roles of Authority: Thespian Biography and Celebrity in Eighteenth-Century Britain* (2003) that those earliest biographies, dating from the *Account of the Life of Coppinger* in 1695, were unremarkable from a technical standpoint, generally pandering to the perception of actors as criminals or providing unsophisticated sketches of their subject rather than being sustained, book-length biographies.
4   Cibber, *Apology*, 60.
5   Cibber's concerns for the obstacles represented in general by the impermanence of the theatre, and more specifically by theatrical biography itself, were compounded as the genre matured. His implied requirement of first-hand spectatorship was not always feasible in situations where biographers of actors who were active in the late eighteenth century felt compelled to offer a history of the stage from the Restoration to the end of their subject's life.
6   Hazlitt, "On Actors and Acting," 243.
7   Taylor, *Archive and the Repertoire*, 18.
8   Ibid., 19.
9   Carlson, *Haunted Stage*, 8.
10 Generally, the novel would seem to be a good parallel for questions of originality, not the least because of the demand for something new implied by the generic term "novel." However, the relationship of truth to the novel has been explored exhaustively by a number of talented scholars, and the novel's inclusion within the realm of creative art is certain. In contrast, theatrical biography, which originated only a few decades prior to the novel, enjoys a very constricted popularity among present-day scholars, and is a better means of elucidating the temporal aspects undergirding artistic competition.
11 See Adam Sisman's relatively recent book *Boswell's Presumptuous Task* (2000) and John B. Radner's *Johnson and Boswell* (2013); both texts have been described as biographies of Samuel Johnson's biography—or, more appropriately, of Boswell's art.

12   Paulin, "Sidetracks." The description of Hazlitt is Heather McPherson's (McPherson, *Art and Celebrity in the Age of Reynolds and Siddons*, 10).

13   James L. Clifford, author of *Biography as an Art: Selected Criticism, 1560–1690* (1962) speculates that eighteenth-century readers would have perceived biography as a "technique" of historical writing. He writes that biography was contemplated as potentially a scientific genre, but "not widely recognized as a literary genre" (ibid., 76).

14   Marcus, *Auto/biographical Discourses*, 255.

15   Boswell, *Life of Johnson*, 1: 4.

16   Taylor, *Archive and Repertoire*, 19.

17   Perry, Roach, and West, *First Actresses*, 67. In *Multiple Authorship and the Myth of the Solitary Genius* (1991), Stillinger argues that no work is produced without reference to earlier works and the participation of numerous influences. Bate, a biographer as well as a scholar, argues in *The Burden of the Past and the English Poet* (1970) that the period from the Restoration to the 1830s, the "long eighteenth century," was the first period to have enough recent literature (from the Renaissance, initially) to feel a strong sense of competition with more "contemporary" or accessible authors, rather than solely contending with the distant precedent of Greek and Roman literature. See also Harold Bloom's *Anxiety of Influence* (1973) for more about the relationship between proximity and competition.

18   Carlson, *Haunted Stage*, 83.

19   See the editorial preface to Maria Edgeworth's *Castle Rackrent* (1800), possibly the first "historical novel," in which the author, in the guise of an editor, declares the biographer's advantage over the historian in illustrating truth. Indirectly pointing to the pervasive appeal of theatrical biography in particular, the editor avails himself of a theatrical metaphor: "After we have beheld splendid characters playing their parts on the great theatre of the world, with all the advantages of stage effect and decoration, we anxiously beg to be admitted behind the scenes, that we may take a nearer view of the actors and actresses" (Edgeworth, *Castle Rackrent*, iv).

20   See Heather McPherson's *Art and Celebrity in the Age of Reynolds and Siddons* (2017), in which McPherson argues that portraiture engendered the type of deeply image-conscious celebrity that still prevails today. In doing so, she traces the symbiosis between theatre and portraiture that magnified not just individual performers' fame, but ideas about fame, patriotism, cultural politics, and of course, proper acting.

21   The vocabulary of painters, specifically that of Joshua Reynolds, was borrowed by those who wished to critique acting but lacked field-specific terminology (West, *The Image of the Actor*, 149). West notes that "the ideas and language of Reynolds was also used both directly and indirectly" to categorize styles of acting and endow them with moral authority (112–113). Reynolds is responsible for perhaps the most well-known portrait of the actress Sarah Siddons, *Siddons as the Tragic Muse* (1784). West notes that Reynolds's theories on drapery informed not only critiques but also stage practices, furthering the interlink between theatre and painting.

22   In their introduction to *The First Actresses: Nell Gwyn to Sarah Siddons* (2011), Gillian Perry, Joseph Roach, and Shearer West convincingly argue that painting undergirded theatrical biography directly, as in instances where Thomas Davies's analysis of an actor's onstage antics was informed by an existing painting of a thespian; the biographer (possibly unwittingly) described the scene *as the painting depicted it* rather than from his own memory. This upends the earlier assumption that a painting could serve as

a legitimate source corroborating what Davies described as being witnessed firsthand (Perry, introduction to *First Actresses*).

23   Sherman, "Garrick among Media," 971.

24   Ibid.

25   Marcia Pointon posits that the "preoccupation with authenticity [...] originates in the eighteenth century and may be seen as a legacy of the antiquarian researches" like that conducted by George Vertue in identifying "authentic" portraits of Milton, or, as I would point out, by Boaden himself, whose work on the authenticity of portraits identified as Shakespeare, as well as his work on the Ireland Shakespeare forgeries, undoubtedly colored his approach to the material aspects of biography and his insistence on authenticity (Pointon, *Hanging the Head*, 67).

26   Annibel Jenkins, writing a biography of Elizabeth Inchbald in 2015, comments on Boaden's "predictable [...] chauvinist" attitude in assuming that women could not partake of classical education, an opinion that undoubtedly colored his view of the actresses about which he wrote (Jenkins, *I'll Tell You What*, 484). Additionally, as Jim Davis points out, Boaden "tended to be prejudiced about what actresses might or might not be permitted to do" (Davis, *Comic Acting and Portraiture*, 7). One of Boaden's more widely quoted views is his assessment of Siddons as Hamlet: "Were she *but* a man, she would exceed all that man has ever achieved in Hamlet" (*Memoirs of Mrs. Siddons*, 1:259). Boaden makes an inevitable cameo in Kristina Straub's (1999) article for *Feminist Theory and the Body: A Reader* about eighteenth-century cross-dressing onstage. Boaden was highly critical of gender ambiguity. He criticized aging or overweight actresses. Perhaps most provokingly, Boaden makes the case that the ideal woman would "avoid the pen of history" to pursue the pleasures of anonymous domesticity, a striking comment for a biographer acting *as* the pen of history on behalf of female thespians (Boaden, *Memoirs of Mrs. Siddons*, 1: xiv).

27   Theatrical biography, particularly in Boaden's hands, seems to be a rather conservative enterprise, in contrast to the more progressive efforts of autobiography.

28   See examples of female autobiography by Colley Cibber's daughter, Charlotte Charke (1755), George Anne Bellamy (1785) and of course Mary Robinson (1801). For contemporary criticism that shines further light on eighteenth-century actresses through their own words, see Laura Engel's *Fashioning Celebrity: Eighteenth-Century British Actresses and Strategies for Image Making (2011)*.

29   In the Chapter 3, I briefly discuss Elizabeth Inchbald's participation in writing prefatory biographies (brief biographical sketches preceding edited editions of authors' works). Throughout this investigation, I distinguish between prefatory biographies, capsule biographies (works of one paragraph to perhaps five pages), pamphlets (under seventy pages or so) and full-length or book-length biographies (often multivolume).

1 "Davies's Name [...] in Fame's Brightest Page Shall on Garrick Attend": From Anonymous to Personalized Participation in the *Memoirs of the Life of David Garrick*

1   J. R., "On Reading Memoirs," 494.

2   Boswell writes of Johnson's feelings for Garrick, "His being outstripped by his pupil in the race of immediate fame as well as of fortune, probably made [Johnson] feel some

indignation, as thinking that whatever might be Garrick's merits in his art, the reward was too great when compared with what the most successful efforts of literary labour could attain" (Boswell, *Life of Johnson*, 1: 90).

3   Johnson, *Rambler No. 60*. This essay outlines the most desirable features of biography and addresses some common pitfalls; Johnson's *Idler No. 84* opines that the best biography is that written by the subject himself and published after his death. For Johnson, specificity and truthfulness, with an emphasis on the private life and everyday events in a man's life, are the supreme goals of biography.

4   Berkowitz, *David Garrick*, 80. For a wonderful scholarly discussion of Johnson and his continued fascination for readers, please see Helen Deutsch's *Loving Dr. Johnson* (2005).

5   Davies makes no secret of his obligation to Dr. Johnson, for a debt to Johnson was a credit to its possessor. Davies's advertisement from a later edition of 1781 immediately accords to Johnson any pleasure the reader might feel in perusing the *Life of Garrick*. "To the same excellent friend I am indebted for several diverting anecdotes in this narrative; and I heartily wish I could boast of farther assistance from one so able to give it," writes Davies, whose praise of Johnson threatens to eclipse his own authority.

6   Wanko comments on Garrick's remarkably good timing in his arrival on the London stage: he came at a moment when newspapers were becoming popular tools to negotiate an actor's relationship with his audience (Wanko, *Roles of Authority*, 188). In *The Player's Passion: Studies in the Science of Acting* (1985), Joseph Roach also remarks on the status of acting when Garrick arrived—compared to Thomas Betterton's debut eighty years earlier. In the 1740s, Roach notes, people were beginning to consider acting a science, and Garrick's sensibilities were particularly well-suited to capitalize on the appetite for changing acting styles. Stuart Sherman argues that Garrick in particular evoked "biographies of a length and substance no earlier actor had prompted, theatrical memoirs by colleagues and critics, and scrapbooks" (Sherman, "Garrick among Media," 977). These memorials were popular because of Garrick's unusual theatrical achievement, and were made feasible by Garrick's relationship with the press.

7   Churchill's satirical poem, *The Rosciad*, features a particularly unflattering description of Davies's performance in *Cymbeline*: "He mouths a sentence as curs mouth a bone" (Boswell, *Life of Johnson*, 2: 186.) The precise reason for Davies's early retirement from the stage is not agreed upon by historical sources: James Boaden cites a letter from Garrick to Davies about Churchill, but other evidence suggests that Davies was driven from the stage at least in part by Garrick's "warmth of temper" (Toothill, *Stages of Celebrity*, 32).

8   Davies published and distributed a number of notable works within the genres of classics, history, and memoir, including a collection of Lillo's plays, *Robinson Crusoe*, Johnson's *Miscellaneous and Fugitive Pieces* (this he did without permission), and of course his own *Memoirs of the Life of David Garrick*.

9   Brack, "Davies, Thomas."

10   *A Genuine Narrative of the Life and Theatrical Transactions of Mr. John Henderson* is just under seventy pages long; by contrast, the Davies's *Memoirs of the Life of David Garrick* necessitated two volumes of over four hundred pages each.

11   Wanko, *Roles of Authority*, 169. Although the two-volume work was "compact and cheaply produced," Matt Toothill believes that accessibility aided the *Life of Garrick* in its continued popularity (Toothill, *Stages of Celebrity*, 29).

12   It is said that his love of high-quality volumes damaged Davies's competitive edge; with continued references to the honesty and kindness of Tom Davies, "gentleman," it is also likely that he may have been lax about collecting payment for his wares from customer-friends. Certainly, he was sensitive to criticism and eager to please.

13   Davies, *Life of Garrick*, 1: x.

14   Wanko, *Roles of Authority*, 191.

15   Davies was the printer and bookseller of James Granger's *Biographical History of England* (1769), a catalogue of portraits that ushered in the eighteenth-century vogue for "collecting heads" and pasting or mounting them into existing books, and it was Davies who facilitated this interest by providing twenty copies of the 1769 original and the 1774 supplement to Granger's *History* with blank pages interleaved "for the convenience of such gentlemen as may chuse to place the heads near to the lives in your work" (Pointon, *Hanging the Head*, 53, 59). See James Raven's *Publishing Business in Eighteenth-Century England* (2014) for a nuanced look at the variable relationships among booksellers, publishers, printers, bookseller-publishers, and bookseller-financiers.

16   Although the *Life of Garrick* provided significant financial recourse for Davies, he must have significantly mismanaged his windfall, for Johnson had to arrange a subscription for Davies's *Dramatic Miscellanies* only a few years later, and it seems to be understood among the patrons of more than four hundred copies that the proceeds from the work were deeply in demand by an increasingly ill Davies in order to guarantee the security of his wife.

17   Davies mentions in the preface to his *Dramatic Miscellanies* that Mrs. Garrick had disapproved of the *Life of Garrick*, noting that she refused Davies's offer to work with him on a second volume that might have better pleased her. Wanko makes a crucial miscalculation when she asserts that "it seems as though Davies had little choice" but to take on Garrick as a subject, as it implies remarkably limited volition on the part of a man who, while in need of income, would still have a choice of theatrical or literary subjects about which to write (Wanko, *Roles of Authority*, 191).

18   Stone, "David Garrick," 4.

19   We repeatedly see David Garrick contrasted with his predecessors, such as the Restoration-age Thomas Betterton; with veterans toward the end of their careers, such as James Quin; and with his direct contemporaries Spranger Barry and the currently much less known Henry Mossop.

20   The futility of making comparisons in the present age because of the great number of thespians is not lost on me, and the understanding that these comparisons will only become more obsolete with time may be part of the charm and frustration of theatrical biography as an enterprise (or cinematic biography, to a lesser degree).

21   Some scholars object to claims that Garrick invented the natural declamation style for which he was known: in fact, he was the most gifted practitioner of a theory espoused by Charles Macklin, Garrick's acting tutor, a famous actor in his own right, and the subject of this project's second chapter.

22   Burnim, "An Introduction to Garrick." The Folger Shakespeare Library (Washington, DC) holds the largest collection of Garrickiana in the world. Garrick is the most represented figure at the Folger, after Shakespeare himself, which should suggest Garrick's importance not only to folks in the eighteenth century but also to Shakespeare scholars.

23   Byrn, *Repository of Wit*, 26.

24   For example, Garrick is satirized in Tobias Smollett's *The Adventures of Peregrine Pickle* (1751) and *The Adventures of Roderick Random* (1748). In *The History of Tom Jones*,

a Foundling (1749), Fielding memorably describes the actor's portrayal as Hamlet encountering his father's ghost, and the pedant Partridge's negative critique suggests the brilliance of Garrick's ability (Fielding, *Tom Jones*, 313–17).

25 From the 1701 anonymous biography of the comedian Jo Haynes, one of the earliest examples of the genre (more akin to a pamphlet than a "full-length" biography at any rate, and unlisted in Bryan's *Bibliography and Index to Theatrical Biographies*), through the 1730s, when theatrical biography had its first moderate wave of popularity, the majority of offerings employ pseudonyms or do not reference an author. Theatre historian Benjamin Victor's well-received 1733 *Memoirs of the Life of Barton Booth* was published anonymously "by an Intimate Acquaintance of Mr. Booth, By Consent of His Widow," and a number of "named" biographies like William Oldys's *Memoirs of Mrs. Anne Oldfield* (1731) or O'Bryan's *Authentic Memoirs of, Mr. Robert Wilkes* (1732) employ pen names. Exceptions include a 1729 biography of James Spiller, "Interspers'd [with] Much of the Poetical History of His own Times," attributed to "George Akerby, Painter," and an unsuccessful biography of Booth in a volume of *Lives and Characters of the Most Eminent Actors and Actresses* by Theophilus Cibber, Colley Cibber's son (1753). Even the then relatively well-known 1710 biography by Charles Gildon on Thomas Betterton was not formally attributed.

26 See Pat Rogers's "Edmund Curll and the Publishing Trade" for a rather balanced look at Curll's career, including his business practices, lawsuits, and how, retrospectively, this "unspeakable" villain also performed "heroic services in antiquarian studies" (215; 217–18).

27 The binary of fact/fiction will be challenged in Chapter 2, with the appearance of a wildly fictional biography of Charles Macklin that is much more akin to a novel. Also, please see the Epilogue for a brief discussion of potentially fictive anecdotes to reveal truths, and the role of fiction or near-fiction in scholarly biography.

28 One review of *The Juvenile Adventures of David Ranger* is accompanied by a marginal note in pencil, perhaps made by a disappointed scholar who had thought he had uncovered a new account of Garrick's pretheatrical existence: the note reads, succinct and weighty in its simplicity, "novel."

29 Besides being a "ramble" novelist, Edward Kimber was an established editor and compiler. Originally trained as a bookseller's apprentice, Kimber shares some distinct similarities of background with Thomas Davies.

30 "Article XV," 655.

31 "Article XIX," 379.

32 Ibid.

33 Kimber, *David Ranger*, 1: 283. Indeed, the mention of actual theatrical figures was characteristic of novels at the time.

34 Even at its earliest points, *David Ranger* repeatedly cues itself as a novel, its narrator describing laying down "at the feet of that awful tribunal [...] the ensuing sheets," hoping that the work would find "the same favour with which they have smiled on my contemporaries, the universal Dr. – , the multiloquacious Henry F – , or that poetical, critical, physical, political novelist Dr. – " (Ibid., 1: 5).

35 "Article XV," 655–56.

36 The rather dismissive reviewer seems at odds with public assessment of *David Ranger*. Simon Dickie declares, "These 'ramble' novels, as we might call them, were clearly written for an educated urban audience with considerable disposable income," appealing to both men and women. Kimber's *Life and Adventures of Joe Thompson* (1750) was

"one of the great unacknowledged best-sellers of eighteenth-century fiction" (Dickie, "Joseph Andrews," 285).

37   Gerald M. Berkowitz and I both confidently identify Leonato and Davies as the same man (Berkowitz, *David Garrick*, 69). While Berkowitz does not offer a rationale for why he believes Davies to be Leonato, the shared writing style is evident even during a superficial read.

38   Leonato, "Eulogium," 304.

39   "The only correct speaker our playhouses could boast of, was Quin, but he was utterly unfit for the great and animated characters of tragedy," Leonato asserts ("Eulogium," 304). Similarly, while writing under his own name in *Life of Garrick*, Davies says that Quin, who "understood propriety in speaking better than any other actor of the time [...] was utterly unqualified for the striking and vigorous characters of tragedy; he could neither express the tender nor violent emotions of the heart" (Davies, *Life of Garrick*, 1: 28). The last two phrases appear verbatim from Leonato's account.

40   Leonato, "Eulogium," 304; Davies, *Life of Garrick*, 1: 42.

41   Leonato, "Eulogium," 305; Davies, *Life of Garrick*, 2: 79.

42   Leonato, "Eulogium" 305; Davies, *Life of Garrick*, 1: 113.

43   Perhaps he started small, writing a sample-sized eulogium under a pseudonym to see whether interest was generated before he launched the full biography.

44   As to why Davies chose the name Leonato, it was a good Shakespearean name, featured in *Much Ado About Nothing*. To frame oneself as a Shakespearean character seems appropriate for a narrator talking about Garrick, who was credited with "reviving" Shakespeare. But why not Leontes, from the *Winter's Tale*, or Leonatus, from *Cymbeline*? The latter name was mistakenly transcribed by biographical critic Stone. As Davies had played Leonatus to Garrick's Cymbeline onstage, that name, in the context of a writing about Garrick, could have served as a cipher for Davies's identity (Stone, "David Garrick," 29). Leonato, the name he actually selected, links with Garrick's portrayal of Benedick in *Much Ado About Nothing*, most notably in his first performance after marrying Eva Marie Veigel in 1749. Is Davies suggesting that he is playing Leonato to Garrick's Benedick? Perhaps the role of Leonato was chosen not to suggest Davies's relationship with Garrick, but Davies's relationship with the narrative of Garrick's life, or his biographical craft. Leonato is a character at the margins, but not a marginal character, center-stage even in times of absentia: his presence permeates the play, and indeed, the connections between people and progression of events are centered on him (Blasingame, "Shakespeare Character Analysis"). As weaver of Garrick's life narrative, Davies might have used "Leonato" to allude to the power of a biographer to shape perceptions by fostering connections and promoting teleologies. However, Leonato's work is firmly proto-biography in terms of its short length, limited comprehensiveness, reliance on anonymity, and obvious novelty in terms of medium.

45   Wanko, *Roles of Authority*, 189.

46   Toothill, *Stages of Celebrity*, 11. Toothill points out that the very phrase "living embodiment" dictates that the mantle of authority be surrendered upon death (16). The Jubilee itself, structured to preserve the memory of a dead actor-author, undoubtedly was self-serving for Garrick, who probably had a didactic intent in showing the people how to keep a fallen thespian "alive" for future generations.

47   Old Comedian, *The Life and Death of David Garrick*, 9.

48   Ibid., 13.

49   Ibid., 14–15.

50   Please also see Judith Pascoe's *The Sarah Siddons Audio Files: Romanticism and the Lost Voice*, in which the author tests a number of ways of seeking to "experience" Siddons's voice as her audience would have been able to: Pascoe's conclusion is that it is no longer possible, particularly as current audiences (auditors) have a markedly different relationship to auditory effects than Siddons's original audience had.

51   Old Comedian, *Garrick*, 16.

52   Ibid., 17.

53   "The Life of David Garrick, Esq., the Celebrated English Roscius [By the Old Comedian]" Review, *Westminster Magazine*, April 1779, 196.

54   The "Biographical Anecdotes of Mr. Garrick" does not appear on Stone or Bryan's lists of legitimate Garrick biography, which may be interpreted as a neglect of newspaper biographies or a comment on the comparatively meager length of what was called an "Anecdotal Life." Alternatively, the "Biographical Anecdotes" may have been overlooked by more modern scholars as one of hundreds of fragmentary anecdotal accounts that were wildly popular in the later eighteenth and early nineteenth centuries.

55   Please see N. D. Norman's study of the rise of celebrity obituary in the popular press, *From a Record of Death to a Memory of Life* (2008), a trend that he locates as emanating from the *Gentleman's Magazine*, under the auspices of the "editor" Sylvanus Urban. His theory is that obituary-biographies became more subjective and moralistic as the number of solicited pieces outweighed those written by editors more faithful to the "voice" of the magazine.

56   Norman, *Record of Death*, 17.

57   For example, the May installment records the story of Dr. Hill, who once wrote a pamphlet accusing Garrick of frequently mispronouncing the letter "I" "as *furm* for *firm*, *vurtue* for *virtue*, and others." Garrick responded with a witty epigram that "deserves to be preserved," in which the actor wishes that the letters "both have their due/And that *I* may never be mistaken for *U*" ("Biographical Anecdotes of the Late Mr. Garrick" (II)," 227).

58   Ibid., 118.

59   If we look at earlier full-length biographies, we see that Cibber, in his autobiography; Curll's sham pseudoautobiography of Betterton less than a year after Cibber's work; and the anonymous 1766 *Life of Mr. James Quin* (which brackets a much smaller historical scope coinciding with Quin's theatrical career) had formulated and adapted the same tactic of a theatre history, but Davies appears to have popularized this approach in biography.

60   Davies is almost universally referred to as Garrick's "first biographer" or "first historian" (the terms were interchangeable in this context for an eighteenth-century audience). I wish to claim not only that Davies was Garrick's first major historian, but also that he was the father of mature thespian biography. Certainly, theatrical biography had existed as a concept since 1695. As mentioned earlier, Wanko cites the *Life of Matthew Coppinger*, an actor, as the first example of English theatrical biography (unsurprisingly, anonymous). She also recognizes a distinction between that style of actor-criminal narrative and the actor as a figure of interest sans the attraction of crime. She cites Charles Gildon's *Life of Betterton*, 1710, as its first occurrence (although it bears noting that, as a precursor to the bait-and-switch tactic of Kimber's *David Ranger*, Gildon's *Life of Betterton* has very little to do with the life of Betterton, per

se, lacking facts about Betterton in favor of dialogue about good acting—supposedly based on Betterton's style). Moreover, Gildon did not initially claim authorship of the work. While Joseph Roach (*Cities*, 94) considers Gildon's work to be the first full-length theatrical biography "in its entirety because it is also a poetics of orature [...] a life not of the actor's career but of his bodily art," I contend that basic biographical facts are an inalienable feature of biography.

61   Cibber, Davies, and the English poet–historian Benjamin Victor are staples of theatrical biography, their names and material peppering many theatrical biographies that otherwise pretend to have sprung, fully formed and unresearched, from the mind of the author. Victor was a barber from London, later the manager of the Theatre Royal of Dublin. Like Cibber in England (1730 to his death in 1757), Victor was the 1755 poet laureate in Ireland. Victor wrote the *Memoirs of Barton Booth* anonymously in 1733, and his magnum opus, *The History of the Theatres of London* in three volumes, from 1761 to 1771. This latter work is repeatedly cited by theatrical biographers. Victor also wrote an autobiography prefacing his own *Dramatic Works* (1774).

62   Wanko, *Roles of Authority*, 191.

63   Davies seems to suggest that the ideal history would be one that is read by a mass audience, and his approach reflects that belief. Although Davies's *Life of Garrick* is in two volumes exceeding eight hundred pages total, his textual apparatus is quite light, and his references to supporting documentation are minimal.

64   Davies, *Life of Garrick*, 2: 94.

65   Ibid. 2: 95–96.

66   Cooke, *Memoirs of Charles Macklin*, 33.

67   Ibid., 33–34; the original quote is found in Davies, *Dramatic Miscellanies*, 1: 8.

68   A key criticism of Davies's *Life of Garrick* was his tendency to allude to good material that he saved for the *Dramatic Miscellanies*, which he had begun planning prior to the *Life of Garrick*.

69   Davies, *Life of Garrick*, 2: 336.

70   Ibid., 2: 192.

71   Ibid., 2: 363.

72   Ibid., 2: 366.

73   Ibid., 2: 207.

74   Ibid., 2: 215.

75   Ibid., 2: 336.

76   Ibid.,1:30.

77   Urban, "Article XII," 88.

78   The discreet revelation of authorship of *Massinger* meets with the reviewer's encouragement: "To this uncommon character we are glad to find that he has now added that of author, and has also delivered proposals for 'Miscellaneous Notes and Observations on several Plays of Shakespeare, with a critical review of his characters, and those of many eminent dramatic poets, as represented on the stage by Mr. Garrick and other celebrated comedians; with anecdotes of authors, actors, &c'" (Urban, "Article XII," 88).

79   Davies, *Life of Garrick*, 1: 62.

80   Ibid., 1: 63.

81   Ibid, 1: 64. The description of Garrick as Hamlet may have had much more immediacy to its first readers, who of course could have recalled Garrick's performance for themselves. Such a line of thought is supported by Pascoe's contention that

eighteenth-century and early nineteenth-century audiences had a much more developed memory for performance because they did not rely on the technologies that we do today for preserving memories (Pascoe, *Siddons Audio Files*, 16).

82 "Memoirs of the Life of David Garrick, Esq., Interspersed with Characters and Anecdotes of His Theatrical Contemporaries." Review, *Westminster Magazine*, 277.

83 Ibid., 278.

84 Ibid.

85 Ibid.

86 If this characterization of Davies as a penurious opportunist seems inordinately harsh, it is difficult to quibble with the reviewer's last objection: Davies's misguided attempt to classify David Garrick as superior to the Roman Roscius by virtue of Garrick's dealings with the upper classes (consider the earlier anecdote about Garrick's visit to the French thespian Preville). No such records of Roscius's dining schedule exist—therefore, Davies's musings are irrelevant if patriotically driven speculation at best.

87 J. R., "On Reading Memoirs," 494.

88 Ibid.

89 Ibid.

90 Surely the poet intends a parallel between Garrick's relationship with Shakespeare, by whose genius and authority he himself derived his reputation; Davies, then, acquires the crowning jewel in his own reputation as the historian of Garrick, benefiting from the actor's genius and authority, and, albeit mediated, Shakespeare's.

91 The criticism of Davies as simply riding on Garrick's coattails foreshadows all the commentaries about the source of Boswell's genius in the *Life of Johnson* as actually belonging to Johnson himself rather than to Boswell; the essayist was suggested to have flowed, unmediated by any Boswellian intelligence or useful additions, through Boswell's pen onto the page.

92 It also raises the possibility that, at some point, biographers might join poets and actors arm in arm on Pindus.

93 In the midst of these responses is a modest pamphlet-style *David Garrick* in 1807, which turns out to be a bait-and-switch philosophical rambling about acting theory, a throwback to the biographies of Betterton but with the added novelty of a named author, James Smyth. Smyth makes a proto-Romantic individualist out of Garrick, and makes himself the enthusiastic receiver, able to divine Garrick's dreams and ambitions, translating the biographer's job into a sibyl-poet-philosopher figure. For our purposes, the importance of Smyth's work, beyond simple taxonomy, is to note the more explicitly Romantic philosophical permutation of Curllian bait-and-switch.

94 We can see in the introduction to the "Anecdotes of the Late David Garrick, Esq," that an earlier, unrelated "anecdotal life" of the actor had appeared in that same magazine in October 1776 by "F," only a few months after Davies's first attempt at Garrick biography as Leonato. I am not attempting to catalogue the exhaustive list of biographical sketches of Garrick, but merely give a representative picture of the most prominent trends.

95 Davies, *Life of Garrick*, 1: 52.

96 "Anecdotes of the Late David Garrick (I)" 255; Davies, *Life of Garrick*, 1: 45.

97 Davies, *Life of Garrick*, 1: 46.

98 Anecdotes stripped of narrative through lines, introductory materials, and transitions necessarily take away valuable real estate for the author to make his own mark, especially in achieving a semblance of mastery in telling a story of significant length. On the other hand, a properly executed anecdote is also an art form.

99 Prior to his biography of Garrick, Murphy was responsible for collecting Fielding's work and supplementing it with an introductory biography in 1762, followed by *An Essay on the Life and Genius of Samuel Johnson* (1792), which accompanied Murphy's edition of the collected works of Dr. Johnson.

100 "Article XIV," 637.

101 Some people have speculated that there wasn't much to Garrick when he was out of the spotlight (Wanko, *Roles of Authority*, 196). Alternatively, see Chapter Four of Julia Fawcett's *Spectacular Disappearances* for her argument that Garrick's insistence on professionalism was a means of preserving his private life from eager spectators.

102 "Article XIV," 637.

103 "Article X," 189. This reviewer is not as brusque as his fellow critic at the *British Critic*, commending Murphy on his impressively thorough appendix but faulting him for less criticism and instruction than had been expected.

104 Ibid., 190.

105 Ibid., 193.

106 These reviews, as a rather representative sample, suggest why a chapter on theatrical biography of Garrick largely belongs to Davies. This does not mean, however, that his competitor's work is unworthy of analysis. Murphy's work reads more like Cibber's than like a Curllian hodgepodge, especially in the prominent role that the author himself plays (though admittedly, Murphy is far more restrained—and less relevant—than Cibber). There is a consistent narrative voice and certain attempts at philosophy, criticism, wit, and comprehensive history.

107 Murphy, *Life of David Garrick*, 2: 152–53. Probably taking a cue from Davies's earlier squeamishness about intruding on Garrick's sabbatical, Murphy anticipates disappointment from his audience and attempts to deflect it first through evoking pragmatics and then genre: "An account of his tour [...] *will not be expected* in this place. We have no materials, and if they were in our possession, they would not be of a colour with the present work, which is *the history of Garrick in his profession*" [my italics] (Murphy, *Life of David Garrick*, 2: 14–15).

108 Wanko, *Roles of Authority*, 202; Murphy, *Life of David Garrick*, 2: 154. In contrast to Murphy's biography of himself and Garrick as great British theatrical authors, Wanko says that the protagonist of Davies's *Life of Garrick* might actually be the English theatre itself, rather than Garrick (196). In both instances, we can see that Garrick always seems to need a costar, most likely to fill in the spaces that might otherwise be filled with revelations of private life.

109 Testifying to the increasingly competitive spirit between biographers, Davies's name arises in the context of Murphy's self-righteous indignation over the earlier biographer's treatment of a conflict between Murphy and Garrick over a play that the manager initially rejected. Murphy devotes a whole chapter to rehabilitating his own image (and, at least in his own mind, Garrick's), sniping that "a very lame and imperfect account has been published by different authors, who do not seem to have had authentic information" (Murphy, *Life of David Garrick*, 1: 330). In truth, Davies sides with Murphy in his account of the play; he says that Garrick made a gross error in judgment in not accepting Murphy's play (Davies, *Life of Garrick*, 2: 213), suggesting not only that Davies was aware of Garrick's weaknesses, but also that Murphy was not altogether interested in relaying an honest representation of Davies's account.

110 Murphy, *Life of David Garrick*, 1: 104.

111 Ibid., 1: 365.

112 Ibid., 2: 175–76.

113 Ibid., 2: 175.

114 Ibid., 1: 160–61.

115 While the copious plot summary and analysis is additional evidence for Wanko's claim that Murphy's Garrick is an author-actor rather than an actor-author, it also suggests a degree of defensiveness on the part of Murphy against Davies. Davies is charged with random tangents, so Murphy ceases the tradition of following minor thespians' life sketches to their demise despite being in the middle of a larger narrative. Davies is charged with not incorporating enough philosophy or criticism even though he had clearly bracketed instances in which he would be providing further commentary in the *Dramatic Miscellanies*, so Murphy seeks to combine in one two-volume *Life of David Garrick* what Davies took one two-volume *Life of Garrick* and one three-volume *Dramatic Miscellanies* to do.

116 "Article X," 195.

117 An advertisement by the editor, dated 1807, describes the continued popularity of Davies's biography, explaining that editing was required simply to update the volumes with "facts and anecdotes [that] have transpired [and] which, as illustrative of this Biography, the Proprietors were of opinion should be collected, for the purpose of rendering the Work more complete" after twenty-seven years (Jones and Davies, *Life of Garrick*, 1: xi.)

118 According to John Nichols, editor of the *Gentleman's Magazine*, Jones had developed a strong reputation for taking primarily intact narratives and editing them in such a manner that the works appeared to the public "with every advantage" (Nichols, *Literary Anecdotes*, 665). For Jones, preserving Davies's product is more important than following current fashion—he is acknowledging the continued popularity of Davies's narration. Further framing Davies's writing as valuable, Jones adopts the editorial practice that developed in early eighteenth-century criticism dealing with classics, delineating the words of an important primary text from the editor's commentary through marks of reference. Pope did so with Homer's *Iliad*; for Jones to do so with Davies's *Garrick* suggests a certain authority to Davies's words. Unlike Pope and other commentators, however, Jones keeps his editorial apparatus quite sparse, with most pages unmarked by an editorial hand.

119 Jones and Davies, 1: 16.

120 Ibid., 1:11.

121 The view that Davies promotes of Garrick was not, contrary to the reviews, utterly positive: actually, Davies spent a decent amount of time expounding on Garrick's weaker characteristics, especially in the penultimate section of the biography, the character sketch. Furthermore, although Wanko declares Davies's biography to be universally unobjectionable, we can recall that Eva Marie Garrick had found the characterization of her husband most unfair.

122 The story, which was much repeated, is that Woffington, enjoying a tryst with Garrick, heard another gentleman with whom she was involved entering the home. Garrick having fled rapidly, the gentleman is surprised to find a man's wig in the floor. He demands to know the meaning of the wig; Woffington, coolly composed, explained that it was her own, for use in an upcoming breeches role. Perhaps not worried about proving himself a gentleman, or alternatively recognizing the need to preserve a historical connection that would be lost by more chaste biographies, Murphy made the relationship clear to anyone who hadn't already been quite aware.

123 Jones and Davies, *Life of David Garrick*, 1: 229.

124 Ibid., 1: 380.

125 The almost thirty offerings in Murphy's appendix included numerous prologues and epilogues, letters written by Garrick to Smollett and to the newspaper, some poetic odes about Garrick, the contents of his will, and, forming a significant chunk, the entire play-by-play of Garrick's battle with Macklin.

126 "Article CX," 718.

127 Sherman, "Garrick among Media," 977.

128 Greetham, *Textual Scholarship*, 135.

129 To speak of anyone in the 1780s as "grangerizing" the *Life of Garrick* is accurate but anachronistic, as, according to the *OED*, the term only came about in 1882, despite the evident occurrence of such activity in the eighteenth century. The word took on a pejorative meaning for critics who objected to the destruction of some books to provide illustration for other books, or disliked the expansion of a contained text into often unwieldy repositories of loosely related scraps. See the Folger Library's brilliant webpage on extra-illustrated works about Garrick.

130 Due to markings by an interested librarian, we can see that the extra-illustrator of the copy under discussion heavily relied upon a text called *Worthies of Britain*, presumably a large volume replicating engravings of important figures. By the 1880s, publishers began to openly advertise the desirability of a particular text to a "grangerizer," either as providing a central source from which to harvest portraits, or having blank backs on pages to facilitate the desire of owners to paste in their own illustrations, the latter of which Davies did when reprinting Granger's work in 1774 (Pointon, *Hanging the Head*, 59).

131 Murray, Caroline, "Letter of Provenance."

132 Charlotte of Mecklenberg, Queen, and Thomas Davies. *Memoirs of the Life of David Garrick*. See "Front matter."

133 Marcia Pointon, in her 1993 study of eighteenth-century British portraiture, *Hanging the Head*, notes that portraiture was a conservative, as well as nationalistic enterprise, helping eighteenth-century Britain "compensate [...] for its shortcomings with other European nations"; similarly, the collecting of 'heads' was actually figured by Granger as a specifically Protestant enterprise (*Hanging the Head*, 79, 55, 59). Pointon traces the links between portraiture, physiognomy, the collection of "heads," and political satire, observing that the very act of collecting heads was political: "[The] symbolic structure [of privileging head as metonym for body] must be understood in its relation to a hierarchical process in which society's disparate parts are inscribed in a hegemonic order" (56).

134 The phenomenon of grangerizing drove up the price of "heads," with "scarce heads not worth three pence" selling for five guineas; books that had been extra-illustrated, in turn, sold for approximately five times the value of unaugmented works (Pointon, *Hanging the Head*, 59, 58).

135 Roach, *Cities*, 76. It should be noted, as Roach does, that the mingling of actors with kings had already reached a key moment when Thomas Betterton was buried in Westminster Abbey among kings in 1710, with Richard Steele observing in the *Tatler* 2: 424 that "there is no Difference in the Grave between the Imaginary and the Real Monarch" (Roach, *Cities*, 84).

136 Pointon, *Hanging the Head*, 58.

137 Ibid., 56.

138 More information about the item under discussion can be found in the Folger catalogue, item W.b.471.

139 *Scrapbook of David Garrick*, 45.

140 Ibid., 39.

141 Intriguingly, the scrapbooker's skill seems to progress as his project continues: he develops a system of flaps where readers have access not only to both sides of the page that he's added, but to the original text underneath.

142 Strictly speaking, the *Life* was not built on a single copy of the French text, as several pages of the text appeared identical: thus, it was more likely that the owner acquired a number of leaves from several copies, perhaps enticed by the generous size of the margins of the original, the texture of its leaves, or other features of the physical book that made it a desirable base text.

143 Those lives appearing on the verso or, in some cases, underneath a flap on the recto, include: Villiers (thrice). Howard. Hume (twice). George II (twice). Inigo Jones (twice). Johnson (twice). Fairfax. Fox. George I. George III. Dobson. Vandyke. Steele. Thurloe. Churchill. Cromwell (twice). Percy. Charles I. Reynolds. Manners (thrice). Russel (thrice). Raleigh (twice). Locke (thrice). Lelys. Lambert. Newton. Charles Edward Stuart. More. James Stuart.

144 Although I have already given my rationale for centering this chapter on Davies, rather than on Murphy, those readers interested in Murphy's *Life of David Garrick* should know that the text also forms the entire basis for a number of extra-illustrated editions which are quite worthy of study, though outside the scope of the present project.

145 Davies, *Life of Garrick*, 1: 100.

146 Murphy, *Life of David Garrick*, 1: 66; *Scrapbook of David Garrick*, 27.

147 I am indebted to one of my anonymous manuscript reviewers for this excellent summation of scrapbooking's allure.

148 Pointon, *Hanging the Head*, 67. Similarly, Pointon explains that portrait collectors prior to the 1770s were less concerned with authenticity of the faces they collected than that the portrait seemed "to bridge the chasm between material existence and the interiority of the individual rather than as a means of recording the physical appearance of a particular historical person" (62).

149 See Wanko for an analysis of the significance of Booth's autopsy in the *History of the Theatres of London and Dublin* by Benjamin Victor.

150 *Scrapbook of David Garrick*, 81. As noted earlier, the vogue for collecting signatures seems to have arisen simultaneously with an interest in scrapbooking: even Queen Charlotte, who did not deign to post actual scraps in her extra-illustrated copy of Davies, did include a handful of signatures from noble persons.

151 A research librarian at the Folger verified the divergent penmanship.

152 Some scrapbooks incorporate the entire memento, as in the case of another anonymous scrapbook at the Folger, which proudly offers an official death notice of Eva Marie Garrick, complete with black-edged mourning paper.

153 If the academy has not yet produced a paper about Wikipedia as the direct inheritance of Edmund Curll, I have found my next project.

154 Brack, O.M., "Davies, Thomas," *Oxford Dictionary of National Biography.*

155 Boswell, *Life of Johnson*, 1: 447.

156 Ibid., 2: 494.

157 Ibid., 1: 745; 1: 248.

158 Ibid., 1: 476. And, of course, he was always in need of money: in the surprisingly frequent cameos of Tom Davies in the narrative, several remark on Johnson's charitable
reaction to "his poor friend's narrow circumstances" (Ibid., 1: 460).

159 "Article CX," 717.

160 Fitzgerald, *Life of Garrick*, 2: 284. Percy Fitzgerald's impressive biographical cache
included David Garrick (1868), the Kembles (1871), Catherine Clive (1888), the
Sheridans (1886), Henry Irving (1893), and Samuel Foote (1910). Counted among
Fitzgerald's seven memoirs pertaining to the theatre is his autobiographical *Memoirs
of an Author* (1895), suggesting the monumental rise in the status and importance of
the individual biographer that had occurred in the past century, certainly in part
attributable to the efforts of Thomas Davies.

161 Boswell says that Murphy had claimed to be present at the famous first meeting
between Boswell and Johnson, but that Thomas Davies, and not Murphy, was
there: he would have remembered if Murphy had been. This small note contrib-
utes to a strong sense of Murphy attempting to take over Davies's claims to fame/
association, first with Garrick in the dueling biographies, and then even at a high
point in Davies's personal life. Like Garrick, Johnson becomes a point of contesta-
tion. Davies wrote fairly extensively about—and for—Johnson in the *Life of Garrick*,
Murphy wrote an "Essay on the Life of Johnson," and of course, Boswell wrote *Life
of Samuel Johnson*. I am intrigued by this palpable desire to possess Samuel Johnson: in
Boswell, Murphy, and Davies (the latter of whom didn't even write a biography
about Johnson), we see three biographers locked in a competition for proximity to
Johnson and biographical authority via Johnson.

2 His Work, My Words: Anxiety and Competition in the Posthumous Lives of Charles Macklin, Comedian

1 Those biographies were discussed in Chapter 1 of the present work. Currently, Garrick
boasts the greatest number of biographies of any eighteenth-century thespian, and
has been a consistently popular subject of study. Macklin, on the other hand, enjoyed
a brief renaissance of interest with Edward Abbott Parry's *Charles Macklin* (1891) as
one installment of a planned collectable set of thespian biographies; he became the
focus of his first (and only) full-length monograph "scholarly" biography in 1960 at
the hands of William Worthen Appleton in *Charles Macklin: An Actor's Life*.

2 Seeing biography as more like an encyclopedia than a novel, I believe, is rooted in a
privileging of fiction over fact as innately more creative, thus more "artistic."

3 Paulin, "Sidetracks."

4 Carlson, *Haunted Stage*, 8.

5 Macklin likely got inspiration for his serious portrayal of the formerly comical
Shylock from Rowe's 1709 biography of Shakespeare, in which Rowe claims that
"though we have seen that play received and acted as a comedy, and the part of the
Jew performed by an excellent comedian [Thomas Doggett], yet I cannot but think
it was designed tragically by the author. There appears in it such a deadly spirit of
revenge, such a savage fierceness and fellness, and such a bloody designation of cruelty and mischief, as cannot agree either with the style or characters of comedy"
(Rowe, *Shakespear*, 1: xix–xx).

6   Cooke, *Memoirs of Charles Macklin*, 89–90.

7   Macklin, *Autograph List by Charles Macklin of Correspondence with George Colman*.

8   Braudy, *Frenzy of Renown*, 384.

9   Cooke, *Memoirs of Charles Macklin*, 90.

10   Of Macklin's autobiographical intentions, Cooke writes in his introduction to *Memoirs of Charles Macklin*, "Those who know the human heart, know that such resolutions only shewed he was the dupe of his own irresolution. He had not courage sufficient to undertake a work of so much labour and retrospection." (ix). See Macklin's *Commonplace Book, 1778–1790*, one of several that survive, which indicates some of the likely content of his autobiography, had it been undertaken.

11   A collection called *The Autograph Papers of Charles Macklin* at the Folger holds a Sotheby's record of provenance that markets the papers as including an outline of Macklin's intended autobiography, most of the rest of which was lost in a shipwreck (see Y.d.515(8)). Correspondingly, Kirkman states of the accident, "It was not Mr. Macklin alone that had to lament the loss; the Stage, and the whole of the dramatic world, suffered very materially by the shipwreck: the merciless waves destroyed his Treatises on the *Science of Acting*, on *The Works of Shakespeare*, on *Comedy*, *Tragedy*, and many other subjects, together with several manuscripts of infinite value to the British Theatre" (Kirkman, *Memoirs*, 2: 46–47).

12   Palfrey and Stern, *Shakespeare in Parts*, 68.

13   Worthen, *Idea of the Actor*, 73.

14   Roach, *Cities of the Dead*, 94–95.

15   Campbell, *Life of Mrs. Siddons*, 36. Judith Pascoe's efforts to replicate the audience experience of hearing Siddons points to the limitations of this type of "recording"; she notes that Siddons's repertoire features several key screams, "but you can't read a scream in any event, except in comic books (A-A-A-A-A-A-H-H-H!!!) (Pascoe, *Siddons Audio Files*, 2011, 68). While I can read the provincial "tum te tum" that Campbell records, and my mind imitates the sound as I read, I have no way of knowing how close to reality my imagination comes. As Pascoe suggests, this interpretative gap might not have been so pronounced for people who either saw Siddons herself, or actresses in the Siddonian tradition.

16   *The Laureat*, 35. The author notes that Colley's call for a "harse" "highly delighted some, and disgusted some of his Auditors; and when he was kill'd by Richmond, one might plainly perceive that the good People were not better pleas'd that so execrable a Tyrant was destroy'd, than that so execrable an Actor was silent."

17   Campbell, *Life of Mrs. Siddons*, 250.

18   Worthen, *Idea of the Actor*, 72.

19   Ibid.

20   Carlson observes that subsequent actors often "stressed their difference from their absent originals by not knocking over the chair" (*Haunted Stage*, 167). Intriguingly, the biography of Betterton by Charles Gildon is largely given over to an acting treatise supplying very detailed directions for how to represent the passions. For example, Gildon writes, "You must never let either of your Hands hang down, as if lame or dead; for that is very disagreeable to the Eye, and argues no Passion in the Imagination […] in Swearing, Attestation, or taking any solemn Vow or Oath, you must raise your Hand" (*Life of Betterton*, 77).

21   See Shearer West's *The Image of the Actor* for further discussion of points in painting.

22   Campbell, *Life of Mrs. Siddons*, 187.

23 We recall efforts to encapsulate Mrs. Siddons's genius merely through several signature screams and, in one or two cases, the withholding of expected screams (Pascoe, *Siddons Audio Files*, 68).

24 Roach, *Cities of the Dead*, 3.

25 Cibber, *An Apology*, 114; Campbell, *Life of Mrs. Siddons*, 84.

26 Palfrey and Stern, *Shakespeare in Parts*, 69.

27 Campbell, *Life of Mrs. Siddons*, 263, 169.

28 Carlson, *Haunted Stage*, 27.

29 Cibber, *Apology*, 21.

30 Ibid., 15. Cibber's relationship to originality/truthfulness was influenced by his dual nature as subject/author, which he played to his advantage. A discussion of the complications raised by autobiography is outside the scope of this dissertation; please see Felicity Nussbaum's *The Autobiographical Subject* (1989) and Laura Marcus's *Auto/biographical Discourses* (1994) for further insight.

31 Congreve, *Authentic Memoirs*, "Preface."

32 Ibid.

33 Ibid.

34 Congreve, *Authentic Memoirs*, 10.

35 Ibid., 60. Congreve joined Johnson and Macklin in his cultural bias: he commends Macklin's play *The Man of the World* for excelling in spite of its reliance on "the deformities of the Scottish speech" (*Authentic Memoirs*, 54).

36 Boswell, *Life of Samuel Johnson*, 2: 580–81.

37 F. A. Marshall, "Introduction" to *Works of William Shakespeare*, 3: 249.

38 Kirkman even had a prompt-book in the form of Congreve's biography; just as the prompt-book both aided and constrained an actor's innovations, so too did a previous biography.

39 Macklin's fourth biographer, Parry, suggests that some people believed Kirkman to be Macklin's illegitimate son, a notion that opens up the floor for further debate about "ownership" of Macklin's story (Parry, *Charles Macklin*, 3).

40 Kirkman writes of Macklin's intended memoir: "He resolved to give the material to some person, on whom he could depend, for the purpose of compiling and throwing them into form" (Kirkman, *Memoirs*, 1: 3). Like Cooke after him, Kirkman characterizes himself as a compiler; the description of "throwing" materials suggests a diffidence that undercuts the writing self as a "biographer." Nonetheless, Kirkman stresses the importance of his selection: "With this view he made choice of the author, conceiving, as it is hoped the reader will, that a near relation, bred up, and living for upwards of twenty years with him; acquainted from his infancy with his descent, family, and connections; and enabled by daily observations to trace out, and truly delineate his character, would be more likely than any other person to write a history recommended by truth and fidelity; objects, in Mr. Macklin's opinion, far superior, in intrinsic value, to all the graces and beauties which the highest embellishments of style could bestow upon it" (Kirkman, *Memoirs*, 1: 3). The project changes—a mere compiler need not add his own material—and Kirkman's role grew from a compiler to an artist capable of "delineat[ing] his character" and "writ[ing] a history."

41 Kirkman, *Memoirs*, 1: 318.

42 Ibid., 1: 362.

43 Bratton, *New Readings in Theatre History*, 103.

44 Parry, *Charles Macklin*, i.

45   Appleton, *Charles Macklin: An Actor's Life*, 2–4. The inclusion of an archival dimen-
     sion does not prohibit an author from achieving originality: on the contrary, Stauffer
     locates one of the first early modern biographies in the early seventeenth century,
     claiming that *Izaak Walton's Lives*, a series of four prefatory biographies published
     between 1640 and 1672, turned raw archival materials "into those artistic and indi-
     vidual compositions which are unmistakably his own" (Stauffer, *English Biography before
     1700*, 265).

46   Parry, *Charles Macklin*, 5.

47   Similarly drawing upon a predecessor while disparaging the source, as we will see in
     Chapter 3, Siddons's second biographer, Campbell, writing in 1834, genially thanks
     his "brother biographer, Mr. Boaden" for the reminiscences that he borrows from
     the earlier account of Siddons, written in 1827. Nonetheless, he is not above cri-
     tiquing Boaden's work. For example, he notes, "I have strong doubts with regard to
     this anecdote" (Campbell, *Life of Mrs. Siddons*, 36), elevating his own credibility at his
     "brother's" expense, attempting to overcome the ghost of his predecessor.

48   Perhaps it was reflective of the philosophical principle that a man's character cannot
     be fixed or known until he is deceased. Having access to a full narrative before pro-
     nouncing the final judgment on character allows the assessor to avoid any embarrass-
     ment if the subject/character proves inconsistent later in life. It should be noted that
     Johnson endorsed the character sketch, but as a summation tool, rather than depriv-
     ing the narrative of characteristic flavor.

49   Stauffer, *English Biography before 1700*, 273. It is interesting to consider how biogra-
     phers divided narration and description: Stauffer writes that the narrative part was
     "dynamic and progressive" while the portrait/character is "static and final" (ibid.,
     269). Portrait, according to Stauffer, is "without incidence and all elements of chro-
     nology" (271). In keeping with the tendency to force a comparison between biography
     and other genres or art forms, the larger narrative is play-like, full of motion and inci-
     dence, often driven by chronology or cause-and-effect, whereas a character sketch sets
     up permanent traits independent of the world in which the character lives (more like
     a portrait—fixed). Biography is not as static as a painting due to its ability to pinpoint
     multiple important moments.

50   Although Congreve's discussion of Macklin as Shylock, which appeared in chronolog-
     ical order relative to the actor's career, lacked specifics, this may be in part attributable
     to Congreve's commitment to the eighteenth-century preference for division outlined
     earlier: sustained "character sketches" at the end of a heavily narrative biography.
     Thus, Congreve may have felt that to perform a detailed critique of Macklin "in char-
     acter" at the chronological point that Macklin achieved prominence in the role would
     impede the plot or narrative thrust. The struggle between the highlights of one's life
     in chronological order, like those featured in the *Oxford Dictionary of National Biography*
     (DNB), and anecdotes, pithy moments of characterization, manifests itself in a range
     of solutions that suggest anecdote's role as a substitution for the more sustained char-
     acter sketch. For example, the *Theatrical Monitor, or Green Room Laid Open* (1767–68), a
     series of collected capsule theatrical biographies, each about four pages long, sepa-
     rated narrative from anecdotes and jests by design, so that "character" began to be
     represented almost solely through anecdote, although a more traditional character
     would have included physical description, others' perceptions, and a direct assessment
     of moral qualities, as found in a character sketch. Cooke's memoir of Macklin empha-
     sized anecdote so significantly that he included that word in the title and decried an

attempt at a traditional narrative biography. At its most extreme, anecdotes existed entirely out of surrounding context, jumbled together in books held together only by the common theme of anecdotes, with each anecdote bluntly unrelated to its neighboring selections in character, purpose, or scenario: narrative was subsumed by anecdote. At its best, anecdote could combine with narrative and character to amplify both, but anecdote also threatened both elements, able to become a tool of subversion acting against the unification of the biographical impulse.

51   Congreve, *Authentic Memoirs*, 44. Additionally, Congreve borrows from an account of Foote's, a description of how Macklin, as an acting coach, required his pupils to practice their lines as though in normal conversation, commanding, them to use "more force, but preserving the same accent" as their everyday speech pattern (22–24). This gives a clue, albeit not a strong one, to how Macklin acted onstage.

52   Ibid., 45.

53   Ibid., 58.

54   Ibid., 59.

55   It is interesting that, while Kirkman's title page only recognizes Macklin's male colleagues, the contents of his text include a number of his female colleagues as well, though rarely with the same sharpness of detail.

56   Kirkman, *Memoirs*, 1: 1.

57   Fielding, *Tom Jones*, 67.

58   Ibid., 68.

59   Kirkman, *Memoirs*, 1: 2.

60   Ibid., 1: 59.

61   Fielding, *Tom Jones*, 68. Other similarities between *Tom Jones* and Kirkman's *Memoirs of Macklin* include the degree of digression appropriate to a history. *Tom Jones's* narrator states, "Reader, I think proper, before we proceed any further together, to acquaint thee that I intend to digress, through this whole history, as often as I see occasion, of which I am myself a better judge than any pitiful critic whatever; and here I must desire all those critics to mind their own business, and not to intermeddle with affairs or works which no ways concern them; for till they produce the authority by which they are constituted judges, I shall not plead to their jurisdiction" (33). Just as Fielding often addresses his reader, Kirkman refers to this ideal reader frequently, offering, for example, to "lay before the reader" criticisms (2: 259), "present the reader" with letters (2: 329), and trust that "the reader will be able to form some idea" from collected conversations (2: 416).

62   Kirkman, *Memoirs*, 1: 60.

63   Ibid., 1: 71.

64   Ibid., 1: 79–80.

65   Ibid., 1: 82.

66   Macklin had the advantage, at least for posterity, of beginning life as a foreign and provincial speaker. His pronunciation was apparently so jarring that his first manager suggested that he spend some time touring with lesser theatres before applying for the London stage. Kirkman shares an anecdote in which Macklin, assaying the role of Friar Lawrence, was told by his manager (who was playing Romeo) that "if he could cut three or four inches more of the brogue from his tongue, he would speak the part well. Macklin replied, he wished he could; but observed, that cutting off tongues was a dangerous experiment – if not, it would certainly be more practiced […] for there were some who would be much more inoffensive actors, if they had no tongue at all."

STAGING MEMORY AND MATERIALITY

Kirkman records that Manager/Romeo "took Macklin by the hand [...] observing he was a clever fellow" (1: 64). While he may have tempered his brogue, Macklin had a distracting verbal tic of overusing the honorific "Sir," which persists in every dialogue supplied for him by Kirkman and Cooke, and appears to serve as a presumed mark of conversational authenticity. In one such instance, Cooke admits to staging a particularly dramatic conversation after it has been presented: "We have thrown the above conversation into dialogue, for the purpose of better elucidating the two characters: it is in substance what we have often heard from Macklin, animated by those looks of terror and alarm, which no man could assume better than himself" (Cooke, *Memoirs of Charles Macklin*, 84). Macklin's comparatively brief lines include four "Sir's": "Sir, I have no time to trifle [...] I can't wait, by G – d, Sir [...] No trifling, Sir! [...] Well, Sir, I'll give you the meeting."

67 The number of "missing" decades prior to Macklin's ascent to the stage depends upon which date of Macklin's birth one chooses to accept.

68 Kirkman, *Memoirs*, 1: 85–86.

69 Ibid., 1: 87.

70 Ibid., 1: 88–89, my italics.

71 Ibid., 1: 90.

72 Cooke, *Memoirs of Charles Macklin*, ii.

73 Ibid., ii–iii.

74 In Chapter 3, we will see Boaden attempt to weave a larger theatrical history around John Philip Kemble, a tactic that obscures his main character. Boaden would go on to adjust his formula for his next biography, the *Memoirs of Mrs. Siddons*. The balance of individual to group biography was difficult to master within a single text.

75 Cooke, *Memoirs of Charles Macklin*, "The Opinion of this Work," 3.

76 Cooke, *Memoirs of Charles Macklin*, 136.

77 A veteran actor, J. Moody, writes on behalf of the book, declaring, "His [Cooke's] Digressions (by far the best Part of the Work) are the Digressions of a Gentleman" (Cooke, *Memoirs of Charles Macklin*, "Advertisement," 2).

78 Cooke, *Memoirs of Charles Macklin*, 28.

79 Ibid., 122.

80 Ibid., 177.

81 Cooke also affords Spranger Barry's wife, an actress, a capsule biography, in which Mrs. Barry was given a domestic narrative rather than a tour of her theatrical contributions, while Spranger had the honor to be included for his theatrical doings and his personal life remained offstage. See Kristina Straub's *Sexual Suspects: Eighteenth Century Players and Sexual Ideology* (1992) for further discussion of gendered issues, as well as Cheryl Wanko's chapter on Lavinia Fenton for the unsettling dynamics of biography focused on female thespians, in *Roles of Authority*.

82 Although Kirkman disapproved of Davies, Garrick's first biographer, for what he claimed was an overly worshipful attitude, Cooke evidently esteemed Davies as a model for successful biography. We can recall from Chapter 1 that at Cooke's first opportunity to create the vision of an actor's prowess for his readers, Cooke evades the pressure by literally co-opting Davies's more successful performances in the *Memoirs of the Life of David Garrick* and *Dramatic Miscellanies*.

83 Cooke, *Memoirs of Charles Macklin*, 181.

84 Ibid., 284–85.

85 Ibid., 92–93.

86 Cooke records that Macklin "used to dwell with delight on his [Booth's] performance of the Ghost in *Hamlet*, which he made very awful and pathetic. In this performance he used cloth shoes (soles and all) that the sound of his step should not be heard on the Stage, which had a characteristical effect" (*Memoirs of Charles Macklin*, 16).

87 Parry, *Charles Macklin*, 87.

88 Kahan argues that the actor Edmund Kean, about whom many anecdotes involving boxing circulated, was rather adversarial onstage with his costars, and self-consciously tapped into the anecdotes about his boxing prowess in order to inform his onstage persona. See Jeffrey Kahan, *The Cult of Kean* (2006).

89 Congreve, *Authentic Memoirs*, 16.

90 Kirkman, *Memoirs*, 1: 188.

91 Ibid., 1: 192.

92 Ibid., 1: 193.

93 Ibid., 1: 202.

94 Edward Abbott Parry, the nineteenth-century cut-and-paste biographer, who has a tendency to present as many versions of Macklin's foibles as he finds interesting, chooses to combine the best of Congreve and Kirkman (unfortunately he had nothing from Cooke, who was more concise and reliable than Kirkman and more florid than Congreve). Parry begins with a dry recitation of the basic narration, supplementing the known accounts with the revelation of "a letter [...] expressing his deep sorrow" that Macklin supposedly wrote to the manager of the theatre, Drury Lane (Parry, *Charles Macklin*, 27). Parry provides Thomas Arne's account from Kirkman verbatim, and includes portions of Macklin's own defense. Parry shows his awareness of Kirkman's multiple accounts, but seems to only see the need for one eyewitness account, as the other accounts primarily corroborate the information given by Arne. He sums up two other arguments on behalf of Macklin and adds a quick aside about the state of manslaughter as a legal concept during the preceding century.

95 Congreve, *Authentic Memoirs*, 35–37.

96 Kirkman, *Memoirs*, 1: 359–61; Cooke, *Memoirs of Charles Macklin*, 203; Parry, *Charles Macklin*, 95–96.

97 Kirkman, *Memoirs*, 119.

98 Cooke, *Memoirs of Charles Macklin*, 200–01.

99 The other three anecdotes were the long-anticipated Foote ones, referenced but not provided by Congreve or Kirkman. First, an uncharacteristically brief Macklin anecdote: Macklin is preparing to start his lecture and finds that Foote is still holding court in the back of the room. Cooke describes that Macklin "therefore cried out, with some authority, 'Well, Sir, you seem to be very merry there; but do you know what I am going to say now?' 'No, Sir,' says Foote; 'Pray, do you?'" Cooke records that the quip stunned Macklin into silence "for some minutes." The second anecdote is longer, with Foote attempting to stop an interminable lecture on the origins of dueling: the wit interrupts to note that drunkenness leads to quarreling, which leads to dueling, "and so there's an end of the chapter" (Cooke, *Memoirs of Charles Macklin*, 209). Macklin was not able to resume his lecture, and let everyone go home. Finally, of Macklin's famous dumb-show, the actor explains that he learned the serving techniques from James, Duke of York, who invented the signals for use of the fleet. "'Very apropos! indeed,' says Foote, 'and good poetical justice; as from the fleet they were taken – so to the Fleet both master and signals are likely to return'" (209). Cooke remarks that Foote went too far when he set up a mockery of Macklin

at the theatre at Haymarket, "where neither cut so good a figure as they did in the British Inquisition" (209). Parry manages to dredge up three entirely different Foote anecdotes surrounding the British Inquisition. "The simple went to learn, the witty to laugh and sneer, the learned to wonder at Macklin's folly," prefaces Parry. One joke from Foote's Haymarket routine sees Foote pretending to be Macklin tutoring a classics student, expounding upon how Roscius, the greatest Roman actor, could never have played Shylock. The next joke that Parry records, also in dialogue, is Foote's imitation of Macklin telling an improbable story about the Prince of England expressing admiration for Macklin's acting. In telling the story, Foote uses Macklin's speech patterns and delivery in order to make the transaction sound like Macklin was telling the story. Foote, as Macklin, pretending to be the Prince, declares, in Macklin's characteristic speech pattern: " 'Sir, if I were not the Prince – ha – hum – you understand? – I should wish to be Mr. Macklin!' Upon which I [Foote, in the guise of Macklin] answered, 'Royal Sir, being Mr. Macklin, I do not desire to be the—' " Foote notes that Macklin, who was part of the audience of this joke, could no longer contain himself, but, starting up, he stretched his body forward and shouted, " 'No, I'll be d—d if I did!' " This anecdote captures not only the real Macklin's inability to take a joke, but also his stubborn decision to attend a show that was designed to mock his "Inquisition." The biographer notes that the "burlesque [...] probably did as much as anything to bring Macklin's experiment to a speedy termination" (Parry, *Charles Macklin*, 98). Parry concludes his showcase of Foote's wit by sharing an incomprehensible paragraph that Foote astutely penned and presented to Macklin in the midst of the latter's discourse on memory, with hopes that the lecturer would demonstrate his superior technique by repeating it from memory. The paragraph, dubbed "immortal nonsense" by Parry, is preserved for posterity; Parry notes, however, that "how Macklin took this ridiculous jest history does not relate [...] if he read and repeated it, his system of memory must have been a very complete one indeed" (98).

100 Congreve, *Authentic Memoirs*, 45. Henry Mossop, who died at an early age, was slated to be a serious rival to David Garrick if he could have had time to overcome his legendary stiffness. Parry relates the advent of "Barryists and Mossopists," fans who preferred one or the other of those two actors; he gives praise to Mossop for superior learning, but notes Mossop's "over-deliberation both in speech and action," citing the phrase "Mossop's minute-guns" (*Charles Macklin*, 117). Equally illuminating is Cooke's description, borrowed from Charles Churchill, of Mossop as "The Distiller of Syllables": "the frequent resting of his left-hand on his hip, with his right extended, has been often ludicrously compared to the handle and spout of a teapot," notes Cooke disapprovingly (*Memoirs of Charles Macklin*, 258). Of course, the Eight Kings poem, depicting eight famous actors as Macbeth, is consistent with these characterizations.

101 Parry replicates the poem that Congreve gave us, and repeats one of Cooke's criticisms—that Macklin lectured, rather than performed, Macbeth. He also adds one viewer's opinion that "Macklin's [Macbeth] was certainly not marked by studied grace of deportment, but he seemed to be more earnest in the character than any actor I have subsequently seen" (Parry, *Charles Macklin*, 161).

102 Cooke, *Memoirs of Charles Macklin*, 286.

103 Ibid., 289.

104 "Anecdotes of Charles Macklin," 418.

105 The move of anecdote into a single scene, detached from a larger narrative, evokes opportunistic and transgressive possibilities: unmoored from surrounding

frameworks or assessments, anecdote can transition from being an integral part of a philosophical meditation on the character under discussion to being simply an easily traded, cheaply consumed commodity. After all, anecdotes took very little space to print and could mingle promiscuously in a hodgepodge collection that lacked organization even by the remarkably loose eighteenth-century standards. This combination of unmediated and disorganized snippets meant that such compilations did not take very much energy to edit and could largely be reused from edition to edition, with some updated or new material supplanting the old chestnuts after several editions. Anecdotes thrived in the rich soil of newspapers, where editors had precious little space and little time, and where readers received a comparatively high bang for their buck, so to speak, in being able to trade anecdotes—which were brief and memorable—about specific public players and thus seem to be in the know.

106 For more information on marginal annotation, see H. J. Jackson's *Marginalia: Readers Writing in Books* (2001).

107 Cossart's copy of *Memoirs of Charles Macklin* was bound with a similarly annotated copy of Harley's *Life of Master Betty* (1804), the story of the precocious child actor whose meteoric rise to fame was only matched by his sudden fall from favor.

108 Ballantyne writes to an unspecified addressee who "desire[s] me to give you a conversation that passed between Mr. Macklin, the comedian, and me." Ballantyne offers a dialogue between himself and Macklin in which the veteran engages in an extended monologue, explaining that his last name was originally M'Laughlan, but that in the process of transitioning over to the more Anglicanized Macklin, a caller came to his lodgings and asked for M'Laughlan since he "had forgot to tell him I had changed my name." The landlady was appalled, as she believed that she had contracted the flat to a man named Macklin: "She said I must quit her apartments, for she had no good opinion of a man that went by two names," says Macklin. Although this anecdote is not particularly significant, Ballantyne's verification of it is designed to boost its value as true rather than yet another tall tale.

109 Cossart and Cooke, *Memoirs of Charles Macklin*, 90–91.

110 Ibid., 46. In another instance, Cossart corrects Cooke for identifying Macklin as an Englishman. "Irishman" is carefully written in the margin next to the inaccurate description (*Memoirs of Charles Macklin*, 406).

111 Cossart and Cooke, *Memoirs of Charles Macklin*, 79.

112 Ibid., 90.

113 Ibid., 161.

114 Ibid., 406.

115 Ibid., 407.

116 Cooke's account is built on an assumption of the lost glory years of theatre, versus Cossart's forward-looking optimism. Cossart's views clash with Kirkman's, too; Cossart insists that he is qualified to judge the worthiness of performers because he has seen them all in performance, whereas Kirkman claimed that at a certain point there was no practical use for, or even possibility of, comparisons between thespians over time.

117 A large quantity of Cossart's notes pertain to the section about the *Beggar's Opera*, suggesting just as much, if not more, interest in that play than in the parts pertaining more directly to Macklin, who was not part of the original cast.

118 See Victor's *History of the Theatres*.

119 See Jacky Bratton's *New Readings in Theatre History* for an astute discussion of how anecdotes passed down by theatre folk in particular, with their capacity for mimicry

and interest in storytelling, transcended the original event; the passing down of often outrageous or questionably valid tales contrasts with Cossart's commitment to factual accuracy. Cossart was willing to deconstruct the mythos surrounding Macklin, a legacy of tall tales that Macklin himself had certainly encouraged.

3 Epistolary Resurrections: James Boaden and the Rise of the Professional Thespian Biographer

1   Boaden, *Mrs. Jordan*, 2: 5.

2   Boaden seems to see a connection between his employments: weighing the possibility that he might have seen Mrs. Jordan as a ghost in London one day, he writes, "I have had, it is true, some ghostly intercourse, as a dramatic poet, but Voltaire, no mean authority as a poet, has never rendered by his Semiramis a noon-day spectre either terrible or credible" (Ibid., 2: 306).

3   Boaden, *An Inquiry*. Boaden writes, "While these sheets are passing through the press, I am shocked and grieved with the intelligence, that my excellent friend has departed this life, at an age that allowed a reasonable hope of many years of honourable retirement. At no very distant period, I hope to deliver to the public a work, the object of which is to record his progress in the art which he professed, and also to display his personal character as it unfolded itself during an intimacy of nearly thirty years. Fortunately the materials before me are at once abundant and authentic" (*Kemble*, v).

4   The *Correspondence of David Garrick* was a collection of letters with an accompanying prefatory biography, and thus not a true full-length biography like the four other works under discussion.

5   Boaden, *Siddons*, 1: ix–x.

6   Ibid., 1: xii–xiii.

7   Boaden, James, *Kemble*, 46.

8   For those interested in more material collectable artifacts, the playbill was a popular alternative: such documents might trace the trajectory of the thespian, and represent a collector's own attendance and investment, but did not capture the actor's art beyond noting the time, place and subject thereof.

9   A number of anecdotes seem to have been "verified" by appearing in multiple, unrelated works; on the other hand, the easy propagation of anecdotes also makes their authenticity as a function of widespread repetition suspect. As with letters, there is an innate not always logical sense in which restriction or privacy seems to make something more valid. Boaden's approach to anecdote, repeating only those things he claims to have participated in or heard directly, hinges on the credibility of his reputation. However, an independent account such as Boaden's (with no other living witnesses) is equally if not more suspect than a story reported by many people. Thus, the logic behind whether an anecdote is verifiably true is fraught with contradictions. Boaden appears not to have entertained the possibility that his word as a gentleman would not be sufficient to vouch for the legitimacy of a given anecdote.

10   Boaden, James, *Kemble*, 297.

11   Critics quibbled with Garrick about his pronunciation of specific words and lines through personal letters, with "Ignoto" writing that in the word "tropically [...] that *o*, I imagine, should be pronounced short, as we pronounce the word in *logical*" (*Private Correspondence of David Garrick*, 1: 11). Another correspondent, signed as "Well Wisher

and Admirer," takes Garrick to task for "several false pronunciations [...] chiefly [...] *matron, Israel, villain, appal[sic] Horatio, wind:* which you pronounced, *metron, Iserel, villin, appeal, Horetio;* and the word *wind* you pronounced short" (1: 12). Even offstage, Garrick's delivery was noted, with one observer commenting on the quality of his voice during a reading at a church service (Daggett, *Sounds of English,* 43).

12   Steele, *Essay,* 47. Steele's stratagem did not take into account the effects of different spaces—see Pascoe's *Sarah Siddons Audio Files,* particularly Chapter 8, for an excellent discussion of the way that particular venues mutated Siddons's voice.

13   Halliday, *Language and Education,* 71.

14   Davies and many other biographers had advanced an openly moral purpose to their writings—Boaden was hardly a vanguard in that. However, Boaden was able to be much more invasive about his subject's social, religious, and political lives because of the increased access to privileged, presumably private, documents.

15   Boaden's approach to biography is rather modern, given his interest in multiple subjects, the gathering of large archival bodies of letters to and by a subject, the practice of citations, the eschewing of unsubstantiated gossip in favor of eyewitness accounts, and field research into less-accessible parts of a subject's life, such as visiting the site of Mrs. Inchbald's childhood home.

16   Following Siddons's death, Boaden did produce a "supplement" in subsequent editions of the memoir, addressing her last four years.

17   Boaden, *Siddons,* 1: xi–xv.

18   Campbell, a much younger man, willingly admitted his limitations as Siddons's biographer: "I am glad that I have far better testimonies than my own to offer in proof of the actress's great triumph," he noted in reference to a character which he had seen Siddons play "in the autumn of her beauty." Campbell says he had imagined that the part would be played by a young lady rather than someone "large, august, and matronly" (Campbell, *Life of Mrs. Siddons,* 100). To compensate for his lack of knowledge about Siddons's earlier years, he borrows from Boaden and "the newspapers of those times." Campbell's admission of his limitations and biases against Siddons's latter-year genius justify Boaden's conviction that a contemporary of hers should write her memoir rather than a youthful admirer seeing her in her decline.

19   Toothill, *Stages of Celebrity,* 46.

20   Boaden, *Jordan,* 2: 178–79. A letter by W. Sherlock, pen name Photius, Junior, dated Feb 6, 1827, shows indignation at Boaden publishing Siddons's life before she was dead. Sherlock notes that Boaden's project would have been appropriate had it been qualified as a "theatrical" life rather than "the" life. Moreover, he took umbrage at a memoir of Siddons that was made "without her having been art or part in the business, or even having (as far as it appears by the context,) a common acquaintance with its modest writer" (Photius, Jr., 119).

21   George IV passed away in 1830; William IV began his reign that same year, receiving his formal coronation in 1831.

22   "Boaden's Life of Mrs. Jordan." Review. *Fraser's Magazine,* 738.

23   Boaden, *Kemble,* iv.

24   The *Memoirs of Mrs. Siddons* was also dedicated to the king, with a review from the *Monthly Magazine, or British Register,* mocking Boaden's "crawling fawningness of the language" of patriotism ("Life of Mrs. Siddons, by James Boaden, Esq." Review. *Monthly Magazine,* 194). The works on Jordan, Garrick and Inchbald came out after his death.

25   Boaden, *Siddons,* 1: xi.

26   Ibid., 1: 9.
27   Ibid., 1: 64–65. Cibber and Davies also remark disgustedly on an uncultured audi-
      ence's applause affecting undisciplined actors.
28   Ibid., 1: 66–67.
29   The most sustained look at *Hamlet* occurs early in the *Life of Jordan*, Boaden's third full
      biography.
30   *Memoirs of the Life of John Philip Kemble* provides some exception to Boaden's tendency
      to promote sound over gesture, as it features a discussion of Kemble's sword, but
      this pertains directly to the ghost and still involves textual criticism. Kemble orig-
      inated a design to lower his sword after "menac[ing] his friends who prevented
      him from following the Ghost" so that he was not pointing a weapon at his father's
      wraith: "Kemble, having drawn it on his friends, retained it in his right hand, but
      turned his left towards the spirit, and drooped the weapon after him—a change both
      tasteful and judicious" (Boaden, *Kemble*, 56–57). Kemble also knelt at the spirit's depar-
      ture, which Boaden approves as marking "the filial reverence [...] Henderson saw it,
      and adopted it immediately,—I remember he was applauded for doing so." So, too,
      in Hamlet's confrontation with Gertrude in her bedchamber, did Kemble "kne[el] in
      the fine adjuration to his mother" and question her without the "unfilial keenness"
      that some Hamlets before had displayed (ibid., 59). These several gestural distinc-
      tions stand out in a sustained investigation of Hamlet that is otherwise overwhelmed
      by text. Even so, the gestural component is bounded by the text that authorizes it,
      Shakespeare's own words.
31   West, *Image of the Actor*, 60–61.
32   When tracking the recurring theme of competition among the biographers discussed
      in this work, it is useful to keep in mind that Congreve, Kirkman, and Cooke (Macklin's
      biographers) were writing within a five-year time span in which Murphy's *Life of David
      Garrick* (1801) marked the midpoint. Davies and Boaden, then, were outliers by at least
      two decades in either direction, with Davies representing the bridge between Cibber's
      and Garrick's styles, and Boaden between Garrick's and Kemble's.
33   Boaden, *Kemble*, 54.
34   Ibid., 54–55.
35   Ibid., 55.
36   Boaden's scholarly approach is not necessarily indicative of his audience; Pascoe com-
      ments that an audience trained to the aural pleasures of Romantic poetry was, above
      all, interested in the *feelings* that Siddons elicited.
37   Boaden, *Mrs. Jordan*, 1: 258–260. Boaden tells a delightful tale about a gaffe commit-
      ted by Guernier, an artist who attempted to depict the banquet scene in Macbeth.
      The eighth ghost in Macbeth's banquet vision, Banquo himself, is described by
      Shakespeare as one "who bears a glass" (a mirror, reflecting Macbeth's horror-addled
      visage). Guernier, fantastically, has depicted Banquo's ghost clutching "a common
      wine glass" (*Mrs. Jordan*, 2: 72–73).
38   However much Boaden admired Shakespeare, Boaden feels that actors should not
      study the First Folio, because Shakespeare himself didn't study much, and therefore,
      "it will be difficult to show that more learning is required for the delivery of a play
      than its composition. The playhouse copy is quite sufficient for the actor. [...] The last
      shelter for pedantry should be the stage" (*Mrs. Jordan*, 2: 167).
39   Boaden, *Kemble*, 65. In the omitted lines, Hamlet considers whether the ghost could be
      hellish, with wicked intent, or otherwise, and resolves to speak to it nonetheless, asking

the ghost in rapid fire a number of questions as to its purpose of return, questions that show Hamlet to be piously concerned about his father's comfort.

40   Ibid., 82.
41   Boaden, *Mrs. Jordan*, 1: 19–20.
42   Boaden, *Siddons,* 1: 103.
43   Boaden, *Kemble,* 44.
44   Ibid., 45.
45   Ibid., 33.
46   Ibid., 34.
47   Ibid., 47.
48   Boaden, *Mrs. Jordan,* 1: 18.
49   The Abington thesis of "restoration by chance" seems antithetical to Boaden's claim of design. Yet Boaden admits to being stymied by his task numerous times, adopting various tactics to overcome the difficulty of translation. Siddons's utterance of line as Lady Macbeth "beggared all description," he says simply (Boaden, *Kemble,* 291). Similarly, he makes no effort to describe Kemble as Coriolanus, one of his signature roles (Boaden, *Mrs. Jordan,* 2: 184). Foreshadowing his increasing dependence on letters and artifacts to stand in for a narrative voice, he offers the cast list for *School for Scandal* but makes no attempt to delineate individual character performances, lamenting, "Why am I not as well able to convey the perfect impression of their performance?" (Boaden, *Siddons,* 1: 100).
50   Having heard the critics' complaints from *Memoirs of the Life of John Philip Kemble,* and being an astute observer of the biographers who had come before him, Boaden attempts to evade criticism about his reliance on scripts: "Whoever attempts to paint the momentary beauties of elocution and personal expression must ask aid from the exact language uttered; the reference from the actor to the poet is perpetual" (*Siddons,* 1: xvi).
51   Boaden, *Kemble,* 35.
52   Boaden, *Mrs. Jordan,* 1: 104; 1: 70.
53   Ibid., 2: 140.
54   Boaden, *Kemble,* 83.
55   Ibid.
56   Ibid., 82.
57   Ibid., 32.
58   Ibid., 19.
59   Ibid., 9. Unusually, Boaden provides two classic bons mots about Voltaire and Le Kain, who are barely incidental to the story of Sarah Siddons; in this case, it is to be imagined that the characters were so foreign and the import so minor that those exceptions were not seen by Boaden to threaten his established persona (Boaden, *Siddons,* 1: 125, 1: 136).
60   Boaden, *Siddons,* 1: vii.
61   "Memoirs of Mrs. Siddons, Interspersed." Review, 184.
62   Boaden, *Kemble,* 408.
63   Ibid., 26.
64   Ibid., 3.
65   Boaden, *Mrs. Jordan,* 1: 275). Another anecdote involves Jordan being criticized as "quite the Duchess" for showing exasperation at a rehearsal. Jordan explains that her interlocutor is not the first "who has condescended to honor me ironically with that title"; earlier the same morning, she had discharged a fiery Irish cook, whom she

describes as banging her wages on the table, shouting, "Arrah now, honey, with this *thirteener*, won't I sit in the gallery?—and won't your Royal Grace give me a *curtsy?*—And won't I give your Royal Highness a *howl*, and a *hiss* into the bargain?" (Ibid., 1: 343). This story seems permissible to Boaden because it was told to Boaden by Reynolds (Boaden inserts the tag "says Reynolds himself" in the midst of the story to secure its lineage), who himself heard it from Jordan.

66   "Memoirs of Mrs. Siddons" Review, 149.

67   Ibid., 153.

68   The digressions, of course, are part of the heritage of theatrical biography, albeit a feature that appears to be falling out of favor since J. Moody claimed in 1804 that William Cooke's "digressions [...] are the digressions of a gentleman," and were, by far, the best part of his biography of Macklin (Cooke, *Memoirs of Charles Macklin, Comedian*, "Advertisement," 2).

69   "Memoirs of Mrs. Siddons, Interspersed ..." Review, 184.

70   "As I paid much attention to Macklin's performances, and personally knew him, I shall endeavor to characterize his acting," writes Boaden, describing the veteran as "essentially manly," with weighty delivery, coldly colourless eyes, and a skill of modulating his voice that could "inveigle as well as subdue" (*Kemble*, 248).

71   Boaden relates that he goes to the theatre to compare Macklin at the age of 89 to Henderson in the role of Shylock—the specificity of detail stresses that Boaden was, in fact, present on a specific night (*Mrs. Jordan*, 1: 117). The encounter is framed even more author-centrically when he notes that he had yet to meet Macklin personally but still felt at that stage that it would be worthwhile to describe him: "Who would not decorate the chambers of memory with portraits painted by the great masters, in living colours, and all the truth of nature?" (Ibid., 1: 118).

72   Boaden, *Kemble*, 249–50.

73   Boswell was known to ask questions of Johnson, more in the style of an interview, in order to furnish good material for the biography he was working on. He was both reviled and begrudgingly admired for the thoroughness of his documentation of Johnson's life, having projected the image of living cheek-to-jowl with him for twenty years in order to get the clearest conception of the man (even though Boswell actually spent long periods apart from Johnson). See *Boswell's Presumptuous Task: The Making of the Life of Dr. Johnson* (2000) by Adam Sisman for a peek at Boswell's calculating approach to biography.

74   Boaden, *Mrs. Jordan*, 2: 99.

75   Boaden, *Siddons* 1: 21–23.

76   Intriguingly, the excellent story about Garrick critiquing Bannister's acting while shaving occurs in Boaden's potentially weakest biography, the impersonal, less documented *Siddons*.

77   We might recall that Davies also marketed himself as a gentleman, and his biography was heralded in large part due to the weight of Davies's own reputation as a good man. He did not, however, stand on as much ceremony about sources and personal involvement as did Boaden, who almost certainly took career cues from Davies.

78   There is a sense in which the sincerity of Boaden's desire to immortalize a single actor is diluted by the serialization of this impulse to commemorate. The more actors Boaden commemorates, the more it seems that his goal is to make a name for himself, rather than for any specific actor.

79   Boaden, *Siddons*, 1: 184–185.

80   "Private Correspondence of David Garrick" Review, 1. The reviewer continues
     to praise Boaden, citing his "diligence in performing his task—a task for which he
     was well qualified, and we render him accordingly our best thanks" for preserving
     a key piece of the "dominion of imagination" (1). By contrast, a reviewer of Percy
     Heatherington Fitzgerald's *Life of David Garrick* (1868) judged *Private Correspondence of
     David Garrick*, edited by James Boaden as bereft of imagination and judgment, result-
     ing in a work "meagre in details, and most colourless and jejune in treatment" ("Life
     of David Garrick [...] by Fitzgerald" Review, 1). While the reviewer's contention that
     a biographer could have written a good work just from knowing Eva Maria and hav-
     ing the letters is interesting, his verdict on Boaden's biography does not take into
     account that Boaden was acting as an editor, not a true biographer. Boaden explicitly
     noted in the "brief précis" of Garrick that he was not going to add any new details or
     interpretations.
81   *The Life of Mrs. Jordan* was a more traditional biography using the actress's letters,
     whereas the Boaden's *Memoirs of Mrs. Inchbald* was almost entirely governed by the
     actress's correspondence and writings. Boaden claims authorship of *The Life of Mrs.
     Jordan*, but signs himself as editor of *Memoirs of Mrs. Inchbald. Inchbald*, then, represents
     the midpoint between epistolary-heavy theatrical biography (*Jordan*) and a collection
     of letters (*Garrick*); Boaden's perception of himself as "editor" of *Inchbald*, even while
     he did significant biographical work to pull the narrative together, suggests his own
     uncertainty in conceiving of his job in relation to collected correspondence.
82   The rise of the novel, with its frequent use of letters, seems to have shaped theatre
     audience's tastes accordingly. See Ian P. Watt's *The Rise of the Novel: Studies in Defoe,
     Richardson, and Fielding* (1957) and Emily Anderson's *Eighteenth Century Authorship and the
     Play of Fiction: Novels and the Theatre, Haywood to Austen* (2009).
83   In his fifth biographical effort, Boaden praises Inchbald's diary for providing evi-
     dence countering unattractive tales of her vanity: he promotes the idea that the diary
     recorded pure unblemished truths, unmeditated upon in anticipation of their place in
     her future fortune (*Inchbald*, 1: 71). Similarly, Boaden records that in a clash between
     newspaper articles and private journals, journals always supersede because of their
     presumed sincerity (Ibid. 1: 22). Boaden highlights the importance of Inchbald's
     diary in reference to her earlier newspaper biographer, Mr. Bellamy: of that account,
     Boaden can approve only of moments where "such particulars are not at variance
     with her written *diary;* which is higher authority than the best recollections that can
     be supplied in conversation, though held for the express purpose of giving correct
     materials to a friend whom she trusted" (Inchbald 1: 254).
84   Boaden, *Mrs. Jordan*, 1: 193. Jordan's identification in letters as "Dora" and sometimes
     as "J. Ford" remind us that "Jordan" was her stage name, and that she had other,
     more intimate names for offstage parts of her life, including "Dora" for friends, and
     "Mrs. Ford" for official correspondences and businesses (her married name). Jordan's
     maiden name was "Bland."
85   Boaden, *Inchbald*, 1: 136.
86   Ibid., 1: 12. Boaden undermines, or at least challenges, his own assertion that hand-
     writing reveals character when he adds that Inchbald's "exterior garb of her candi-
     date farces, ragged paper, rude penmanship, and careless orthography, was not at all
     prophetic of a Dramatic Muse, who should become one of the best supports of com-
     edy, and rank with Centlivre and Cowley" (Ibid., 1: 155).

87   George IV passed away in 1830; William IV began his reign in 1830, receiving his
      formal coronation in 1831.
88   To that end, it is likely that Jordan's executor, Mrs. Phillips, realized the rare possibil-
      ity to generate interest about the letters in her custody. It is difficult to determine why
      Mrs. Phillips didn't produce Jordan's letters sooner after her death, but her delayed
      decision meant that it must have been even more surprising to have Mrs. Jordan
      "speak for herself" through these letters after such a long period of silence.
89   The existence of an autobiography was a big selling point for Boaden, who lovingly
      describes the anticipation of Inchbald's autobiographical memoirs. When word got
      out that Inchbald was writing her own memoirs, Boaden records, she was offered
      one thousand pounds in advance for their publication (*Inchbald*, 2: 57), and peo-
      ple began to wonder how she would portray all of her friends who were still alive
      (*Inchbald*, 2: 63; 2: 75). Eventually, a succession of buyers retracted their offers, and
      Mrs. Inchbald ordered her memoirs burned upon her death, having already burned
      a significant amount of her own papers at the deaths of her sisters in 1815 (*Inchbald*,
      2: 278; 2: 201).
90   *Inchbald*, 2: 280.
91   Ibid., 2: 220.
92   Boaden, *Mrs. Jordan*, 1: iii.
93   Contradictorily, Boaden claims that the "real" Jordan wasn't like the "romps" that
      she played on stage, which seems at odds with his insistence in her raw talent as
      opposed to artifice.
94   Boaden, *Mrs. Jordan*, 2: 228.
95   It does in fact appear that Boaden sought out personal archives for his latter biog-
      raphies. Paradoxically, it seems that very private caches of letters were increasingly
      being made available to specific biographers. Thus, we see Siddons that gave her
      correspondence and memos to her preferred biographer, and Inchbald very self-con-
      sciously shaped the archive of materials that were designed to survive her death.
96   A worthwhile project could be found in addressing the class arguments manifest in
      Boaden's framing of some letters as authentic, as well as the types of content that
      Boaden released from each actor's archive.
97   Boaden, *Siddons*, 2: 273.
98   Boaden's critics suggested that the biographer stole most of his best Siddons material
      from newspapers. The letter that Boaden opaquely leads us to believe that he has
      transcribed may be one such example.
99   Boaden, *Kemble*, xvi.
100   Ibid., xvi.
101   Boaden mentions that Kemble had asked Inchbald to describe Henderson's move-
      ments, costuming, and delivery in the character of Sir Giles, as Kemble believed he
      would be asked to replicate Henderson's performance. "One cannot but regret the
      loss of Mrs. Inchbald's reply to this letter; she was so competent to answer all these
      minute questions by having acted with him," notes Boaden. He graciously offers his
      own observations and opinions in her stead, as "the present writer saw them together
      on stage" (*Inchbald*, 1: 144–46).
102   Boaden, *Mrs. Jordan*, 1: 199–200.
103   Troublingly, Boaden's gentlemanly posture seems compromised by the inclusion
      of a series of letters between Mrs. Jordan and "her confidential friend," with the
      proviso, "These letters are for your eye alone," an order that Boaden indicates (via

footnote) was followed originally by the correspondent, "faithfully obeying the condition attached to their communication" (*Mrs. Jordan*, 2: 251). Boaden's earlier claims of decorum toward the job of a biography and indignation at prying into intimate details of Jordan's life during her pregnancies show in sharp contrast to this letter, apparently safely returned to Jordan and then published, not so privately, in Boaden's biography.

104   Boaden, *Mrs. Jordan*, 2: 209.

105   Ibid., 2: 211.

106   Ibid., 2: 331.

107   In the final pages of Jordan's biography, Boaden adopts the metaphor of himself as a judge, displaying evidence to a jury. While occasionally interjecting his own biased feelings on the case at hand, Boaden positions the reader as the jury to read "his minutes of the evidence" about the personal and professional merits of Jordan. Ostensibly, most biographies make a case for the subject's strong moral character as a dual lodestar alongside acting ability: Boaden's metaphor is particularly troubling because of its association with criminal activity, and as the culmination of a biography that spends precious little time addressing Mrs. Jordan in the public eye as an actress rather than as a respected but slightly scandalous possessor of a scurrilous love life.

108   *Mrs. Jordan*, 1: 186–87.

109   The movement of time is quite dependent on what was new or interesting in Inchbald's life as she presented it in her personal ledger. Thus, Boaden covers the year 1798, uneventful for Inchbald personally, in just five pages. Such personalized treatment is antithetical to that of the *Memoirs of Mrs. Siddons*, where the titular thespian wasn't even on the London stage during some years that were nonetheless heavily chronicled by her biographer.

110   Boaden, *Inchbald*, 1: 62.

111   Ibid., 2: 34.

112   Ibid., 2: 45.

113   Ibid., 2: 70–71.

114   Ibid., 2: 74.

115   Ibid., 2: 187.

116   Ibid., 2: 291–92.

117   Ibid., 2: 289.

118   Boaden, *Inchbald*, 2: 254–55. Moore's parting line wishes upon Inchbald a spectacularly lengthy life-span, and speaks not only to the desire for Inchbald's preservation, but also to the (implicit) preservation of Moore himself, as "one of her contemporaries," alongside her.

119   Boaden, *Inchbald*, 2: 232–35.

120   Ibid., 2: 258–60.

121   Ibid., 2: 257.

122   Inchbald's diary becomes rather depressing (and Boaden's memoir appropriately picks up the somber tone) once she has stopped producing works. This is manifest most clearly in Inchbald's "Retrospective." Starting in 1798 through 1802, each year is designated as "happy" from mildly to wildly so. During this time span, each "happy" year receives the rationale for why it was enjoyable, and then, inevitably, a "but for ..." clause of exception that frequently pertained to her fading looks or declining health, or the passing of a close friend or relative. From 1802 to 1808, only

two years receive positive marks, 1803 being "very happy" and 1807, more in keeping with overall trends, "often very unhappy yet mostly cheerful, and on my return to London nearly happy." Boaden honors the spirit of Inchbald's letters and the factual realities of her decline, but seems to abandon his earlier mantra of variation until the work has concluded, and he presents a few miscellaneous letters that he claims not to have received in time to incorporate into the body of the text, but which "will make the Volume fuller, and have considerable variety as well as interest" (2: 352). One might wish he had realized the potential conflict in expanding a biography of over seven hundred pages, especially when the subject's life reached an undeniable state of drudgery and depression, even according to the subject's own memoranda.

123   The interest in separating biography and criticism seems at odds with the patterns of theatrical biography; the issue may have been the male author's disapproval of a female critiquing him, or a feeling of violation over Inchbald placing a widely published negative opinion about the author's work within that same author's life's story. The author's indignation seems misdirected based on established expectations for biography, particularly for a prefatory biography.

124   "Memoirs of Mrs. Inchbald" Review, 305.

125   Boaden, *Kemble*, 55.

126   Boaden, *Siddons*, 1: 258.

127   Ibid.

128   Ibid., 1: 259.

129   Boaden, *Inchbald*, 1: 120.

130   "Life of David Garrick [...] by Fitzgerald" Review, 1. This review establishes Percy Fitzgerald (M.A., F.S.A.) as the fourth formal biographer after Davies, Murphy, and Boaden. Fitzgerald's biography is called *The Life of David Garrick*, subtitled *from Original Family Papers, and numerous published and unpublished sources*. Fitzgerald, like Boaden, writes a great string of biographies: investigating his work would be a good way to bring the present project into the mid-1800s. Fitzgerald's *Garrick* fell prey to many of the same complaints suffered by Boaden and Campbell: the work was too long, the syntax too permutated, his facts often inaccurate. Even with his own haughtiness toward other men's errors, his sources were not always made clear.

131   Toothill, *Stages of Celebrity*.

132   Boaden, *Siddons*, 1: 146.

133   Ibid., 1: 120.

134   Boaden, *Mrs. Jordan*, 2: 124.

135   Ibid.

136   Boaden, *Inchbald* 1: 137. A contemporary review, "Article IV. *Life of Mrs. Siddons*, by Thomas Campbell," found in the *Quarterly Review*, declares, "Davies knew more of the history of the stage than any man since Colley Cibber" (120). He links Davies to Cibber, and Boaden to Davies, declaring that "the fame of Mrs. Siddons should be rested on the evidence of Davies for her earlier, and on that of Boaden for her later glories; but very little, we are sorry to say, on anything that Mr. Campbell has either written or compiled ("Article IV," 121).

137   Boaden, *Inchbald*, 2: 93.

138   Kennard, *Mrs. Siddons*, v.

139   Ibid., v–vi.

140   "Article IV," 96. The reviewer describes Campbell as "a distinguished poet [...] a man of undoubted genius" but says "it is not given to any man to excel in all the walks of

literature." The conclusion trenchantly declares Campbell, "supposing him to have actually written the book which bears his name—the worst theatrical historian we have ever read" (124).

141   Ibid., 112.

142   Representative examples of Boaden's errors, according to Campbell, include suggesting that Siddons feared Mrs. Crawford as a serious rival in the part of Lady Randolph (Campbell, *Life of Mrs. Siddons*, 124), or that Kemble and Siddons had a feud that precipitated Siddons's retirement (Ibid., 252). Campbell's "sage brother biographer" is admitted to be correct in only two instances—his assessment of Henderson's strengths and Siddons's ability to play Desdemona—in both instances, Campbell relegates Boaden's success to "felicity of expression," suggesting luck rather than general insightfulness (Ibid.). In short, Campbell "bullies the ghost" of his predecessor.

143   "Article IV," 104.

144   Ibid., 105.

145   Ibid., 95.

146   It is apparent that Siddons had not been pleased with her representation in Boaden's *Memoirs of Mrs. Siddons* of 1827; I find it unlikely that she would not have kept abreast of his subsequent work, especially as some critics wrote rather discourteous reviews suggesting that Boaden might have an agenda of systematically picking through the Kemble line as ready source of profit for his biographical enterprise.

147   "The Late Mrs. Siddons," Review. *New Monthly Magazine*, 471.

148   Ibid. The Cambridge University Press website, in service of promoting its 2013 edition of Boaden's *Memoirs of Mrs. Siddons*, evidently conflates Boaden with Campbell in its description of the text, offering a vision Boaden with Campbell in its description of the text, offering a vision of Boaden "closely collaborating with his subject." More appropriately, the description notes an earlier reissuing of Boaden's *Life of Mrs. Jordan*, describing Boaden as having "establish[ed] himself as an authoritative biographer, preferred over others for his intellect and wealth of anecdotes from a lifetime spent within the theatrical world."

149   Ibid., 474.

150   Ibid.

151   Boaden, John, *Illustrations*, "The Dedication." John Boaden was a successful portrait painter, associated with the Royal Academy and the Society of British Artists. He was born in either 1792 or 1793, and died in 1839, the same year of his father's decease.

152   This makes sense if we believe Boaden's claim that the death of Kemble spurred him to write the biography.

153   Boaden, John, *Illustrations*, "Advertisement."

154   Ibid.

155   Perry, Roach, and West, *First Actresses*, 2.

156   See Chapter 2 for a discussion of *pronuntiatio* and *actio*.

157   Perry, Roach and West, *First Actresses*, 26–27, 32–24.

158   Ibid., 135. Boaden populated his biographies with metaphors comparing what he did to painting; recall from earlier in this chapter his description of Macklin, whose death he sought to commemorate: "Who would not decorate the chambers of memory with portraits painted by the great masters, in living colours, and all the truth of nature?" (*Kemble*, 118).

159   McPherson, *Art and Celebrity*, 18.

Epilogue: The Limits of Materially Bound Permanence

1   Kahan, *Cult of Kean*, 9.
2   Menzer spends some time in his coda discussing whether the archive and the anecdote are antithetical, and decides that the opposite of the archive is "absence" (Menzer, *Anecdotal Shakespeare*, 216).

REFERENCES

Akerby, George. *The Life of Mr. James Spiller, the Late Famous Comedian. In which is Interspers'd much of the Poetical History of his Own Times.* Gale: Eighteenth Century Collections Online. First printed London for J. Purser, 1729.

An Account of the Life, Conversation, Birth, Education, Pranks, Projects, and Exploits, and Merry Conceits, of the Famously Notorious Mat. Coppinger. London: T. Hobs, 1695.

Anderson, Emily. 2009. *Eighteenth-Century Authorship and the Play of Fiction: Novels and the Theater, Haywood to Austen.* New York: Routledge.

"Anecdote, n." In *OED Online.* Oxford University Press, March 2013. http://www.oed.com/view/Entry/7367?rskey=jtWSkb&result=1&isAdvanced=false#eid

"Anecdotes of Charles Macklin." *Edinburgh Magazine, or Literary Miscellany* (June 1799): 416–24.

"Anecdotes of the Late David Garrick (I)." *Universal Magazine of Knowledge and Pleasure* 66, no. 461 (May 1780): 252–56.

"Anecdotes of the Late David Garrick (II)." *Universal Magazine of Knowledge and Pleasure* 66, no. 462 (June 1780): 284–86.

Appleton, William Worthen. *Charles Macklin: An Actor's Life.* Cambridge, MA: Harvard University Press, 1960.

"Article IV: Life (sic) of Mrs. Siddons. By Thomas Campbell." Review. *The Quarterly Review* 52, no. 103 (August 1834): 95–124.

"Article X: The Life of David Garrick, Esq., by Arthur Murphy." Review. *The Critical Review, or, Annals of Literature* 32 (June 1801): 189–95.

"Article XIV: The Life of David Garrick, Esq. By Arthur Murphy, Esq." Review. *The British Critic* 17 (June 1801): 637–40.

"Article XV: The Juvenile Adventures of David Ranger." Review. *The Monthly Review, or, Literary Journal, by Several Hands* 15 (1756): 655–56.

"Article XIX: The Juvenile Adventures of David Ranger." Review. *The Critical Review, or, Annals of Literature* 2 (November 1756): 379.

"Article CX: Memoirs of the Life of David Garrick [Ed. Stephen Jones.]" Review. *The Gentleman's Magazine* (August 1808): 717–19.

Bate, W. Jackson. *The Burden of the Past and the English Poet.* Cambridge, MA: Harvard University Press, 1999. [Originally published in 1970.]

Bellamy, George Anne. *An apology for the life of George Anne Bellamy. Late of Covent Garden Theatre. Written by Herself... in five volumes.* London: Printed for the author by the Literary Society, 1785. Gale: Eighteenth Century Collections Online.

Berkowitz, Gerald M. *David Garrick: A Reference Guide.* Boston: G. K. Hall, 1980.

Betterton, Thomas [Edmund Curll]. *The History of the English Stage, from the Restauration to the Present Time ... by Mr. Thomas Betterton.* 1710. Farmington Hills, MI: Gale: Eighteenth Century Collections Online, 2010.

"Biographical Anecdotes of the Late Mr. Garrick. (I)" *The Gentleman's Magazine, and Historical Chronicle* 49 (March 1779): 117–19.

"Biographical Anecdotes of the Late Mr. Garrick (II)." *The Gentleman's Magazine, and Historical Chronicle* 49 (May 1779): 226–28.

Blanchard, Jean Marc. "Of Cannibalism and Autobiography." *Modern Language Notes* 93:4 (May 1978), 654-676.

Blasingame, Dionne. "Shakespeare Character Analysis: The Character of Leonato in Shakespeare's *Much Ado About Nothing*." *Literatures and Foreign Languages* (October 2008).   http://literaturesandforeignlanguages.blogspot.com/2008/10/shakespeare-character-analysis.html

Bloom, Harold. *The Anxiety of Influence: A Theory of Poetry*. New York: Oxford University Press, 1997. First published 1973.

Boaden, James. *An Inquiry Into the Authenticity of Various Pictures and Prints of Shakespeare*. London: Printed for Robert Triphook, 1824.

———. *Memoirs of Mrs. Siddons, Interspersed with Anecdotes of Authors and Actors* [Mrs. Sarah Siddons.] 2 vols. San Bernardino, CA: Ulan Press, 2012. First published in 1827.

———. *The Life of Mrs. Jordan: Including Original Private Correspondence, and Numerous Anecdotes of her Contemporaries. In Two Volumes*. London: Forgotten Books, 2012. First published in 1831.

———. *The Life of John Philip Kemble. Illustrated with Portraits, Autograph Letters, Views, Play Bills, and Original Correspondence*. 8 vol. Extra-illustrated. London: Longman, 1825. The Theatre Collection. Houghton Library, Harvard University.

———. *Memoirs of the Life of John Philip Kemble, Esq.: Including a History of the Stage, from the Time of Garrick to the Present Period. Two Volumes in One*. Charleston, SC: Nabu Press, 2010. First published in 1825.

Boaden, James, editor. *Memoirs of Mrs. Inchbald: Including Her Familiar Correspondence With the Most Distinguished Persons of Her Time, to Which are Added the* Massacre, *and a Case of Conscience, Now First Published from Her Autograph Copies. In Two Volumes*. London: Forgotten Books, 2012. First published in 1833.

Boaden, John. *Illustrations of the Late John Philip Kemble, Drawn on Stone by R. J. Lane, from Pictures Painted in His [Kemble's] Lifetime by John Boaden*. London: J. Dickinson, 1826. The Theatre Collection. Houghton Library, Harvard University.

"Boaden's Life of Mrs. Jordan." Review. *Fraser's Magazine for Town and Country, 1830–1869* no. 12 (January 1831): 736–39.

Boswell, James. *The Life of Samuel Johnson, L.L.D.* 2 vols. London: Printed by Henry Baldwin, for Charles Dilly, 1791.

Brack, O. M. "Davies, Thomas (c.1712–1785)." *Oxford Dictionary of National Biography*. Ed. H. C. G. Matthew and Brian Harrison. Oxford: Oxford University Press, 2004.

Bratton, Jacky. *New Readings in Theatre History*. Cambridge, UK: Cambridge University Press, 2003.

Braudy, Leo. *The Frenzy of Renown: Fame and Its History*. New York: Vintage Books, 1997.

Bryan, George B., editor. *Stage Lives: A Bibliography and Index to Theatrical Biographies in English*. Westport, CT: Greenwood Press, 1985.

Burnim, Kalman A. "An Introduction to Garrick." *Folgerpedia*. The Folger Shakespeare Library, Washington, DC. http://folgerpedia.folger.edu/David_Garrick,_1717%E2%80%931779:_A_Theatrical_Life

Byrn, Lafayette. *The Repository of Wit and Humour, Comprising More than One Thousand Anecdotes, Odd Scraps, Off-Hand Hits and Humorous Sketches.* Arr. M. Lafayette Byrn, M.D. Boston: J.P. Jewitt and Co, 1857.

Campbell, Thomas. *Life of Mrs. Siddons.* Charleston, SC: Nabu Press, 2011. First published in 1834.

Carlson, Marvin A. *The Haunted Stage: The Theatre as Memory Machine.* Ann Arbor: University of Michigan Press, 2001.

Charke, Charlotte. *A narrative of the life of Mrs. Charlotte Charke, (youngest daughter of Colley Cibber, Esq.).* London: Printed for W. Reeve, 1755. Gale: Eighteenth Century Collections Online.

Charlotte of Mecklenburg, Queen, Consort of George III, and Thomas Davies. *Memoirs of the life of David Garrick, esq., interspersed with characters and anecdotes of his theatrical contemporaries: the whole forming a history of the stage which includes a period of thirty-six years. A new edition.* London: Printed for the author, 1780.

Churchill, C. (Charles). *The Rosciad.* 4th ed. London, 1741. Gale: Eighteenth Century Collections Online.

Cibber, Colley. *An Apology for the Life of Colley Cibber: With an Historical View of the Stage During His Own Time.* Edited by B. R. S. Fone. Ann Arbor: University of Michigan Press, 1986. First published in 1740.

Cibber, Theophilus. *Lives and Characters of the Most Eminent Actors and Actresses of Great Britain and Ireland, from Shakespear [sic] to the present time.* London: Printed for R. Griffiths, 1753. Gale: Eighteenth Century Collections Online.

Clifford, James L. *Biography as an Art: Selected Criticism, 1560–1690.* Oxford, UK: Oxford University Press, 1962.

Congreve, Francis Asprey. *Authentic Memoirs of the Late Mr. Charles Macklin, Comedian.* Farmington Hills, MI: Gale ECCO, 2010. First published in 1798.

Cossart, J. J. [annotator] and Cook [Cooke], William. *Memoirs of Charles Macklin, Comedian. With the Dramatic Characters, Manners, Anecdotes, &c. of the Age in which He Lived: Forming an History of the Stage During almost the Whole of the Century...* London: Printed for J. Asperne by T. Maiden, 1804. Annotations ca. 1806. The Folger Shakespeare Library, Washington, DC.

Cooke [Cook], William. *The Elements of Dramatic Criticism, containing a History of the Stage ... Concluding with General Instructions for Succeeding in the Art of Acting.* London: Printed for G. Kearsly and G. Robison, 1775. Gale: Eighteenth Century Collections Online.

———. *Memoirs of Charles Macklin, Comedian. With the Dramatic Characters, Manners, Anecdotes, &c. of the Age in which He Lived: Forming an History of the Stage During almost the Whole of the Century...* London: Printed for J. Asperne by T. Maiden, Charleston, SC: Nabu, 2011. First published in 1804.

Daggett, Windsor Pratt. *The Sounds of English: Orthographic Texts and Phonetic Transcriptions.* Daggett Studio, 1928.

"Davies, Thomas." *Dictionary of Literary Biography, Volume 142: Eighteenth-Century British Literary Biographers,* edited by Steven Serafin. New York: Hunter College Press, 1994.

Davies, Thomas. *Dramatic Miscellanies: Consisting of Critical Observations on Several Plays of Shakespeare with a Review of His Principal Characters, and Those of Various Eminent Writers, as Represented by Mr. Garrick, and Other Celebrated Comedians, with Anecdotes of Dramatic Poets, Actors, &c. In Three Volumes.* London: Printed for the Author, 1783–84. Gale: Eighteenth Century Collections Online.

————. *A Genuine Narrative of the Life and Theatrical Transactions of Mr. John Henderson, Commonly Called the Bath Roscius.* London, 1777. Gale: Eighteenth Century Collections Online.

————. *Memoirs of the Life of David Garrick, Esq. Interspersed with Characters and Anecdotes of His Theatrical Contemporaries...*, 2 vols. Charleson, SC: Nabu Press, 2012. First published in 1780.

————. *Some Account of the Life and Writings of Philip Massinger.* London, 1789. Gale: Eighteenth Century Collections Online.

Davis, Jim. *Comic Acting and Portraiture in Late-Georgian and Regency England.* Cambridge, UK: Cambridge University Press, 2015.

Deutsch, Helen. *Loving Dr. Johnson.* Chicago: University of Chicago Press, 2005.

Dickie, Simon. "Joseph Andrews and the Great Laughter Debate." In *Studies in Eighteenth-Century Culture,* edited by Catherine Ingrassa and Jeffrey S. Ravel, 271–332. Baltimore, MD: Johns Hopkins University Press, 2005.

Diderot, Denis. *The Paradox of Acting.* Piccadilly, UK: Chatto and Windus, 1883. First published in 1830.

Dobson, Michael. *The Making of the National Poet: Shakespeare, Adaptation and Authorship, 1660–1769.* Oxford, UK: Clarendon Press, 1992.

Edel, Leon. "BIOGRAPHY: A Manifesto." *Biography* 1, no. 1 (1978): 1–3.

Edgeworth, Maria. *Castle Rackrent.* London, 1800. Gale: Eighteenth Century Collections Online.

Engel, Laura. *Fashioning Celebrity: Eighteenth-Century British Actresses and Strategies for Image Making.* Columbus: Ohio State University Press, 2011.

The Extra-illustrated Life of David Garrick by Davies, 1780. David Garrick Collection. The Folger Shakespeare Library, Washington, DC.

Fawcett, Julia. *Spectacular Disappearances: Celebrity and Privacy, 1696–1801.* Ann Arbor: Michigan University Press, 2016.

Fielding, Henry. *Tom Jones.* Edited by John Bender and Simon Stern. Oxford, UK: Oxford University Press, 2008. First published in 1749.

Fitzgerald, Percy Heatherington. *The Life of David Garrick; from Original Family Papers.* 1868. Google Play.

Garraty, John A. *The Nature of Biography.* New York: Knopf, 1957.

Garrick, David. *Private Correspondence of David Garrick with the Most Celebrated Persons of His Time ... and a New Biographical Memoir of Garrick.* Edited by James Boaden. 2 vols. London: Henry Colburn and Richard Bentley, 1831–1832.

————. *Private Correspondence of David Garrick, with the Most Celebrated Persons of His Time: Now First Published from the Originals, and Illustrated with Notes, and a New Biographical Memoir of Garrick.* 2 vols. London: Henry Colburn and Richard Bentley, 1831–1832. Extra-illustrated. The Theatre Collection. Boston, MA: Houghton Library, Harvard College.

————. *The Sick Monkey, a Fable.* London: printed for J. Fletcher, 1765. Gale: Eighteenth Century Collections Online.

Gildon, Charles. *The Life of Mr. Thomas Betterton.* Farmington Hills, MI: Gale: Eighteenth Century Collections Online Eighteenth Century Collections Online, 2010. First published in 1710.

Granger, James. *A Biographical History of England, from Egbert the Great to the Revolution ....* 4 vols. London: Printed for T. Davies, 1769. Gale: Eighteenth Century Collections Online.

"Grangerize, v." In *OED Online.* Oxford University Press, July 2014. http://www.oed.com/view/Entry/80726?redirectedFrom=Grangerize#eid

Granville, George [Baron Lansdowne]. *The Jew of Venice. A Comedy.* London, 1701. Gale: Eighteenth Century Collections Online.

Greetham, D. C. *Textual Scholarship: An Introduction.* New York: Garland, 1994.

Halliday, M. A. K. *Language and Education, Volume 9.* Edited by Jonathan J. Webster. New York: Bloomsbury Academic, 2007.

Hazlitt, William. "On Actors and Acting." *The Round Table: A Collection of Essays.* Vol. 2. London: Longhurst, Hurst, Rees, Orme, and Brown, 1817.

Hill, John. *The Actor: A Treatise on the Art of Playing. Interspersed with theatrical anecdotes, critical remarks on plays, and occasional observations on audiences.* London: Printed for R. Griffiths, at the Dunciad, in St. Paul's Church-Yard, 1750. Gale: Eighteenth Century Collections Online.

Holmes, Richard. *Sidetracks: Explorations of a Romantic Biographer.* New York: Pantheon, 2000.

Jackson, H. J. *Marginalia: Readers Writing in Books.* New Haven, CT: Yale University Press, 2001.

Jenkins, Annibel. *I'll Tell You What: The Life of Elizabeth Inchbald.* Lexington: University Press of Kentucky, 2015.

Joe Miller's Jests or, the Wits Vade-Mecum. Compiled by John Mottley. London, T. Read, 1744. Gale: Eighteenth Century Collections Online. First published in 1739.

Johnson, Samuel. "Idler No. 84: Biography How Best Performed." *Samuel Johnson: Selected Poetry and Prose,* edited by Frank Brady and W. K. Wimsatt, 268–70. Berkeley: University of California Press, 1977.

———. "The Rambler No. 60: The Dignity and Usefulness of Biography." *Samuel Johnson: Selected Poetry and Prose,* edited Frank Brady and W. K. Wimsatt, 181–85. Berkeley: University of California Press, 1977.

Jones, Stephen [ed.] and Thomas Davies. *Memoirs of the Life of David Garrick, Esq. Interspersed with Characters and Anecdotes of His Theatrical Contemporaries...* Charleston, SC: Nabu, 2011. First published in 1808.

J. R. "On Reading Memoirs of the Life of David Garrick, Esq., by Mr. Davies." *The Town and Country Magazine, or, Universal Repository of Knowledge, Instruction, and Entertainment* 12 (September 1780): 494.

Kahan, Jeffrey. *The Cult of Kean.* Aldershot, UK and Burlington, VT: Ashgate Publishing, 2006.

Kelly, Ian. *Mr. Foote's Other Leg: Comedy, Tragedy, and Murder in Georgian London.* London: Picador, 2013.

Kennard, Nina H. *Mrs. Siddons.* Edited by John H. Ingram. Charleston, SC: Nabu Press, 2010. Originally published 1887.

[Kimber, Edward]. *The Juvenile Adventures of David Ranger, Esq.: From an Original Manuscript found in the Collections of a Late Noble Lord. In Two Volumes.* London: printed for P. Stevens, 1757. Gale: Eighteenth Century Collections Online.

[Kimber, Edward]. *The Life and Adventures of Joe Thompson. A Narrative Founded on Fact. Written by Himself.* Vol. 1–2. Dublin, 1771. Gale: Eighteenth Century Collections Online.

Kirkman, James Thomas. *Memoirs of the Life of Charles Macklin, Esq.* 2 vols. Amazon Digital Services, 2013. First published in 1799.

The Laureat: Or, the Right Side of Colley Cibber, Esq. London: Printed for J. Roberts, 1740. Gale: Eighteenth Century Collections Online.

"The Late Mrs. Siddons." Review of Life of Siddons by Thomas Campbell. *The New Monthly Magazine and Literary Journal* 41, no. 164 (August 1834): 471–74.

Leonato [Thomas Davies]. "Eulogium on Mr. Garrick's Leaving the Stage. From the *St. James's Evening Post.*" *Gentleman's Magazine, and Historical Review* 46 (July 1776).

"The Life and Death of David Garrick Esq., the Celebrated English Roscius [By the Old Comedian]." Review. *The Westminster Magazine* (April 1779): 196.

"Life of David Garrick ... by Fitzgerald." Review. *The Quarterly Review* (July 1868).

"The Life of David Garrick; from Original Family Papers ... by Percy Fitzgerald." Review. *The Quarterly Review* (September 1868): 1–25.

"The Life of Mr. James Quin, Comedian." London, Printed for S. Bladon, 1766. Gale: Eighteenth Century Collections Online.

"The Life of Mrs. Siddons, by James Boaden, Esq." Review. *Monthly Magazine, or British Register* 3, no. 14 (February 1827): 194–95.

Macklin, Charles. *Autograph List by Charles Macklin of Correspondence with George Colman* [manuscript], 1772–1773. The Folger Shakespeare Library, Washington, DC.

Macklin, Charles. *Autograph Papers of Charles Macklin* [manuscript], 1754?-1787. David Garrick Collection. The Folger Shakespeare Library, Washington, DC.

———. *Commonplace Book* [manuscript], 1778–1790. The Folger Shakespeare Library, Washington, DC.

———. *Four Comedies by Charles Macklin*, edited by J. O. Bartley. London: Sidgwick & Jackson, 1968.

Marcus, Laura. *Auto/biographical Discourses: Theory, Criticism, Practice.* Manchester, UK: Manchester University Press, 1994.

Marshall, F. A. "Introduction." *The Works of William Shakespeare, Vol. 3.*, edited by Henry Irving, Frank Albert Marshall, and Edward Dowden. London: Blackie & Son, 1888.

McPherson, Heather. *Art and Celebrity in the Age of Reynolds and Siddons.* University Park: Pennsylvania State University Press, 2017.

"Memoirs of the Life of David Garrick, Esq., Interspersed with Characters and Anecdotes of His Theatrical Contemporaries [by Davies]." Review. *The Westminster Magazine* (May 1780): 277–79.

"Memoirs of Mrs. Inchbald [by Boaden]." Review. *The Athenaeum* 290 (May 18, 1833): 305–6.

"Memoirs of Mrs. Siddons [by Boaden]." Review. *Robins's London and Dublin Magazine* (February 1827): 147–54.

"Memoirs of Mrs. Siddons, Interspersed with Anecdotes of Actors and Authors [by Boaden]." Review. *The National Magazine, and General Review* 1, no. 3 (January 1827): 183–86.

Menzer, Paul. *Anecdotal Shakespeare: A New Performance History.* London: Bloomsbury Publishing, 2015.

Murphy, Esq., Arthur. *An Essay on the Life and Genius of Samuel Johnson, LL.D.* London: printed for T. Longman, etc. 1792. Gale: Eighteenth Century Collections Online.

———. *The Life of David Garrick, Esq.* Dublin: Brett Smith, 1801.

Murray, Caroline. "Letter of Provenance, by Caroline Murray." In Charlotte of Mecklenburg, Queen, Consort of George III, and Thomas Davies. *Memoirs of the life of David Garrick, esq., interspersed with characters and anecdotes of his theatrical contemporaries: the whole forming a history of the stage which includes a period of thirty-six years. A new edition.* London: Printed for the author, 1780.

Nichols, John. *Literary Anecdotes of the Eighteenth Century: Comprizing [sic] Biographical Memoirs of William Bouyer, Printer.* Vol. 2. London: Printed for the Author, 1812.

Norman, N. D. *From a Record of Death to a Memory of Life: The Rise of the Biographical Obituary in the Gentleman's Magazine.* MA thesis. Virginia Tech. Scholar Library: Blacksburg, VA, 2008.

Nussbaum, Felicity. *The Autobiographical Subject: Gender and Ideology in Eighteenth-Century England.* Baltimore, MD: John Hopkins University Press, 1989.

O'Bryan, Daniel. *Authentic Memoirs or, The life and character of the most celebrated comedian, Mr. Robert Wilkes.* London: Printed for S. Slow, 1732. Gale: Eighteenth Century Collections Online.

Old Comedian. *The Life and Death of David Garrick, Esq., the Celebrated English Roscius.* Second edition. London, 1779. Gale: Eighteenth Century Collections Online.

Oldys, William. *Memoirs of Mrs. Anne Oldfield.* London, 1741. Gale: Eighteenth Century Collections Online.

Palfrey, Simon, and Tiffany Stern. *Shakespeare in Parts.* Oxford, UK: Oxford University Press, 2007.

Parry, Sir Edward Abbott. *Charles Macklin.* Charleston, SC: BibloBazaar, 2011. First published in 1891.

Pascoe, Judith. *The Sarah Siddons Audio Files: Romanticism and the Lost Voice.* Ann Arbor: University of Michigan Press, 2011.

Paulin, Tom. "Sidetracks: Explorations of a Romantic Biographer." Review. *The Guardian,* July 2000.

Perry, Gillian, Joseph Roach, and Shearer West. *The First Actresses: Nell Gwyn to Sarah Siddons.* London: National Portrait Gallery, 2011.

Philological Society of London. "Memoirs of Charles Macklin [by Cooke]" Review. *The European Magazine and London Review* 47 (January 1805): 49–50.

Photius, Jr. [W. Sherlock] "Boaden's Life of Mrs. Siddons, Feb. 6, 1827. Review." *Letters on Literature* by Photius, Junior. Vol. 1. Brussels: Printed by Adolphe Wahlen, 1836.

Pointon, Marcia. *Hanging the Head: Portraiture and Social Formation in Eighteenth-Century England.* London: Paul Mellon Centre BA, 1993.

Radner, John B. *Johnson and Boswell: A Biography of Friendship.* New Haven, CT: Yale University Press, 2013.

Raven, James. *Publishing Business in Eighteenth-Century England.* London: Boydell Press, 2014.

Roach, Joseph R. *Cities of the Dead.* New York: Columbia University Press, 1996.

Robinson, Mary. *Memoirs of the late Mrs. Robinson, written by herself. With some posthumous pieces* … London: Printed by Wilkes and Taylor for R. Phillips, 1801.

Rogers, Pat. "Edmund Curll and the Publishing Trade." *Producing the Eighteenth-Century Book: Writers and Publishers in England, 1650–1800.* Edited by Laura L. Runge and Pat Rogers, 215-234. Newark, DE: University of Delaware Press, 2009.

Rowe, Nicholas. "Some Account of the Life &c. of Mr. William Shakespear [*sic*]." *The Works of Mr, William Shakespear, in six volumes, adorn'd with cuts. Revis'd and corrected, with an account of the life and writings of the author.* 6 vols. London: Printed for Jacob Tonson, 1709. Gale: Eighteenth Century Collections Online.

Scrapbook of David Garrick / Life of Garrick [manuscript.] David Garrick Collection. The Folger Shakespeare Library, Washington, DC.

Schiff, Stacy. "The Dual Lives of the Biographer." *New York Times,* November 24, 2012.

Sheridan, Thomas. *Verses to the Memory of Garrick. Spoken as a Monody, at the Theatre Royal at Drury Lane.* London: Published by T. Evans, 1779. Gale : Eighteenth Century Collections Online.

Sherman, Stuart. "Garrick among Media: The '*Now* Performer' Navigates the News." *PMLA* 126, no. 4 (October 2011): 966–82.

Siddons, Sarah. *Papers of Sarah Siddons* [manuscript], 1778–1832. The Folger Shakespeare Library, Washington, DC.

Sisman, Adam. *Boswell's Presumptuous Task: The Making of the Life of Dr. Johnson*. London: Penguin, 2000.

Smollett, Tobias. *The Adventures of Peregrine Pickle, in which are included Memoirs of a Lady of Quality*. 3 vols. London, 1751. Gale: Eighteenth Century Collections Online.

———. *The Adventures of Roderick Random*. 2 vols. London, 1748. Gale: Eighteenth Century Collections Online.

Smyth, James. *David Garrick*. London, 1807. San Bernardino, CA: University of Toronto Libraries, 2014.

Stauffer, Donald. *The Art of Biography in Eighteenth-Century England*. Princeton, NJ: Princeton University Press, 1941.

———. *English Biography before 1700*. Cambridge, MA: Harvard University Press, 1930.

Steele, Joshua. *An Essay Towards Establishing the Melody and Measure of Speech, to be Expressed and Perpetuated by Peculiar Symbols*. London: Printed by W. Bowyer and J. Nichols, for Jay Almon, in Piccadilly, *1775*. Gale: Eighteenth Century Collections Online.

Stillinger, Jack. *Multiple Authorship and the Myth of Solitary Genius*. New York: Oxford University Press, 1991.

Stone, Jr., George Winchester. "David Garrick and the Eighteenth-Century Stage: Notes toward a New Biography." *In Search of Restoration and Eighteenth-Century Theatrical Biography: Papers Read at a Clark Library Seminar*, January 25, 1975. Los Angeles: William Andrews Clark Memorial Library, 1975.

Straub, Kristina. "The Guilty Pleasures of Female Theatrical Cross-Dressing." In *Feminist Theory and the Body: A Reader*, edited by Janet Price and Margrit Shildrick, 423-431. New York: Routledge, 1999.

———. *Sexual Suspects: Eighteenth Century Players and Sexual Ideology*. Princeton, NJ: Princeton University Press, 1992.

Taylor, Diana. *The Archive and the Repertoire: Performing Cultural Memory in the Americas*. Durham, NC: Duke University Press, 2003.

Taylor, Gary. *Reinventing Shakespeare*. New York: Weidenfeld & Nicolson, 1989.

Theatrical Monitor, or, The Green Room Laid Open no. 1–18 (October 1767–April 1768) London, W. Bingley and S. Bladon, 1768.

Toothill, Matthew. *The Stages of Celebrity*. MA thesis. University of Birmingham, 2013. eTheses.

Urban, Sylvanus. [pseudonym.] "Article XII: Some Account of the Life and Writings of Philip Massinger." Review. *The Gentleman's Magazine, and Historical Chronicle* 49 (February 1779). London: Printed for D. Henry, 1779.

Victor, Benjamin. *The History of the Theatres of London and Dublin, from the year 1730 to the Present Time*. Vols. 1–2, 1761–1771. London: printed for T. Davies. Gale: Eighteenth Century Collections Online.

———. *Memoirs of the Life of Barton Booth, Esq*. London, printed for John Watts, 1733. Gale: Eighteenth Century Collections Online.

Walton, Izaak. *Izaak Walton's Lives of John Donne, Henry Wotton, Richard Hooker, and George Herbert*. 1640–1678. Ed. Henry Morley. London: George Routledge and Sons: 1888. Google Books.

Wanko, Cheryl. *Roles of Authority: Thespian Biography and Celebrity in Eighteenth-Century Britain.* Lubbock: Texas Tech University Press, 2003.

Watt, Ian. *The Rise of the Novel: Studies in Defoe, Richardson, and Fielding.* Whitefish, MT: Kessinger Publishing, 2010.

West, Shearer. *The Image of the Actor: Verbal and Visual Representation in the Age of Garrick and Kemble.* New York: St. Martin's Press, 1991.

Winston, James [compiler]. *David Garrick, A Collection of Engravings, Manuscripts, Playbills* [manuscript], ca. 1830. The Folger Shakespeare Library, Washington, DC.

Worthen, William. *The Idea of the Actor.* Princeton, NJ: Princeton University Press, 1984.

INDEX

CPSIA information can be obtained
at www.ICGtesting.com
Printed in the USA
LVOW10*2356250118
564064LV00002B/11/P

9 781783 086665